Mastering
APA Style
Instructor's Resource Guide

Sixth Edition

Mastering
APA Style

Instructor's Resource Guide

American Psychological Association • *Washington, DC*

Third Printing, September 2009

Published by
American Psychological Association
750 First Street, NE
Washington, DC 20002
www.apa.org

To order
APA Order Department
P.O. Box 92984
Washington, DC 20090-2984
Tel: (800) 374-2721; Direct: (202) 336-5510
Fax: (202) 336-5502; TDD/TTY: (202) 336-6123
Online: www.apa.org/books/
E-mail: order@apa.org

In the U.K., Europe, Africa, and the Middle East, copies may be ordered from
American Psychological Association
3 Henrietta Street
Covent Garden, London
WC2E 8LU England

Typeset in Sabon, Univers, Futura, and Rockwell by Circle Graphics, Columbia, MD

Printer: Goodway Graphics, Springfield, VA
Cover Designer: Naylor Design, Washington, DC
Production Manager: Jennifer L. Macomber
Senior Editor, APA Style: Anne W. Gasque

Printed in the United States of America
Sixth Edition

Contents

Preface

The *Publication Manual of the American Psychological Association* is used not only by psychologists but also by educators, sociologists, nurses, business professionals, criminologists, and numerous others as a guide to structuring their writing. The style elements described in the *Publication Manual,* which have come to be called *APA Style,* are used increasingly as a standard format for writing student papers, laboratory reports, and journal articles. Hundreds of scholarly journals and magazines in the United States and other countries require authors to use APA Style, and professional editors who copyedit those articles edit according to its standards.

Teachers and publishing professionals responsible for training people to use APA Style have often relied on their own ingenuity to develop materials to use in teaching it. But teaching others the stylistic conventions set forth in the sixth edition of the *Publication Manual of the American Psychological Association*—for example, how to format a reference, create a table, or use italics—can be an onerous and time-consuming task. *Mastering APA Style* is the American Psychological Association's answer to the expressed need of both instructors and those who need to learn APA Style.

For Academic Instructors

The exercises and tests in *Mastering APA Style* have been developed over more than a decade and have been tested where it counts—in the classroom. All of the students who participated in field tests of the module achieved mastery. They were able to identify and remediate their own deficiencies more effectively than students who did not use the module. In time, the students made an important discovery: that *Mastering APA Style* made it easy for them to learn APA Style, good writing skills, and other course requirements effectively and simultaneously. In addition, the quality of the students' writing improved with the use of *Mastering APA Style.*

By using the feedback from the exercises and tests in the module, instructors are able to identify problems that all students are having and to devote a minimal amount of class time to remediate the problem, or they can more easily assign relevant parts of the *Student's Workbook and Training Guide* for additional review. Most important, because instructors need to spend less time providing line-by-line feedback about style to individual students, they have more time to give productive feedback about the organization and content of students' papers.

For Publishing Professionals

The exercises in the *Student's Workbook and Training Guide* have been structured to both teach style and provide examples of good writing through individual sentences and larger selections of text. The examples are drawn from psychological literature because that is the field we know best.

Regardless of the setting in which you use the module, its contents and instructional procedures can be used effectively. However, it may be necessary to modify some of the techniques we recommend for the training of publishing professionals. Copy editors must know APA Style thoroughly. It is their function to correct others' use of it and to support the author's efforts to communicate with his or her audience. Both inexperienced and experienced writers depend on the copy editor to identify and fix writers' errors.

In training copy editors, a different kind of orientation may be necessary, and the trainer may want to monitor performance more directly, which is often possible because the training is more individualized and the goal is of higher priority than in the academic setting. The orientation might note why APA Style is used in the publication to be edited as well as exceptions to and special applications of APA Style required in the text. Keeping in mind that copy editors edit the written work of professionals who may not know APA Style thoroughly, the mastery that copy editors must have is likely to be even greater than that attained by an accomplished writer. The copy editor must have mastery of all aspects of style. To ensure that the trainee learns as effectively and accurately as possible, the trainer will probably want to review all exercises and practice tests and to administer and score at least two forms of mastery tests. The trainer may also develop additional tests and review the trainee's copyediting of actual manuscripts over a period of weeks or months.

Mastering APA Style has followed its own developmental path. It was originally conceived by Charles J. Walker and Harold Gelfand about four years before the publication of the third edition of the *Publication Manual*. They created the first set of mastery materials, field tested them in lab courses, and improved the materials on the basis of feedback from students and colleagues. The books they initially created were updated and refined and have now been used with the third, fourth, and fifth editions of the *Publication Manual*. The current edition was thoroughly updated by Anne Woodworth Gasque to match the style changes put in place with the sixth edition of the *Publication Manual*. We are grateful for the creative contributions of each of these individuals.

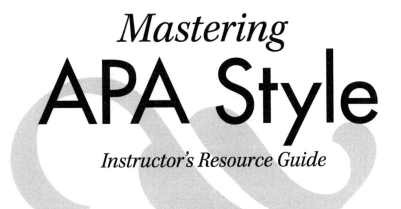

Mastering
APA Style

Instructor's Resource Guide

The Purpose of
Mastering APA Style

Learning effective means of communicating ideas and information is a prerequisite to being able to share ideas with and learn from others. As instructors, we are partly responsible for teaching students these communicative skills as well as the facts and processes of our fields of expertise. One way we do this is to have our students submit written assignments as part of the requirements for successfully completing a course. To adequately prepare these writing assignments, students must develop a writing style. For most students, it is easier to adopt a style developed and perfected by others than to develop their own.

Style encompasses uniform standards and formats for capitalization, punctuation, spelling, word division, use of terms, and so forth. These style elements may vary from one language to another and even from one group to another within the same language. For example, the style used for writing an analysis of English novels takes one form, whereas the style used to report on a chemistry project takes another. Commonalities are established in a particular style of writing because the function of style is to facilitate communication by providing a common ground for understanding among members of a particular scientific or professional community.

If students want to advance professionally in subsequent courses, graduate work, and a career, they must adopt the language of their professional community. Because our community is the behavioral sciences, we start our students on the path to professionalism by requiring them to use the writing style acceptable to the behavioral science community, namely APA Style.

What Is APA Style?

The formalization of APA Style began in 1928, when a group of editors and business managers of anthropological and psychological journals met to discuss the form of journal manuscripts and to write instructions for their preparation. Over the years, the components of style accepted by psychologists and other behavioral scientists were refined, and articles about style were published in the APA journal *Psychological Bulletin*.[1,2] In 1952, a 60-page supplement to the articles in

---

[1]Bentley, M., Peerenboom, C. A., Hodge, F. W., Passano, E. P., Warren, H. C., & Washburn, M. F. (1929). Instructions in regard to preparation of manuscript. *Psychological Bulletin, 26*, 57–63.

[2]Anderson, J. E., & Valentine, W. L. (1944). The preparation of articles for publication in the journals of the American Psychological Association. *Psychological Bulletin, 41*, 345–376.

Psychological Bulletin was published.[3] That supplement was the first publication to carry the title *Publication Manual of the American Psychological Association* and marked the beginning of recognized APA Style.

The *Publication Manual* is a compendium of the guidelines known as APA Style; it is a reference book and was neither designed nor intended to be a textbook or how-to manual. As with any reference work, there is an art to using the *Publication Manual*. Dictionaries, for example, offer much more than the definition and pronunciation of words. A wealth of information can be found in a dictionary, including the origin of words, nuances of meaning, word division, and the location of major cities. However, one needs to be familiar with the dictionary and to practice using it to be aware of all of the kinds of information it offers and to use it expediently.

Books and articles on how to use various reference materials abound, but until 1990 none existed that dealt exclusively with using the *Publication Manual*. We created *Mastering APA Style* to fill that void, and it has been updated to reflect changes made in the sixth edition.

The Challenges Faced by Those Who Teach APA Style

Teaching—and learning—should be rewarding for both instructors and students. Ideally, courses should generate in students some enthusiasm that sparks their own excitement about the field of study and should lead them to become actively involved in the scientific process, even if only a few of those students go on to become professionals in that field. Unfortunately, the requirement that students know and apply APA Style to complete their writing assignments can hamper the educational process. Much time may be spent correcting papers and giving feedback about technical matters of form and style, time that could otherwise be devoted to the paper's substance and the conceptual and methodological issues relevant to the course. The benefits of using APA Style are probably not immediately apparent to students; your insistence that they use it may cause them to feel that you emphasize form more than content, a feeling that you may share.

Let's be honest: The motivation for requiring students to use APA Style in preparing the papers they submit is also somewhat selfish. Future uses aside, as instructors, we want our students to use APA Style now, in our courses, so that we and our students can reap the very benefits that APA Style is intended to provide: to improve our comprehension and evaluation of their work and to enhance the learning value of the feedback that we give them.

When students do attain mastery of APA Style, the rewards are apparent to us and to them. The difficulty, and the challenge, is getting them to that point, and we understand why it is so difficult. Up to the time that most students enter fields of study that require the use of APA Style, they have been required to write using stylistic conventions that probably differ from those used in APA Style (or, in many cases, their instructors were lax in requiring adherence to any stylistic convention). When they enter a course in which APA Style is required, students are required to learn and use a style that not only is new and different but also has been developed on the basis of a more scientific and precise approach to writing, a form that is typically foreign to them. Thus, the requirement that written assignments be prepared in and conform to APA Style poses a challenging learning task, in addition to the other challenges that the course already offers.

The responsibility for teaching APA Style has never been clearly defined; traditionally it has fallen on the instructor of the first laboratory or research methods course. One approach that instructors have taken has been to give the students the entire responsibility for learning APA Style.

---

[3]American Psychological Association, Council of Editors. (1952). *Publication manual of the American Psychological Association*. Washington, DC: American Psychological Association.

Students are instructed to buy a copy of the *Publication Manual* and to use it to write their papers. The results, as you might expect, are seldom satisfactory. Students struggle with learning the conventions on their own, interpret and apply the guidelines in different ways, and turn in papers that are riddled with mechanical errors and inconsistencies. Often they spend so much time worrying about the mechanical details that they have little time to evaluate and refine the content. Instructors are then faced with the time-consuming task of providing corrective feedback; both you and your students may resent having to spend time on stylistic issues at the expense of subject matter.

Many instructors assume some or all of the responsibility for teaching APA Style and have used a variety of techniques to do so in effective and efficient ways. Some instructors supply students with written models (e.g., sample articles or papers that use APA Style correctly). Other instructors actually guide students through the *Publication Manual* and point out those sections that have particular relevance for them, or they give students lists of other resources that will help them learn APA Style. Some instructors spend much time giving written feedback on papers, perhaps by correcting stylistic errors or by citing the section of the *Publication Manual* that pertains to the error. The fact is, however, that regardless of how involved you become in teaching APA Style, the process is time-consuming, disruptive to the teaching of substantive content, fraught with frustration for both instructor and students, and too often only marginally successful.

The challenges that you face when you take on the task of teaching APA Style may be summarized as follows:

1. Students have different levels of expertise in using various writing styles: Some are familiar with another style, whereas others have no experience using any style guide. Thus, you may have to tailor your curriculum to address students' different skill levels.
2. Students who come to their first course to focus on the subject matter of their chosen course of study may be overwhelmed by also having to learn a set of style rules. You are faced with the difficulty of successfully integrating the teaching of APA Style with the course content.
3. Regardless of how much responsibility you assume for teaching APA Style, much of your time will be devoted to matters of style, time that could be spent on course content.
4. Because there has been no systematic method for teaching APA Style in depth, instructors and students have had to reinvent the wheel—that is, develop their own approach. There also has been no official tool to enable mastery of APA Style.

How *Mastering APA Style* Can Help You, the Instructor

Mastering APA Style offers a systematic way of teaching and learning APA Style so that neither you nor your students are unduly burdened by the task. The process of mastering APA Style is outlined in Table 1. *Mastering APA Style* is intended to minimize the amount of time spent by students who are learning and instructors who are teaching APA Style. Broadly defined, the goals of the module are as follows:

- to serve the teaching needs of instructors in any field who give any of a variety of writing assignments to their students;
- to serve the needs of instructors who have different amounts of time and skill available to devote to teaching the use of APA Style; and
- to provide an organized, systematic, and effective way for students to learn and achieve mastery and for instructors to teach.

Table 1

The Process of Mastering APA Style

Step and learning activity	Function
Prewriting phase	
1. Familiarization tests	Assess baseline knowledge Define learning tasks
2. Learning exercises	Teach basic skills Reinforce application skills
3. Integrative exercises	Teach self-editor skills Reinforce basic skills
4. Practice tests	Diagnose learning weaknesses Forecast mastery test performance
5. Mastery tests	Assess knowledge and application skills Provide formative feedback for additional learning
6. Review exercises	Provide a remedial learning activity Rehearse integrative processes
Writing phase	
7. Structured paper writing	Instructor feedback assists further learning of style and technical composition
8. Free paper writing	Instructor feedback helps perfect logic and technical composition

Mastering APA Style is a training module that consists of two companion volumes: The *Student's Workbook and Training Guide* and the *Instructor's Resource Guide*. Although the fundamental goal of the module is identical for students and instructors—achieving mastery of APA Style—the focus of the two volumes is different. Each volume was written specifically to address the needs of its audience.

The *Student's Workbook and Training Guide*

In the introduction to the *Student's Workbook and Training Guide,* we explain what style is in general and what APA Style is in particular. We thoroughly describe the rationale for using APA Style, focusing on what is in it for the student. This material is essential reading: It provides the impetus for learning by showing students how APA Style will benefit them personally. We then describe the teaching materials contained in the workbook and provide clear instructions for how to use the materials. If the workbook is effective and students use it as they are instructed, the amount of time spent teaching APA Style should be greatly reduced.

The contents of the *Student's Workbook and Training Guide* are almost entirely different from those of the *Instructor's Resource Guide*. For example, only the workbook contains the familiarization tests and the practice tests, the exercises, and detailed instructions for taking tests and completing exercises. Thus, you must read both books thoroughly.

The *Student's Workbook and Training Guide* is divided into two sections: the term paper unit and the research report unit. Students are instructed to always begin with the term paper unit, taking the familiarization test to assess their basic knowledge of APA Style. On the basis of their scores, students can determine the areas (e.g., punctuation, grammar, numbers) in which they need the most practice. Students then move on to the learning exercises, which cover various style points. The right-hand page contains "draft" exercises that may or may not need correcting; the particular style point being targeted is shaded. The left-hand page shows the corrected version. Students can write answers directly in the workbook. At the end of each set of exercises on a specific topic, there are integrative exercises. These exercises, which consist of a paragraph or page of text that students are instructed to edit, incorporate the style points that students should have learned while doing the learning exercises.

After completing the integrative exercises, students take a practice test to determine whether they need more help learning style points or are ready to take a mastery test. If they require more help, students can do the review exercises. Students move on to the research report unit and complete it in the same manner that they completed the term paper unit.

The *Instructor's Resource Guide*

In the preface of this guide, we explain how *Mastering APA Style* was developed. Chapter 2 offers advice and instructions for using the training module in your courses. We also describe ways to integrate teaching APA Style with course content, to motivate students, and to administer mastery tests and give feedback, and we suggest other resources and materials that you can use. The mastery tests, answer sheets and feedback reports, and answer keys are in Chapter 3. The master test files (a list of questions contained in the tests) can be found in Chapter 4. Instructors can find additional questions for some topic areas in the Related Resources section of the APA Style website (www.apastyle.org).

What's new in APA Style?

Visit

www.apastyle.org

How to Teach APA Style

Instructor's Preparation

Deciding How You Will Use the Training Module

It is important to decide how actively you will use this training module to teach APA Style. To make this decision, you will need to assess the time and skill that you have available as well as the needs and skills that each new group of students brings to the learning task. The *Student's Workbook and Training Guide* is designed for self-instruction. It does not contain the mastery tests that are in the *Instructor's Resource Guide*; therefore, it is possible to assign the *Student's Workbook and Training Guide* as independent study. However, the more support you can offer to students and the more involved you become in this learning task, the more likely students are to be motivated to achieve the goals of the module. Their level of commitment to the task will mirror your own; therefore, whatever your level of involvement, it is important to convey to students your own belief that learning APA Style is valuable.

Your involvement can take different forms and occur on different levels, such as the following:

- *Free independent study.* Assign the *Student's Workbook and Training Guide* as independent study. That is, have students take the familiarization tests, do the exercises, and take the practice tests outside of class, at their own pace. You may spend a small amount of class time on strategic issues, such as giving an overview of the workbook; setting goals and standards; and most important, administering mastery tests. We have found that free independent study works well with graduate students and advanced undergraduates.
- *Guided independent study.* Have students work independently, but assign deadlines for completing units. In this manner, you can help ensure that students will adequately prepare themselves before their writing assignments are due. You might schedule class times at regular intervals for discussing goals or particular style points, how to use the workbook, and so forth. You might think of other ways to support students without actually having to devote class time to APA Style issues (e.g., have students pair up with a classmate whom they can meet with regularly for study sessions).
- *Fully integrated learning.* Integrate the training module into the course. For example, include goals, assignments, and test dates for learning APA Style in the course syllabus alongside

deadlines for course content. Designate class dates on which particular APA Style issues will be discussed or on which only APA Style will be discussed. Coordinate APA Style assignments with other course assignments so that achievements complement each other. For example, set goals for completing the term paper unit before the first term paper is due. We have found this approach to work the best with the majority of students.

Even if you expect students to work independently, it will be useful to provide them with adequate background on both APA Style and the module to enable them to use the workbook effectively. One of the easiest ways to accomplish this is to devote class time at the beginning of the course to presenting an overview or introduction. To prepare such an overview, first acquaint yourself and your students with the module.

To begin, read the table of contents for both volumes and have students read the table of contents for the workbook. The chapter titles and section headings describe clearly and succinctly the content of each volume. It is also useful to have students read Chapters 1 and 2 of the workbook and look at the exercises and tests at least briefly before you give your overview.

The importance of this kind of preparation cannot be overemphasized. Your own familiarity with the materials will help you integrate APA Style instruction into your courses, set goals and deadlines, anticipate potential problems, and thus save yourself a lot of time. Familiarizing students with the materials can help them see even before they begin that the work is broken into manageable units; that feedback will be available to them immediately; that learning will take place preemptively (i.e., before papers are due); and that mastery can be achieved by the end of the course, if not sooner.

What to Tell Your Students During Orientation

The *Student's Workbook and Training Guide* includes a section outlining the benefits of APA Style for students ("Why Should You Use APA Style?"). It is important for students to understand and internalize the reasons for learning APA Style, beyond the fact that it is a requirement; by doing so, they motivate themselves to learn. Self-motivation is a more powerful incentive than any you could provide. You can play an important role, however, in motivating students and in creating conditions for them to motivate themselves by giving them an orientation to APA Style and to *Mastering APA Style*. Chapters 1 and 2 of the *Instructor's Resource Guide* and the *Student's Workbook and Training Guide* include a great deal of information that you can use. The following checklist, which highlights some of the points made in these chapters, may assist you in developing your own presentation at the beginning of your course:

- Describe what the *Publication Manual* contains and how it is arranged. Clarify the distinction between a reference book and a how-to book, emphasizing that the *Publication Manual* is the former.
- Give a brief, realistic, and enthusiastic talk about the value of learning APA Style, focusing on the benefits that students will derive. (Refer to the section "Why Should You Use APA Style?" in the *Student's Workbook and Training Guide*.)
- Explain how *Mastering APA Style* is designed to help students learn APA Style. You might point out, for example, that it teaches by hands-on practice, provides feedback in the workbook, and allows students to pace themselves.
- Emphasize that good writers are usually good at editing their own work. One role of a critical reader or editor is to identify stylistic errors and suggest improvements in a manuscript. Students (and authors) rely on such feedback regardless of whether the editor is a course instructor, a

mentor, a committee, or a journal editor. To become good writers, students must learn to anticipate the reactions of an editor; doing so will significantly reduce the need for the editor to comment on or demand changes in the presentation of the manuscript. Essentially, then, the goal is for students to become their own editors and to learn to think critically while writing.

- Make students aware that other resources are available to help them learn to write more effectively, develop a learning style that works for them, and use the workbook (e.g., sample manuscripts, other style guides, and their peers). (Direct them to www.apastyle.org for other resources.)
- Specify your level of involvement in teaching APA Style and define deadlines and goals. Explain that although the workbook is designed for self-study, it is important to pace the learning so that it can be applied to writing assignments.
- Explain the kinds of feedback and reinforcement available to students, including test answer keys, APA codes citing the applicable section of the *Publication Manual,* feedback versions of exercises, as well as any input that you or other resources may provide.
- Distinguish between fundamental style knowledge and secondary style knowledge. Examples of fundamental style rules, which students should be able to apply from memory, are those for punctuation, grammar, and so forth. Some secondary style rules are used infrequently and do not have to be memorized, but students are expected to know how to locate them when the need arises.
- Point out that the order in which the workbook materials are used will be different for each student, depending on prior knowledge and skills and current needs.
- Describe how credit or grades, if any, are given.
- Explain the concept of mastery and the criteria for demonstrating it.
- If you plan to use mastery tests, explain their use, how they will be graded, and so forth.
- Invite students to share their experiences and to offer comments and suggestions as they use the workbook.

Setting Goals and Standards of Performance

Mastery as a Prerequisite

We urge you to administer the familiarization tests and the mastery tests yourself to let students know you are serious about the task. Require students to first master the unit on term papers, as reflected in their successful completion of the term paper mastery test, before they are allowed to submit their first written assignment. A similar requirement should be set for mastery of the unit on research reports before the students submit written assignments using those skills. In both cases, students should be required to demonstrate mastery at least 2 days prior to the due date of the assignment to underscore the expectation that students' mastery will be reflected in their work. To fit that timing, you may have to schedule administrations of the mastery test several times before that 2-day cutoff.

Some students (and instructors) may find requiring demonstrated mastery before an assignment is due to be intimidating; however, we have found that this alternative works (students do meet the deadline!) and is more effective than allowing students to submit a written assignment and then subtracting points for not achieving the mastery criterion. Not requiring demonstrated mastery before the assignment due date typically results in students' turning in work that is fraught with errors and that requires a great deal of work (for you as well as for the student) to correct. It is more effective to accept written assignments late, once mastery on the test has been achieved, and then to subtract points on the basis of the degree of lateness of submission. If you accept assignments late, you may want to set a cutoff date after which no points will be awarded for the assignment.

Standards of Performance

Set a rigorous standard (e.g., 80% on Term Paper Mastery Test 1) for acceptable mastery before the first written assignment can be submitted. To qualify for submitting the second written assignment, require students to achieve a higher level (e.g., 90%) of performance on another term paper mastery test (e.g., Term Paper Mastery Test 2).

Consistent with the focus on mastery, set no limit on how many times or how frequently a student may take the tests, subject to an announced schedule of when the tests may be taken. However, do not give a student the same mastery test repeatedly. These tests are designed to be given in the following order if a student does not achieve criterion: Mastery Test 1, Mastery Test 2, Mastery Test 3, Mastery Test 4, Mastery Test 1, and so forth.

Follow the same procedure for research report mastery, setting the criterion initially at 80% and then at 90% for mastery tests before submission of subsequent written assignments using the style components categorized as being for research reports.

Grades and Awarding Credit

Consistent with the mastery approach and with the view that the students are developing their skills as a means to achieve the goal of effective writing, students' grades in the course should not be based directly on test or exercise performance. Rather, the incentive for mastery of APA Style should be that mastering APA Style will qualify them for turning in a written assignment and that their grades on their written assignments will reflect the mastery they achieved.

Because we as instructors know that students generally get the best results if they do the exercises, we have been tempted to provide incentive by having students turn in their exercises and then grading them. However, we have learned that such a practice is counterproductive. The students learn to read the items—at best—and simply copy the correct answers from the feedback to the exercise section of their workbook. One way of providing incentive for working through the exercises is to check that the students are using the workbook—even to award points for it—regardless of the accuracy of their performance.

Administering Tests
Familiarization Tests and Practice Tests

The *Student's Workbook and Training Guide* contains two types of tests (familiarization tests and practice tests) for each of the two units (term paper and research report). The familiarization tests help students to identify the areas of style that they are unfamiliar with and direct them to the sections of the *Publication Manual* that pertain to those style issues. The practice tests help students assess the level of mastery they have obtained after completing the exercises. The feedback that students garner by grading their own tests helps them to decide whether they need more work or are ready to take a mastery test. All of the material relating to these tests is contained only in the *Student's Workbook and Training Guide*.

Although these tests are designed so that students can administer them to themselves (or can ask a classmate to administer them), you may decide to administer these tests yourself or at least to provide class time for students to take the tests as a group. The value of administering these tests yourself is that you can gain a sense of where the class stands as a whole. Making the tests a group activity is also a supportive gesture.

Mastery Tests

The mastery tests are only in the *Instructor's Resource Guide,* and you or your assistants are the only ones who should administer them. The mastery tests have two functions: (a) to assess learning level and (b) to diagnose weaknesses and guide further learning. They are the primary means by which you can evaluate a student's readiness to prepare writing assignments; in the case of the student who is not ready, the mastery tests guide and support additional learning.

Chapter 3 of this guide contains eight mastery tests: Term Paper Mastery Tests 1 through 4 and Research Report Mastery Tests 1 through 4. Although the topics covered overlap extensively, and some items appear on more than one test, the individual test items are mostly dissimilar. Thus, memorization of the items on one test will not enable a student to answer the questions on another test. Furthermore, none of the tests cover all of the major style issues; each contains a representative sampling. To retain the integrity of the mastery tests, administer them yourself, and do not allow students to keep the test questions.

The procedure for administering mastery tests is as follows:

- Briefly describe the purpose of the test.
- Give each student a test and a blank answer sheet/feedback report.
- Inform students that unlike the procedure for taking the familiarization tests and practice tests, they may not use the *Publication Manual* during the tests.
- Monitor students during the test.
- Collect all tests and answer sheets and feedback reports.

Answer Sheets/Feedback Reports and Answer Keys

Answer keys for the familiarization tests and practice tests are in the *Student's Workbook and Training Guide;* answer keys for the mastery tests are only in the *Instructor's Resource Guide.*

Grade the mastery tests yourself to maintain the confidentiality of the answers. Feedback is given differently for mastery tests in that students are not told the correct answers. The procedure that we recommend is as follows:

- Grade the mastery tests, and give feedback to students as soon as possible after the test.
- Compare the student's answer sheet/feedback report with the appropriate mastery test answer key, and circle the number of the questions that are incorrectly answered.
- Calculate a grade if grades are being assigned, and write it on the student's answer sheet/feedback report; record the grades on student and class record sheets.
- Give students a blank answer sheet/ feedback report showing their score (or grade) and the items they answered incorrectly. (APA codes for each question are listed beside each answer blank, so students can look up questions they missed.)

Note: Do not allow students to keep the mastery test questions or their corrected answer sheets/feedback reports (give them feedback on blank answer sheets); also do not let students see the *Instructor's Resource Guide* because it contains the mastery tests and the answer keys to them.

Keeping Records and Providing Feedback

It may be helpful to create two types of record sheets: (a) a student record sheet and (b) a class record sheet. Use the student record sheet to record each student's performance. It should provide spaces to record the date on which a student took a test, which test was taken, and the student's score. The scores may be recorded by you or by a student assistant, or by students themselves in the case of the familiarization tests and practice tests. On the class record sheet, you can record the date, which test was taken, and the score for each student in the class. Both record sheets will be useful to you. The student record sheet will allow you to determine a baseline measure of each student's performance, and the class record sheet will reveal the standing of the class as a whole. Furthermore, by keeping a record of which mastery test was taken, you can determine which test to administer next if a student needs to repeat the mastery test several times.

Feedback on performance is extremely useful to students, and the workbook incorporates several forms of feedback:

■ In the *Student's Workbook and Training Guide,* all of the exercises in need of correction appear on right-hand pages; this is called the *draft version.* (Note that not all exercises contain errors: Some are correct as is, and it is up to the student to determine whether that is the case.) The style issue emphasized in a particular question is shaded. The left-hand pages contain the *feedback version* of the same questions (i.e., the corrected style issue is shaded or the statement "correct as is" appears at the bottom of the exercise).

■ Answers to the familiarization tests and practice tests are provided, along with the APA codes that pertain to each question.

■ APA codes are cited for each exercise so that students can consult the *Publication Manual* for review or further information.

The exercises also provide feedback and reinforcement that are less obvious. For example, each exercise not only targets a style issue that may need to be learned but also models how to use APA Style correctly. Furthermore, although an exercise may target only one element of style, other points of style are taught incidentally. The exercises also contain much information about psychology and therefore may be interesting and informative aside from their purpose of teaching APA Style. For example, some of the exercises describe particular research findings.

Once you have oriented students and they are using their workbooks, you may choose not to work directly or in class with students except for administering and scoring mastery tests, giving students feedback on the mastery tests, and keeping record sheets for each student and for the class. However, once students begin writing their own papers, giving feedback regularly and formally is valuable because you not only help them learn the material but also provide them with a role model as editor. Eventually, students learn to edit their own work. Feedback that you give to the whole class is valuable as well. To supply such feedback, you need to observe the students' progress in using the workbook and monitor performance on the practice tests and mastery tests. In this way, you can pinpoint problems being experienced by both individuals and the class as a whole.

It may be appropriate to devote some class time to reviewing a particular style point that is problematic for most students in their papers. As you review and evaluate writing assignments, be sensitive to patterns of incorrect usage and to whether students are trying to apply APA Style mechanically, without thinking about the purpose of the style component. It is also useful to encourage the exchange of feedback between students. Perhaps you can arrange to have more skilled writers work with students who are less skilled. The "master" writer can provide some of the critique that you would provide and act as a tutor for the "apprentice" student. The experience is useful for the more skilled writer as well; he or she will have to think critically to give useful feedback to a fellow student and fulfill the role of editor.

Using the Master Test Files

All of the test items in the module are drawn from a pool of items. Chapter 4 of the *Instructor's Resource Guide* contains all of the items, divided into two categories—term paper and research report—and listed in the order of the sections of the *Publication Manual*. Each question appears with the section of the *Publication Manual* (APA code) addressed by the question, the number of the question in the group of questions provided for that section of the *Publication Manual*, its correct answer, the designated tests that contain the item, and some room for you to record information about the item's use. The files are provided for those who would like to construct additional forms of tests or tests with different mixes of items. Instructors can find additional questions for some topic areas in the Related Resources section of the APA Style website (www.apastyle.org).

Using Other Resources

The *Publication Manual of the American Psychological Association*

It is essential that every student have a copy of the most recent edition (sixth edition) of the *Publication Manual*. The *Publication Manual* is the official repository of information about APA format and style, and it contains the standards for written materials in psychology as well as in many other fields. *Mastering APA Style* is designed to teach about using, not to supplant, the *Publication Manual*. The module does not cover all of the rules, standards, and guidelines that are contained in the *Publication Manual*. It focuses on key elements of style and on teaching, by application, how to use the *Publication Manual* as a resource.

Other Style and Writing Guides

The *Publication Manual* is not exhaustive in its coverage of style guidelines. Students need to be aware that there are other writing and style guides to consult on matters for which the *Publication Manual* does not provide guidance. Many institutions use *The Chicago Manual of Style*[1] as their authority. Some style guides are written for specific disciplines, such as *The Bluebook: A Uniform System of Citation*[2] for the legal profession. These kinds of style guides may be consulted when a special need arises.

The *Publication Manual* devotes two chapters to writing style. Again, although the information in these chapters presents fundamentals of good writing that apply to any kind of writing, the information is not exhaustive and focuses only on the more pertinent issues faced by writers of research articles. Should students discover that they need more assistance in writing, it would be useful for them to know that there are many good books on the topic; some of these are listed on www.apastyle.org. Students can also consult their reference librarian.

---

[1]University of Chicago Press. (2003). *The Chicago manual of style* (15th ed.). Chicago, IL: Author.
[2]*The bluebook: A uniform system of citation* (18th ed.). (2005). Cambridge, MA: Harvard Law Review Association.

Model Manuscripts and Articles

One of the most effective ways to learn is through observing models. You might want to assemble a set of examples of written work (published and unpublished), preferably with content that is relevant to the subject being taught, and distribute it to students. Bad examples can be as instructive as good ones, and you may want to supply some of each (clearly designated as a model to emulate or not emulate). Several kinds of models would be useful for teaching APA Style:

- published articles or book chapters;
- drafts of published articles or book chapters, which students can compare with the final version;
- manuscripts written by other students (so students can gain a sense of where they stand among their peers), with the author masked; and
- written work that illustrates a successful way of handling a complicated or unusual style matter that APA Style does not cover (e.g., atypical references, presentation of case studies).

Supplemental Exercises and Tests

You may want to develop your own exercises to supplement those provided in the workbook. Your experiences teaching APA Style, using this module, and using model manuscripts will probably indicate topics or skills that are not adequately covered, that need to be further explored with your particular class or a particular student, or that might be presented in a better way.

Human Resources

As we have already mentioned, instructors and fellow students can be valuable resources. One of the most important skills a writer can have is the ability to edit his or her own work. Rare is the person who produces a perfect first draft; the ability to revise and to correct errors comes with experience. Many students lack this experience, and it is often difficult to be objective about one's own work. *Mastering APA Style* is written in a way that fosters editorial skills. Students are directed to give themselves feedback by referring to the feedback version of exercises and to relevant sections of the *Publication Manual* and to apply that feedback to new situations.

Instructors and fellow students can provide more opportunities for giving, receiving, and applying feedback. The instructor's feedback is important because the student views it as having authority. However, an equally valuable experience is to encourage the exchange of feedback between students. A student who edits another student's paper gains experience being an editor, can be more objective about the flaws in a manuscript, and can practice giving constructive criticism, all skills that will be useful in editing his or her own work.

Testing Materials and Record Sheets

TERM PAPER MASTERY TEST 1

1. In an introduction, controversial issues may be discussed when relevant; however, an author must

   a. present both sides of the issue.
   b. develop sound ad hominem arguments.
   c. cite authorities out of context.
   d. disguise his or her bias.
   e. do none of the above.

2. If a paper you have written is too long, shorten it by stating points clearly, confining discussion to the specific problem under investigation, writing in the active voice, and

   a. deleting or combining data displays.
   b. using more figures.
   c. developing new theories.
   d. repeating the major points.
   e. Do none of the above.

3. Edit the following by selecting the correct format:

   Scenario and settings. The same action scenario was described in the context of eight different settings, designed to represent the eight physical–social conditions of the experiment.

   a. leave as is
   b. **Scenario and settings:** The same action scenario was described in the context of eight different settings, designed to represent the eight physical–social conditions of the experiment.
   c.   **Scenario and settings.** The same action scenario was described in the context of eight different settings, designed to represent the eight physical–social conditions of the experiment.
   d.   **Scenario and Settings.** The same action scenario was described in the context of eight different settings, designed to represent the eight physical–social conditions of the experiment.

4. Within a paragraph or sentence, identify elements in a series by

   a. Arabic numerals in parentheses.
   b. Arabic numerals underlined.
   c. lowercase letters in parentheses.
   d. lowercase letters followed by a colon.

5. Report your conclusions in

   a. the past tense.
   b. the past perfect tense.
   c. the present tense.
   d. any of the above.

6. Which of the following phrases is an example of economical writing?

   a. absolutely essential
   b. four groups saw
   c. one and the same
   d. the reason is because

7. Identify problems with clarity in the following sentences:

   We read instructions to the students. This was done to reduce experimenter bias.

   a. Both sentences are expressed clearly.
   b. The first sentence is clear, but the second starts with *this,* a vague reference pronoun, and is in the passive voice.
   c. The first sentence uses a first-person pronoun.
   d. Instructions should be read to subjects, not students.
   e. Both sentences are unclear.

8. Edit the following for the use of nonsexist language:

The researcher must avoid letting biases and expectations influence his interpretation of the results.

  a. leave as is

  b. The researcher must avoid letting biases and expectations influence the interpretation of the results.

  c. Researchers must avoid letting biases and expectations influence their interpretation of the results.

  d. Both b and c are correct.

9. Edit the following for language that shows consideration of the reader:

In the past few years, 26 states have changed their constitutions to restrict marriage to one man and one woman. There has been little research on the psychological effects of this political process on homosexual individuals.

  a. leave as is

  b. In the past few years, 26 states have changed their constitutions to restrict marriage to one man and one woman. There has been little research on the psychological effects of this political process on gay individuals.

  c. In the past few years, 26 states have changed their constitutions to restrict marriage to one man and one woman. There has been little research on the psychological effects of this political process on gay men, lesbian women, and bisexual and transgender individuals.

  d. In the past few years, 26 states have changed their constitutions to restrict marriage to one man and one woman. There has been little research on the psychological effects of this political process on deviant individuals.

10. Edit the following for verb tense:

After completing the preliminary battery of rating scales, each worker watched one of the six videotapes of a problem-solving session.

  a. leave as is

  b. After completing the preliminary battery of rating scales, each worker would watch one of the six videotapes of a problem-solving session.

  c. After completing the preliminary battery of rating scales, each worker had watched one of the six videotapes of a problem-solving session.

  d. After completing the preliminary battery of rating scales, each worker was watching one of the six videotapes of a problem-solving session.

11. Edit the following for the use of pronouns:

    The students that were assigned to the delay condition were asked to return at the same time in 3 days.

    a. leave as is
    b. The students who were assigned to the delay condition were asked to return at the same time in 3 days.
    c. The students whom were assigned to the delay condition were asked to return at the same time in 3 days.
    d. The students which were assigned to the delay condition were asked to return at the same time in 3 days.

12. Edit the following for the choice and placement of modifiers:

    Hopefully, the different types of music will induce different levels of arousal in the listeners.

    a. leave as is
    b. The different types of music will, hopefully, induce different levels of arousal in the listeners.
    c. Hopefully the different types of music will induce different levels of arousal in the listeners.
    d. We hope that the different types of music will induce different levels of arousal in the listeners.

13. Edit the following for the use of relative pronouns:

    The pictorial feedback, which was interpreted more rapidly than the verbal feedback, was remembered better.

    a. leave as is
    b. The pictorial feedback which was interpreted more rapidly than the verbal feedback was remembered better.
    c. The pictorial feedback, which was interpreted more rapidly than the verbal feedback was remembered better.
    d. The pictorial feedback that was interpreted more rapidly than the verbal feedback was remembered better.

14. End a complete declarative sentence with a

    a. prepositional clause followed by a question mark.
    b. semicolon.
    c. period.
    d. comma.

15. Edit the following for punctuation:

The participants were introduced to each of the trainers, but they were not allowed to choose their own trainer.

   a. leave as is

   b. The participants were introduced to each of the trainers but they were not allowed to choose their own trainer.

   c. The participants were introduced to each of the trainers; but they were not allowed to choose their own trainer.

   d. The participants were introduced to each of the trainers. But they were not allowed to choose their own trainer.

16. What punctuation should follow *volunteers* in the example below?

The participants in the first study were unpaid volunteers those in the second study were paid for their participation.

   a. comma

   b. colon

   c. dash

   d. semicolon

17. Edit the following for punctuation:

They have agreed on the outcome . . . informed participants perform better than do uninformed participants.

   a. leave as is

   b. They have agreed on the outcome: Informed participants perform better than do uninformed participants.

   c. They have agreed on the outcome: informed participants perform better than do uninformed participants.

   d. They have agreed on the outcome; Informed participants perform better than do uninformed participants.

18. Edit the following for punctuation:

The book—that the client selected to read aloud—was given to the client as a reward for completing the task.

   a. leave as is

   b. The book that the client selected to read aloud was given to the client as a reward for completing the task.

   c. The book, that the client selected to read aloud, was given to the client as a reward for completing the task.

   d. The book (that the client selected to read aloud) was given to the client as a reward for completing the task.

19. Put no space after

    a. the colon in ratios.
    b. periods in the initials of personal names.
    c. periods that separate parts of a reference.
    d. all of the above.
    e. none of the above.

20. Edit the following for highlighted key terms:

    Among the most common types of synesthesia are *colored grapheme synesthesia,* in which black letters and digits induce colored percepts, and *time–space synesthesia,* in which units of time (weekdays, months, digits) are laid out regularly in space (e.g., Simner et al., 2006).

    a. leave as is
    b. Among the most common types of synesthesia are "colored grapheme synesthesia," in which black letters and digits induce colored percepts, and "time–space synesthesia," in which units of time (weekdays, months, digits) are laid out regularly in space (e.g., Simner et al., 2006).
    c. Among the most common types of synesthesia are 'colored grapheme synesthesia,' in which black letters and digits induce colored percepts, and 'time–space synesthesia,' in which units of time (weekdays, months, digits) are laid out regularly in space (e.g., Simner et al., 2006).
    d. Among the most common types of synesthesia are COLORED GRAPHEME SYNESTHESIA, in which black letters and digits induce colored percepts, and TIME–SPACE SYNESTHESIA, in which units of time (weekdays, months, digits) are laid out regularly in space (e.g., Simner et al., 2006).

21. Edit the following for the punctuation of a reference citation in text:

    Basu and Jones, 2007, considered several models of legal regulation in cyberspace.

    a. leave as is
    b. Basu and Jones, in 2007, considered several models of legal regulation in cyberspace.
    c. Basu and Jones [2007] considered several models of legal regulation in cyberspace.
    d. Basu and Jones (2007) considered several models of legal regulation in cyberspace.

22. Edit the following for punctuation:

Clients on the waiting list who were assigned to the delayed-treatment condition (whose mean age and educational level (see Table 2) did not differ from those assigned to the immediate-treatment condition) were asked to return in 6 weeks.

 a. leave as is
 b. Clients on the waiting list who were assigned to the delayed-treatment condition [whose mean age and educational level (see Table 2) did not differ from those assigned to the immediate-treatment condition] were asked to return in 6 weeks.
 c. Clients on the waiting list who were assigned to the delayed-treatment condition (whose mean age and educational level [see Table 2] did not differ from those assigned to the immediate-treatment condition) were asked to return in 6 weeks.
 d. Clients on the waiting list who were assigned to the delayed-treatment condition (whose mean age and educational level, see Table 2, did not differ from those assigned to the immediate-treatment condition) were asked to return in 6 weeks.

23. Of the following examples, which represents correct hyphenation?
 a. randomly-assigned participants
 b. higher-scoring students
 c. self-report technique
 d. all of the above

24. Do not capitalize
 a. names of laws, theories, and hypotheses.
 b. trade and brand names.
 c. references to a specific department within a specific university.
 d. all of the above.
 e. b and c.

25. Select the alternative that corrects the error of abbreviation in the following sentence. (Assume that the abbreviations are being used for the first time in text.)

The TAT was given to all LH women after they watched 30 hours of TV commercials.

 a. The Thematic Apperception Test (TAT) was given
 b. to all left-handed (LH) women after
 c. they watched 30 hr of
 d. television (TV) commercials
 e. a, b, and c

26. Which Latin abbreviations are used correctly in the following example?

    Not all traditional sex role expectancies (e.g., women may cry, men should not cry) transfer into all organizational cultures, i.e., an organization's social environment. Some organizations punish traditional sex role behavior in women but not in men in military organizations, heavy industries, etc.

    a. e.g.
    b. i.e.
    c. etc.
    d. all of the above
    e. none of the above

27. When citing the source of a direct quotation that you found on the web,

    a. it is not necessary to give source information in text because it will be given in the reference list.
    b. in online material without pagination, the citation should include information to help readers locate the quotation, such as a paragraph number or heading followed by paragraph number.
    c. the citation is enclosed in parentheses after the final period of the quotation if the quoted passage is set off in a block and not put in quotation marks.
    d. b and c are correct.

28. Edit the following for the citation of a reference in text:

    Using a version of Barr et al.'s (2003) SPC procedure, Townsend, 2007, preexposed infants to a new pair (instead of to the same pair) of puppets for 1 hr per day on successive days. One member of each new pair had been preexposed the day before, whereas the other member was novel. In Phase 1, Townsend, 2007, preexposed 6-month-olds to a different pair of puppets on each of 2 days (A + B, B + C).

    a. leave as is
    b. Using a version of Barr et al.'s (2003) SPC procedure, Townsend (2007) preexposed infants to a new pair (instead of to the same pair) of puppets for 1 hr per day on successive days. One member of each new pair had been preexposed the day before, whereas the other member was novel. In Phase 1, Townsend preexposed 6-month-olds to a different pair of puppets on each of 2 days (A + B, B + C).
    c. Using a version of Barr et al.'s (2003) SPC procedure, Townsend (2007) preexposed infants to a new pair (instead of to the same pair) of puppets for 1 hr per day on successive days. One member of each new pair had been preexposed the day before, whereas the other member was novel. In Phase 1, Townsend (ibid.) preexposed 6-month-olds to a different pair of puppets on each of 2 days (A + B, B + C).
    d. Using a version of Barr et al.'s (2003) SPC procedure, Townsend (2007) preexposed infants to a new pair (instead of to the same pair) of puppets for 1 hr per day on successive days. One member of each new pair had been preexposed the day before, whereas the other member was novel. In Phase 1, Townsend (see Townsend, 2007) preexposed 6-month-olds to a different pair of puppets on each of 2 days (A + B, B + C).

29. Edit the following for the citation of a reference in text:

    Connell & Wellborn (1991) have stressed the importance of children's involvement in deciding what they would like to learn and do.

    a. leave as is
    b. J. P. Connell and J. G. Wellborn (1991) have stressed the importance of children's involvement in deciding what they would like to learn and do.
    c. Connell, and Wellborn (1991) have stressed the importance of children's involvement in deciding what they would like to learn and do.
    d. Connell and Wellborn (1991) have stressed the importance of children's involvement in deciding what they would like to learn and do.

30. Order the citations of two or more works within the same parentheses in order of their

    a. appearance in the reference list.
    b. importance.
    c. dates of publication.
    d. status as printed or electronically published works.

31. Edit the following for the citation of a specific part of an Internet source:

    One explanation might be similar to that of another fibromyalgia study (Verbunt, Pernot, & Smeets, 2008), in which the level of disability participants perceived had more to do with their mental health status and less to do with their physical condition (PDF page 4).

    a. leave as is
    b. One explanation might be similar to that of another fibromyalgia study (Verbunt, Pernot, & Smeets, 2008), in which the level of disability participants perceived had more to do with their mental health status and less to do with their physical condition (n.p.).
    c. One explanation might be similar to that of another fibromyalgia study (Verbunt, Pernot, & Smeets, 2008), in which the level of disability participants perceived had more to do with their mental health status and less to do with their physical condition (Discussion section, para. 1).
    d. One explanation might be similar to that of another fibromyalgia study (Verbunt, Pernot, & Smeets, 2008), in which the level of disability participants perceived had more to do with their mental health status and less to do with their physical condition (http://www.hqlo.com/content /pdf/1477-7525-6-8.pdf).

32. Cite personal communications that are not archived or recoverable

    a. in the text.
    b. in the reference list.
    c. Do not cite personal communications.
    d. Do a and b.

33. Edit the following for ordering the references in a reference list. Choose the sequence of numbers that indicates the correct order of the four references. (Note: The numbers are not part of APA Style but are used here for brevity.)

   1. Steege, M. W., Brown-Chidsey, R., & Mace, F. C. (2002). Best practices in evaluating interventions. In A. Thomas & J. Grimes (Eds.), *Best practices in school psychology IV* (pp. 517–534). Washington, DC: National Association of School Psychologists.

   2. Steege, M. W., & Brown-Chidsey, R. (2005). Functional behavioral assessment: The cornerstone of effective problem solving. In R. Brown-Chidsey (Ed.), *Assessment for intervention: A problem solving approach* (pp. 131–154). New York, NY: Guilford Press.

   3. Stokes, T. F., & Osnes, P. G. (1988) The developing applied technology of generalization and maintenance. In R. Horner, G. Dunlap, & R. L. Koegal (Eds.), *Generalization and maintenance: Life-style changes in applied settings* (pp. 5–19). Baltimore, MD: Brookes.

   4. Stokes, T. (1992). Discrimination and generalization. *Journal of Applied Behavior Analysis, 25,* 429–432.

   a. leave as is (i.e., 1, 2, 3, 4)
   b. 2, 1, 3, 4
   c. 2, 1, 4, 3
   d. 3, 2, 1, 4

34. The general rule to follow in alphabetizing surnames that contain articles and prepositions (e.g., Ibn Abdulaziz, von Helmholtz) is to

   a. alphabetize letter by letter.
   b. always treat the prefix as part of the middle name.
   c. treat the prefix as part of the surname if it is commonly used that way or as part of the middle name if it is not customarily used that way.
   d. a and c are correct.

35. Edit the following for the application of APA reference style:

Guimard, P., & Florin, A. (2007). *Les évaluations des enseignants en grande section de maternelle sont-elles prédictives des difficultés de lecture au cours préparatoire?* [Are teacher ratings in kindergarten predictive of reading difficulties in first grade?]. *Approche Neuropsychologique des Apprentissages Chez l'Enfant, 19,* 5–17.

   a. leave as is

   b. Guimard, P., & Florin, A. (2007). Les évaluations des enseignants en grande section de maternelle sont-elles prédictives des difficultés de lecture au cours préparatoire? [Are teacher ratings in kindergarten predictive of reading difficulties in first grade?]. *Approche Neuropsychologique des Apprentissages Chez l'Enfant, 19,* 5–17.

   c. Guimard, P., & Florin, A. (2007). Les évaluations des enseignants en grande section de maternelle sont-elles prédictives des difficultés de lecture au cours préparatoire? ("Are teacher ratings in kindergarten predictive of reading difficulties in first grade?") *Approche Neuropsychologique des Apprentissages Chez l'Enfant, 19,* 5–17.

   d. Guimard, P., & Florin, A. (2007). Les Évaluations des Enseignants en Grande Section de Maternelle Sont-elles Prédictives des Difficultés de Lecture au Cours Préparatoire? [Are Teacher Ratings in Kindergarten Predictive of Reading Difficulties in First Grade?]. *Approche Neuropsychologique des Apprentissages Chez l'Enfant, 19,* 5–17.

36. In entries in the reference list,

   a. periods are used to separate major elements (e.g., names of authors, dates, titles).

   b. a comma is used to separate the name of a periodical from volume and page number information.

   c. brackets are used to indicate nonroutine information that is important for identification and retrieval.

   d. punctuation may vary in format according to the type of source.

   e. All of the above are correct.

37. Edit the following for formatting a reference entry:

Axelman, A., & Shapiro, J. L. (2007). Does the solution warrant the problem? [Review of the DVD *Brief therapy with adolescents,* produced by APA, 2007]. *PsycCRITIQUES, 52*(51). doi:10.1037/a0009036

   a. leave as is

   b. Axelman, A., & Shapiro, J. L. (2007). Does the solution warrant the problem? [Review of the DVD *Brief therapy with adolescents,* produced by APA, 2007]. *PsycCRITIQUES, 52*(51). doi:10.1037/a0009036.

   c. Axelman, A., & Shapiro, J. L. (2007). Does the solution warrant the problem? [Review of the DVD *Brief therapy with adolescents,* produced by APA, 2007]. PsycCRITIQUES, 52(51). doi:10.1037/a0009036

   d. Axelman, A., & Shapiro, J. L. (2007). Does the solution warrant the problem? [Review of the DVD *Brief therapy with adolescents,* produced by APA, 2007]. *PsycCRITIQUES 52*(51). doi:10.1037/a0009036

38. Edit the following for line spacing:

Experiment 1

Method

    Participants. The participants were 44 sets of parents who were bringing their firstborn infant children to a well-baby clinic in a university hospital. The ages of the parents ranged from 19 to 38 years.

a. leave as is

b.

Experiment 1

Method
    Participants. The participants were 44 sets of parents who were bringing their firstborn infant children to a well-baby clinic in a university hospital. The ages of the parents ranged

from 19 to 38 years.

c.

Experiment 1

Method

    Participants. The participants were 44 sets of parents who were bringing their firstborn infant children to a well-baby clinic in a university hospital. The ages of the parents ranged from 19 to 38 years.

d.

Experiment 1

Method
    Participants. The participants were 44 sets of parents who were bringing their firstborn infant children to a well-baby clinic in a university hospital. The ages of the parents ranged from 19 to 38 years.

39. Margin size

    a. depends on the style of the typeface.

    b. should always be 1 in. (2.54 cm) at the top, bottom, and sides of the paper.

    c. depends on what section of the paper is being typed.

    d. should be 2 in. (5.08 cm) at the top and bottom and 1/2 in. (1.27 cm) at the left and right sides.

40. Indentation at paragraphs

    a. is not necessary if there is triple-spaced typing between paragraphs.

    b. should be at least 0.5 in (1.27 cm).

    c. is not necessary if block-style typing format is used for the entire page.

    d. is required in all but a few instances.

TERM PAPER MASTERY TEST 1
ANSWER SHEET AND FEEDBACK REPORT

Question Number	Answer	APA Codes	Question Number	Answer	APA Codes
1		2.01–2.05	21		4.01–4.11
2		3.01–3.07	22		4.01–4.11
3		3.02–3.04	23		4.12–4.13
4		3.02–3.04	24		4.14–4.20
5		3.05–3.06	25		4.22–4.30
6		3.08–3.11	26		4.22–4.30
7		3.08–3.11	27		6.03–6.10
8		3.12–3.17	28		6.11–6.21
9		3.12–3.17	29		6.11–6.21
10		3.18–3.19	30		6.11–6.21
11		3.20–3.23	31		6.05, 6.11–6.21
12		3.20–3.23	32		6.11–6.21
13		3.20–3.23	33		6.22–6.25
14		4.01–4.11	34		6.22–6.25
15		4.01–4.11	35		6.27–6.31
16		4.01–4.11	36		6.27–6.31
17		4.01–4.11	37		6.27– 6.31, 7.01
18		4.01–4.11	38		8.03
19		4.01–4.11	39		8.03
20		4.01–4.11	40		8.03

TERM PAPER MASTERY TEST 1
ANSWER KEY

Question Number	Answer	APA Codes	Question Number	Answer	APA Codes
1	a	2.01–2.05	21	d	4.01–4.11
2	a	3.01–3.07	22	c	4.01–4.11
3	c	3.02–3.04	23	c	4.12–4.13
4	c	3.02–3.04	24	a	4.14–4.20
5	c	3.05–3.06	25	e	4.22–4.30
6	b	3.08–3.11	26	a	4.22–4.30
7	b	3.08–3.11	27	d	6.03–6.10
8	d	3.12–3.17	28	b	6.11–6.21
9	c	3.12–3.17	29	d	6.11–6.21
10	a	3.18–3.19	30	a	6.11–6.21
11	b	3.20–3.23	31	c	6.05, 6.11–6.21
12	d	3.20–3.23	32	a	6.11–6.21
13	a	3.20–3.23	33	c	6.22–6.25
14	c	4.01–4.11	34	d	6.22–6.25
15	a	4.01–4.11	35	b	6.27–6.31
16	d	4.01–4.11	36	e	6.27–6.31
17	b	4.01–4.11	37	c	6.27–6.31, 7.01
18	b	4.01–4.11	38	d	8.03
19	a	4.01–4.11	39	b	8.03
20	a	4.01–4.11	40	d	8.03

TERM PAPER MASTERY TEST 2

1. A good title should

   a. include terms such as *A Study of* or *An Experimental Investigation of.*
   b. include abbreviations to keep it concise.
   c. be full explanatory when standing alone.
   d. b and c.

2. Edit the following for the typing of a reference list:

   1. Employee Benefit Research Institute. (1992, February). *Sources of health insurance and characteristics of the uninsured* (Issue Brief No. 123). Washington, DC: Author.
   2. Kaiser Commission on Medicaid and the Uninsured. (2007, January). *Health coverage for low-income children: Fact sheet* (Publication No. 2144-05). Washington, DC: Kaiser Family Foundation.

   a. leave as is
   b. 1. Employee Benefit Research Institute. (1992, February). *Sources of health insurance and characteristics of the uninsured* (Issue Brief No. 123). Washington, DC: Author.
      2. Kaiser Commission on Medicaid and the Uninsured (2007, January). *Health coverage for low-income children: Fact sheet* (Publication No. 2144-05). Washington, DC: Kaiser Family Foundation.
   c. Employee Benefit Research Institute. (1992, February). *Sources of health insurance and characteristics of the uninsured* (Issue Brief No. 123). Washington, DC: Author.

      Kaiser Commission on Medicaid and the Uninsured (2007, January). *Health coverage for low-income children: Fact sheet* (Publication No. 2144-05). Washington, DC: Kaiser Family Foundation.
   d. 1. Employee Benefit Research Institute. (1992, February). *Sources of health insurance and characteristics of the uninsured* (Issue Brief No. 123). Washington, DC: Author.
      2. Kaiser Commission on Medicaid and the Uninsured (2007, January). *Health coverage for low-income children: Fact sheet* (Publication No. 2144-05). Washington, DC: Kaiser Family Foundation.

3. It is important that headings convey to the reader

   a. a sense of style.
   b. the hierarchy of sections via format or appearance.
   c. organization of ideas within a study.
   d. b and c.
   e. all of the above.

4. Articles in APA journals use

    a. centered, boldface, upper and lowercase headings only.
    b. centered, italicized, upper and lowercase headings only.
    c. centered, boldface upper and lowercase headings and flush left upper and lowercase headings only.
    d. a and c.
    e. as many as five levels of headings.

5. A finished report should possess

    a. no recognizable theme or logical structure.
    b. disconnected but logical subsections.
    c. continuity in words, concepts, and thematic presentation.
    d. inferential statistical tests of the data.

6. You can check your writing for smoothness of expression by

    a. looking for sudden shifts in topic, tense, or person.
    b. having a colleague search the paper for abrupt transitions.
    c. reading the paper aloud.
    d. doing all of the above.
    e. doing a and b.

7. Redundancy, wordiness, jargon, evasiveness, and circumlocution contribute to

    a. poor economy of expression.
    b. clear scientific writing.
    c. smoothness of expression.
    d. erudite precision.
    e. a more readable, less pompous style of writing.

8. The best person to select to critique your manuscript is

    a. your spouse or another person whom you know very well.
    b. a colleague who is familiar with your work.
    c. a colleague who does not follow your work closely.
    d. a stranger off the street.

9. Edit the following for the use of nonsexist language:

In the informational intervention, a nurse met briefly with her patient so that she could assess his recent risk behavior and stage-of-change for taking an HIV test.

   a. leave as is

   b. In the informational intervention, a nurse met briefly with his patient so that he could assess her recent risk behavior and stage-of-change for taking an HIV test.

   c. In the informational intervention, a nurse met briefly with her patient so that she could assess his or her recent risk behavior and stage-of-change for taking an HIV test.

   d. In the informational intervention, a nurse met briefly with the patient to assess his or her recent risk behavior and stage-of-change for taking an HIV test.

10. Edit the following for avoiding ethnic bias:

The sample of 400 undergraduates included 250 Black students (125 women and 125 men) and 150 Asian students (75 women and 75 men).

   a. leave as is

   b. The sample of 400 undergraduates included 250 Negro students (125 women and 125 men) and 150 Asian students (75 women and 75 men).

   c. The sample of 400 undergraduates included 250 African American students (125 women and 125 men) and 150 Oriental students (75 women and 75 men).

   d. The sample of 400 undergraduates included 250 Black students (125 women and 125 men) and 150 Oriental students (75 women and 75 men).

11. Edit the following for verb tense:

If the experiment was not designed this way, the results could not be interpreted properly.

   a. leave as is

   b. If the experiment was not being designed this way, the results could not be interpreted properly.

   c. If the experiment was not designed this way, the results have not been interpreted properly.

   d. If the experiment were not designed this way, the results could not be interpreted properly.

12. Edit the following for the use of pronouns:

The volunteer whom the confederate selected had to use nonverbal gestures to convey the emotion to the other volunteers.

   a. leave as is

   b. The volunteer that the confederate selected had to use nonverbal gestures to convey the emotion to the other volunteers.

   c. The volunteer who the confederate selected had to use nonverbal gestures to convey the emotion to the other volunteers.

   d. The volunteer which the confederate selected had to use nonverbal gestures to convey the emotion to the other volunteers.

13. Misplaced modifiers can be avoided by

   a. placing adjectives and adverbs at the end of sentences wherever possible.
   b. placing adjectives and adverbs as close as possible to the words that they modify.
   c. using the word *only* for clarification.
   d. writing in the passive voice.

14. Edit the following for sentence structure:

   We recorded the difference between the performance of subjects who completed the first task and the second task.

   a. leave as is
   b. We recorded the difference between the performance of subjects who completed the first task and those who completed the second task
   c. We recorded the difference between the performance of subjects who completed the first task as well as those who completed the second task
   d. We recorded the difference between the performance of subjects who completed the first task and the performance of those who completed the second task.

15. Edit the following for punctuation:

   Culture change refers to leaving one's indigenous cultural context to spend increasing time in an alternative (e.g., White majority) one—*acculturation* refers to the extent to which those who do so retain their indigenous culture versus adopt the White-majority host culture as a result (Chun, Organista, & Marin, 2003; B. Kim & Abreu, 2001).

   a. leave as is
   b. *Culture change* refers to leaving one's indigenous cultural context to spend increasing time in an alternative (e.g., White majority) one: *acculturation* refers to the extent to which those who do so retain their indigenous culture versus adopt the White-majority host culture as a result (Chun, Organista, & Marin, 2003; B. Kim & Abreu, 2001).
   c. *Culture change* refers to leaving one's indigenous cultural context to spend increasing time in an alternative (e.g., White majority) one; *acculturation* refers to the extent to which those who do so retain their indigenous culture versus adopt the White-majority host culture as a result (Chun, Organista, & Marin, 2003; B. Kim & Abreu, 2001).
   d. *Culture change* refers to leaving one's indigenous cultural context to spend increasing time in an alternative (e.g., White majority) one, *acculturation* refers to the extent to which those who do so retain their indigenous culture versus adopt the White-majority host culture as a result (Chun, Organista, & Marin, 2003; B. Kim & Abreu, 2001).

16. Edit the following for punctuation:

Damage to the left temporal cortex may impair language comprehension; whereas damage to the left frontal cortex may impair language production.

  a. leave as is

  b. Damage to the left temporal cortex may impair language comprehension. Whereas damage to the left frontal cortex may impair language production.

  c. Damage to the left temporal cortex may impair language comprehension, whereas damage to the left frontal cortex may impair language production.

  d. Damage to the left temporal cortex may impair language comprehension—whereas damage to the left frontal cortex may impair language production.

17. Edit the following for punctuation:

These two participants, one from the first group and one from the second, were tested separately.

  a. leave as is

  b. These two participants; one from the first group and one from the second; were tested separately.

  c. These two participants—one from the first group and one from the second—were tested separately.

  d. These two participants [one from the first group and one from the second] were tested separately.

18. Which of the following examples is correctly punctuated?

  a. They have agreed on the outcome, informed participants perform better than uninformed participants.

  b. They have agreed on the outcome; Informed participants perform better than uninformed participants.

  c. They have agreed on the outcome: Informed participants perform better than uninformed participants.

  d. None of the above is correct.

19. Edit the following for punctuation:

The stimuli were six songs—matched for length, complexity of melody, and familiarity of lyrics.

  a. leave as is

  b. The stimuli were six songs: matched for length, complexity of melody, and familiarity of lyrics.

  c. The stimuli were six songs . . . matched for length, complexity of melody, and familiarity of lyrics.

  d. The stimuli were six songs matched for length, complexity of melody, and familiarity of lyrics.

20. Edit the following for the correct way to identify an ironic, coined, or invented expression:

Although we found null results for a Gene × Environment interaction with parental education at the favorable end of the inattention distribution, it is likely that our measure of good attention indicated only an absence of attention problems because it was based on ratings of inattention, not on ratings of good attention.

   a. leave as is

   b. Although we found null results for a Gene × Environment interaction with parental education at the favorable end of the inattention distribution, it is likely that our measure of GOOD attention indicated only an absence of attention problems because it was based on ratings of inattention, not on ratings of good attention.

   c. Although we found null results for a Gene × Environment interaction with parental education at the favorable end of the inattention distribution, it is likely that our measure of *good* attention indicated only an absence of attention problems because it was based on ratings of inattention, not on ratings of good attention.

   d. Although we found null results for a Gene × Environment interaction with parental education at the favorable end of the inattention distribution, it is likely that our measure of "good" attention indicated only an absence of attention problems because it was based on ratings of inattention, not on ratings of good attention.

21. Edit the following for punctuation:

Scores were higher when participants were tested in the same environment as the one in which they learned (the effect of environmental similarity is reflected in the interaction between study environment and test environment).

   a. leave as is

   b. Scores were higher when participants were tested in the same environment as the one in which they learned. (The effect of environmental similarity is reflected in the interaction between study environment and test environment.)

   c. Scores were higher when participants were tested in the same environment as the one in which they learned. (The effect of environmental similarity is reflected in the interaction between study environment and test environment).

   d. Scores were higher when participants were tested in the same environment as the one in which they learned (The effect of environmental similarity is reflected in the interaction between study environment and test environment.).

22. Edit the following for punctuation:

The heated blocks were replaced every 20 min, whereas the frozen blocks were replaced every 2 hr, and the floors were kept clean with a damp cloth (see Ward-Robinson & Honey, 2000, for further details).

   a. leave as is
   b. The heated blocks were replaced every 20 min, whereas the frozen blocks were replaced every 2 hr, and the floors were kept clean with a damp cloth (see Ward-Robinson & Honey (2000) for further details).
   c. The heated blocks were replaced every 20 min, whereas the frozen blocks were replaced every 2 hr, and the floors were kept clean with a damp cloth (see Ward-Robinson & Honey [2000] for further details).
   d. The heated blocks were replaced every 20 min, whereas the frozen blocks were replaced every 2 hr, and the floors were kept clean with a damp cloth [see Ward-Robinson & Honey (2000) for further details].
   e. The heated blocks were replaced every 20 min, whereas the frozen blocks were replaced every 2 hr, and the floors were kept clean with a damp cloth (see Ward-Robinson & Honey [2000], for further details).

23. Edit the following for the spacing of punctuation:

Some therapists select the method of treatment on a case–by–case basis.

   a. leave as is
   b. Some therapists select the method of treatment on a case by case basis.
   c. Some therapists select the method of treatment on a case-by-case basis.
   d. Some therapists select the method of treatment on a case - by - case basis.

24. Which of the following words with a prefix require a hyphen?

   a. compounds in which the base word is an abbreviation (e.g., pre-UCS)
   b. *self* compounds (e.g., self-esteem)
   c. words that could be misunderstood or misread (e.g., un-ionized)
   d. all of the above
   e. none of the above

25. Which of the following examples shows the wrong way to capitalize proper nouns?

   a. All psychology departments are reviewing their instructional effectiveness.
   b. Gardner (2004) has further suggested that a good story overcomes resistances.
   c. Dolphins are pro-Skinnerian.
   d. The study involved whether the presentation of information in preparation for cesarean delivery reduces physiologic reactivity during surgical intervention and enhances postoperative recovery.
   e. None of the above is incorrect.

26. Edit the following for the use of abbreviations to describe a procedural sequence:

    All the men read about (R), danced with (D), or smelled (S) potential romantic partners. The bachelor group received one of four romantic interest arousal sequences: RDS, SDR, RSD, or SRD.

    a. leave as is
    b. read about, danced with, smelled; smelled, danced with, read about; read about, smelled, danced with; or smelled, read about, danced with.
    c. read, danced, smelled; smelled, danced, read; read, smelled, danced; or smelled, read, danced.
    d. read about then danced with then smelled; smelled then danced with then read about; read about then smelled then danced with; or smelled then read about then danced with.

27. Is the Latin abbreviation *i.e.* used incorrectly in the following example?

    Some lonely individuals appear to be shy but are in fact isolated because of social rejection (i.e., are actively avoided and excluded by others).

    a. The parentheses should be removed.
    b. The Latin abbreviation *i.e.* should be *viz.*
    c. The abbreviation *i.e.* should be spelled out as *that is.*
    d. In the above example, *i.e.* is used correctly.

28. When quoting,

    a. provide the author's name in the text.
    b. provide the year in the text.
    c. provide the page citation in the text, or another locator such as paragraph number.
    d. include a complete reference in the reference list.
    e. do all of the above.

29. At the end of a block quote,

    a. cite the quoted source in parentheses after the final punctuation mark.
    b. cite the quoted source in parentheses before the final punctuation mark.
    c. use a footnote with a superscript number and cite the quoted source in the footnote.
    d. insert closing quotation marks before the citation.

30. Edit the following for the citation of a quotation in text:

It has been suggested that "therapists in dropout cases may have inadvertently validated parental negativity about the adolescent without adequately responding to the adolescent's needs or concerns" (Robbins et al., 2003: 541).

a. leave as is

b. It has been suggested that "therapists in the dropout cases may have inadvertently validated parental negativity about the adolescent without adequately responding to the adolescent's needs or concerns" (Robbins et al., 2003, p. 541).

c. It has been suggested that "therapists in the dropout cases may have inadvertently validated parental negativity about the adolescent without adequately responding to the adolescent's needs or concerns" (Robbins et al., second section).

d. It has been suggested that "therapists in the dropout cases may have inadvertently validated parental negativity about the adolescent without adequately responding to the adolescent's needs or concerns" (Robbins et al., PubMed, pp. 7–8).

31. From the examples below, identify the correct forms of citation:

a. In the United States, the American Cancer Society (2007) estimated that about 59,940 cases of melanoma would be diagnosed in 2007.

b. One could conclude that the longer the spacing gap, the greater the long-term retention of previously learned material (Rohrer & Pasher, 2007).

c. In 1997, Purcell found that large social gatherings could compound the difficulty of making new friends.

d. All of the above are correct.

32. Edit the following for the citation of the first mention of a reference in text:

For example, Steinberg, Lamborn, Dornbusch, and Darling (1992) demonstrated that parental involvement had a greater impact on school performance when coupled with authoritative parenting styles.

a. leave as is

b. For example, Steinberg, Lamborn, Dornbusch, & Darling (1992) demonstrated that parental involvement had a greater impact on school performance when coupled with authoritative parenting styles.

c. For example, Steinberg, et al. (1992) demonstrated that parental involvement had a greater impact on school performance when coupled with authoritative parenting styles.

d. For example, Steinberg et al. (1992) demonstrated that parental involvement had a greater impact on school performance when coupled with authoritative parenting styles.

33. Edit the following for the citation of references in text:

The study showed that among workers employed in natural resource, construction, and maintenance occupations, 12.3% of workers employed in farming, forestry, and fishing occupations and 8.1% of those in construction and extraction occupations were classified as working poor (see Table 4; U.S. Department of Labor, 2009; for complete data.)

a. leave as is

b. The study showed that among workers employed in natural resource, construction, and maintenance occupations, 12.3% of workers employed in farming, forestry, and fishing occupations and 8.1% of those in construction and extraction occupations were classified as working poor (see Table 4: U.S. Department of Labor, 2009, for complete data.)

c. The study showed that among workers employed in natural resource, construction, and maintenance occupations, 12.3% of workers employed in farming, forestry, and fishing occupations and 8.1% of those in construction and extraction occupations were classified as working poor (see Table 4; U.S. Department of Labor, 2009, for complete data.)

d. The study showed that among workers employed in natural resource, construction, and maintenance occupations, 12.3% of workers employed in farming, forestry, and fishing occupations and 8.1% of those in construction and extraction occupations were classified as working poor (see Table 4, U.S. Department of Labor, 2009, for complete data.)

34. A reference list

a. cites all works supportive of or contradictory to the text.

b. is a synonym for bibliography.

c. should include only the references cited in the article.

d. should never be used in short articles.

35. Edit the following for ordering the references in a reference list. Choose the sequence of numbers that indicates the correct order of the four references. (Note: The numbers are not part of APA Style but are used here for brevity.)

1. Chamberlin, M. T., & Zawojewski, J. (2006). A worthwhile mathematical task for students and their teachers. *Mathematics Teaching in the Middle School, 12*(2), 82–87.

2. Chamberlin-Quinlisk, C. R. (2005). Across continents or across the street: Using local resources to cultivate intercultural awareness. *Intercultural Education, 16*(5), 469–479.

3. Chamberlin, S. A., Buchanan, & M. Vercimak, D. (2007). Serving twice-exceptional preschoolers: Blending gifted education and early childhood special education practices in assessment and program planning. *Journal for the Education of the Gifted, 30*(3), 372–394.

4. Chamberlin, S. A. (2008). An examination of articles in gifted education and multicultural education journals. *Journal for the Education of the Gifted, 32*(1), 86–99.

a. leave as is (i.e., 1, 2, 3, 4)

b. 1, 4, 3, 2

c. 1, 2, 4, 3

d. 2, 1, 4, 3

36. A reference list entry should have

    a. the author's surname and initials in inverted order (e.g., McMahon, P. M.).
    b. the journal article DOI if available
    c. the author's surname only.
    d. a and b.

37. Edit the following for the application of APA reference style:

    Sillick, T. J., & Schutte, N. S. (2006). Emotional intelligence and self-esteem mediate between perceived early parental love and adult happiness. E-Journal of Applied Psychology, 2(2), 38–48. Retrieved from http://ojs.lib.swin.edu.au/index.php/ejap

    a. leave as is
    b. Sillick, T. J., & Schutte, N. S. (2006). Emotional intelligence and self-esteem mediate between perceived early parental love and adult happiness. *E-Journal of Applied Psychology, 2*(2), 38–48. Retrieved from http://ojs.lib.swin.edu.au/index.php/ejap
    c. Sillick, T. J., & Schutte, N. S. (2006). Emotional intelligence and self-esteem mediate between perceived early parental love and adult happiness. E-Journal of Applied Psychology, 2(2), 38–48. [HTML file]
    d. Sillick, T. J., & Schutte, N. S. (2006). Emotional intelligence and self-esteem mediate between perceived early parental love and adult happiness. *E-Journal of Applied Psychology, 2*(2), 38–48. (no DOI)

38. The use of a uniform typeface and font size

    a. enhances readability for the reviewer.
    b. should not be used for the reference list.
    c. allows the publisher to estimate the page length.
    d. a and c.

39. Edit the following by selecting the correct spacing arrangement:

> Effects of Academic Stress on Interpersonal Relationships
> of Male and Female Students
> Whatever the academic standards of a college or university, there
> always seem to be students who do not meet the standards.

   a. leave as is

   b.

> Effects of Academic Stress on Interpersonal Relationships
> of Male and Female Students

> Whatever the academic standards of a college or university there
> always seem to be students who do not meet the standards.

   c.

> Effects of Academic Stress on Interpersonal Relationships
> of Male and Female Students

> Whatever the academic standards of a college or university there
> always seem to be students who do not meet the standards.

   d.

> Effects of Academic Stress on Interpersonal Relationships
> of Male and Female Students

> Whatever the academic standards of a college or university there

> always seem to be students who do not meet the standards.

40. Identify the numbering error in the following example of the first page of text of a manuscript that has a title page and an abstract page:

Running head: UNDERGRADUATE HELPING SKILLS TRAINING   3

   a. The numbering is correct.
   b. The first text page is numbered with a 1.
   c. A number is not put on the first page.
   d. Page numbers are typed flush with the left margin.

TERM PAPER MASTERY TEST 2
ANSWER SHEET AND FEEDBACK REPORT

Question Number	Answer	APA Codes	Question Number	Answer	APA Codes
1	_____	2.01–2.11	21	_____	4.01–4.11
2	_____	2.11	22	_____	4.01–4.11
3	_____	3.02–3.03	23	_____	4.12–4.13
4	_____	3.02–3.03	24	_____	4.12–4.13
5	_____	3.05–3.06	25	_____	4.14–4.20
6	_____	3.05–3.06	26	_____	4.22–4.29
7	_____	3.07–3.11	27	_____	4.22–4.29
8	_____	3.07–3.11	28	_____	6.03–6.10
9	_____	3.12–3.17	29	_____	6.03–6.10
10	_____	3.12–3.17	30	_____	6.03–6.10
11	_____	3.18–3.19	31	_____	6.11–6.21
12	_____	3.20–3.23	32	_____	6.11–6.21
13	_____	3.20–3.23	33	_____	6.11–6.21
14	_____	3.20–3.23	34	_____	6.22–6.25
15	_____	4.01–4.11	35	_____	6.22–6.25
16	_____	4.01–4.11	36	_____	6.27–6.32
17	_____	4.01–4.11	37	_____	6.27–6.32, 7.01
18	_____	4.01–4.11	38	_____	8.03
19	_____	4.01–4.11	39	_____	8.03
20	_____	4.01–4.11	40	_____	8.03

TERM PAPER MASTERY TEST 2
ANSWER KEY

Question Number	Answer	APA Codes	Question Number	Answer	APA Codes
1	c	2.01–2.11	21	b	4.01–4.11
2	c	2.11	22	a	4.01–4.11
3	d	3.02–3.03	23	c	4.12–4.13
4	e	3.02–3.03	24	d	4.12–4.13
5	c	3.05–3.06	25	e	4.14–4.20
6	d	3.05–3.06	26	a	4.22–4.29
7	a	3.07–3.11	27	d	4.22–4.29
8	c	3.07–3.11	28	e	6.03–6.10
9	d	3.12–3.17	29	a	6.03–6.10
10	a	3.12–3.17	30	b	6.03–6.11
11	d	3.18–3.19	31	d	6.11–6.21
12	a	3.20–3.23	32	a	6.11–6.21
13	b	3.20–3.23	33	d	6.11–6.21
14	d	3.20–3.23	34	c	6.22–6.25
15	c	4.01–4.11	35	b	6.22–6.25
16	c	4.01–4.11	36	d	6.27–6.32
17	c	4.01–4.11	37	b	6.27–6.32, 7.01
18	c	4.01–4.11	38	d	8.03
19	d	4.01–4.11	39	a	8.03
20	d	4.01–4.11	40	a	8.03

TERM PAPER MASTERY TEST 3

1. The introduction of a manuscript

    a. discusses the importance of the problem and why it needs research.
    b. describes in detail how the study was conducted.
    c. describes the sample adequately.
    d. includes information essential to comprehend and replicate the study.

2. In the Results section of a manuscript,

    a. report the data in sufficient detail to justify your conclusions.
    b. include a clear statement of support or nonsupport for your original hypotheses.
    c. provide dates defining the periods of recruitment and follow-up and the primary sources of the potential subjects, where appropriate.
    d. a and c are correct.

3. Edit the following for the format of a reference list:

REFERENCES

Baron, J. B., & Sternberg, R. J. (1987). *Teaching thinking skills: Theory and practice.* San Francisco, CA: Freeman.

Nickerson, R. S., Perkins, D. N., & Smith, E. E. (1985). *The teaching of thinking.* Hillsdale, NJ: Erlbaum.

    a. leave as is
    b.

References

Baron, I. B., & Sternberg, R. J. (1987). *Teaching thinking skills: Theory and practice.* San Francisco, CA: Freeman.

Nickerson, R. S., Perkins, D. N., & Smith, E. E. (1985). *The teaching of thinking.* Hillsdale, NJ: Erlbaum.

    c.

References

Baron, J. B., & Sternberg, R. I. (1987). *Teaching thinking skills: Theory and practice.* San Francisco, CA: Freeman.

Nickerson, R. S., Perkins, D. N., & Smith, E. E. (1985). *The teaching of thinking.* Hillsdale, NJ: Erlbaum.

    d.

References

Baron, J. B., & Sternberg, R. J. (1987). *Teaching thinking skills: Theory and practice.* San Francisco, CA: Freeman.

Nickerson, R. S., Perkins, D. N., & Smith, E. E. (1985). *The teaching of thinking.* Hillsdale, NJ: Erlbaum.

4. Before you begin to write, you should consider

   a. statistical analyses.
   b. length and structure of your paper.
   c. the hypotheses.
   d. all of the above.

5. A heading that is flush left

   a. should be boldface and typed in uppercase and lowercase letters.
   b. should be italicized.
   c. may be typed in all uppercase letters or all lowercase letters depending on the heading's level.
   d. must end with a period.

6. Level 5 headings (indented, boldface, italicized lowercase paragraph headings ending with a period) are used

   a. only when the article requires five levels of headings.
   b. in short articles where one level of heading is sufficient.
   c. after any other type of heading in single-experiment papers.
   d. only in multiexperiment papers.

7. In scientific writing, continuity

   a. is achieved partly by proper use of punctuation marks and transitional words.
   b. is improved by avoiding the use of pronouns.
   c. is enhanced by using many commas.
   d. is not really necessary.

8. Verb tense should

   a. be varied to keep the reader's interest.
   b. never change.
   c. always be the past or past perfect.
   d. be consistent within a section of a paper such as the Results.

9. A writer must be careful when using the pronouns *this, that, these,* and *those.* The writer can eliminate or reduce the vagueness of these pronouns by

   a. using them to modify a noun (e.g., this frenulum, that hypothalamus, these electrodes, those mice).
   b. using them frequently.
   c. clarifying what is being referred to for the reader.
   e. a and c

10. Which of the following is a good strategy for improving writing style?

    a. Revise the first draft after a delay.

    b. Use an outline.

    c. Ask a colleague to review and critique the draft.

    d. Do all of the above.

11. Edit the following for the use of nonsexist language:

    Before an experienced web developer attempts a particular solution, he tries to relate the problem structure to other problems he has solved successfully.

    a. leave as is

    b. Before an experienced web developer attempts a particular solution, he/she tries to relate the problem structure to other problems he/she has solved successfully.

    c. Before experienced web developers attempt a particular solution, they try to relate the problem structure to other problems they have solved successfully.

    d. none of the above

12. Edit the following for avoiding ethnic bias:

    Similarly, in community-based studies of diagnosed psychiatric disorders, uncultured migrant Mexican farmworkers, when compared with native-born Mexican Americans and with non-Hispanic White Americans, exhibited the lowest rates of psychiatric disorder (Alderete, Vega, Kolody, & Aguilar-Gaxiola, 2000).

    a. leave as is

    b. Similarly, in community-based studies of diagnosed psychiatric disorders, low-acculturated migrant Mexican farmworkers, when compared with native-born Mexican Americans and with the non-Hispanic White majority, exhibited the lowest rates of psychiatric disorder (Alderete, Vega, Kolody, & Aguilar-Gaxiola, 2000).

    c. Similarly, in community-based studies of diagnosed psychiatric disorders, low-acculturated migrant Mexican farmworkers, when compared with native-born Mexican Americans and with non-Hispanic White Americans, exhibited the lowest rates of psychiatric disorder (Alderete, Vega, Kolody, & Aguilar-Gaxiola, 2000).

    d. Similarly, in community-based studies of diagnosed psychiatric disorders, low-acculturated migrant Mexican farmworkers, when compared with the more sophisticated native-born Mexican Americans and with non-Hispanic normal White Americans, exhibited the lowest rates of psychiatric disorder (Alderete, Vega, Kolody, & Aguilar-Gaxiola, 2000).

13. Edit the following for grammar:

    The six stimulus were presented to each participant simultaneously.

    a. leave as is

    b. The six stimuli were presented to each participant simultaneously.

    c. The six stimuli was presented to each participant simultaneously.

    d. The six stimuluses were presented to each participant simultaneously.

14. Edit the following for the use of pronouns:

The team achieved a 38% improvement in their scores after undergoing imagery training.

   a. leave as is
   b. The team achieved a 38% improvement in its scores after undergoing imagery training.
   c. The team achieved a 38% improvement in each of their scores after undergoing imagery training.
   d. The team achieved a 38% improvement in scores after undergoing imagery training.

15. Which of the following sentences illustrates the correct use of the word *while* in scientific writing?

   a. Skutley (2003) found that participants performed well, while Jackson (2006) found that participants did poorly.
   b. While these findings are unusual, they are not unique.
   c. Skutley found that participants performed well while listening to music.
   d. All of the above are correct.

16. Edit the following for sentence structure:

Successful problem solvers were both more adept at representing the problem and using heuristics.

   a. leave as is
   b. Successful problem solvers were both more adept at representing the problem as well as using heuristics.
   c. Successful problem solvers were more adept both at representing the problem and at using heuristics.
   d. Successful problem solvers were more adept at both representing the problem and at using heuristics.

17. Edit the following for punctuation:

Optimal-level theories of motivation follow a homeostatic model. Opponent-process theories were advanced to account for addiction and other phenomena.

   a. leave as is
   b. Optimal-level theories of motivation follow a homeostatic model, opponent-process theories were advanced to account for addiction and other phenomena.
   c. Optimal-level theories of motivation follow a homeostatic model—Opponent-process theories were advanced to account for addiction and other phenomena.
   d. Optimal-level theories of motivation follow a homeostatic model; Opponent-process theories were advanced to account for addiction and other phenomena.

18. Edit the following for correct punctuation:

    The floor was covered with cedar shavings and paper was available for shredding and nest building.

    a. The sentence is correct as it stands.
    b. Put a semicolon after *shavings.*
    c. Put a comma after *shavings.*
    d. Put a comma after *floor.*

19. Edit the following for punctuation:

    Thus, the light status for the three trials in the four conditions was on, off, on: off, on, off: on, on, on: or off, off, off.

    a. leave as is
    b. Thus, the light status for the three trials in the four conditions was on, off, on, off, on, off, on, on, on, or off, off, off.
    c. Thus, the light status for the three trials in the four conditions was on, off, and on, or off, on, and off, or on, on, and on, or off, off, and off.
    d. Thus, the light status for the three trials in the four conditions was on, off, on; off, on, off; on, on, on; or off, off, off.

20. Which sentence is correct?

    a. The digits were shown in the following order: 3, 2, 4, 1.
    b. The digits were shown in the following order, 3, 2, 4, 1.
    c. The digits were shown in the following order; 3, 2, 4, 1.
    d. The digits were shown in the following order—3, 2, 4, 1.

21. Edit the following for punctuation:

    The four participants—two in the vicarious condition, one in the direct condition, and one in the control condition—who recognized the confederate as a fellow student were excused from the second part of the experiment.

    a. leave as is
    b. The four participants, two in the vicarious condition, one in the direct condition, and one in the control condition, who recognized the confederate as a fellow student were excused from the second part of the experiment.
    c. The four participants: two in the vicarious condition, one in the direct condition, and one in the control condition: who recognized the confederate as a fellow student were excused from the second part of the experiment.
    d. The four participants . . . two in the vicarious condition, one in the direct condition, and one in the control condition . . . who recognized the confederate as a fellow student were excused from the second part of the experiment.

22. When introducing slang or a coined expression, use

    a. double quotation marks the first time the expression is used.
    b. double quotation marks every time it is used.
    c. dashes every time it is used.
    d. single quotation marks the first time it is used.

23. Edit the following for punctuation:

    The length of utterances increases dramatically between the ages of 18 and 60 months. See Figure 1.

    a. leave as is
    b. The length of utterances increases dramatically between the ages of 18 and 60 months (see Figure 1).
    c. The length of utterances increases dramatically between the ages of 18 and 60 months (see Figure 1.).
    d. The length of utterances increases dramatically between the ages of 18 and 60 months, see Figure 1.

24. Edit the following for spacing and punctuation:

    Physical and psychological measures of the members of the medical emergency staff—nurses and doctors—were taken immediately and 48 hr after the crisis.

    a. leave as is
    b. Physical and psychological measures of the members of the medical emergency staff - nurses and doctors - were taken immediately and 48 hr after the crisis.
    c. Physical and psychological measures of the members of the medical emergency staff-nurses and doctors-were taken immediately and 48 hr after the crisis.
    d. Physical and psychological measures of the members of the medical emergency staff — nurses and doctors — were taken immediately and 48 hr after the crisis.

25. The standard spelling reference for APA journals is

    a. the most recent edition of *Merriam-Webster's Collegiate Dictionary.*
    b. the *British-American Speller.*
    c. the *Random House Dictionary.*
    d. *Merriam-Webster's Collegiate Dictionary* for standard spelling; *APA Dictionary of Psychology* for psychological terms.

26. Identify the example with incorrect use of capitalization:

    a. The conclusion is obvious: forgiveness is not granted to the stronger partner in an inequitable relationship.
    b. The students reviewed the criticism of the article, "Ultrasonic Vocalizations Are Elicited From Rat Pups."
    c. Undergraduates were advised to take an introductory psychology course.
    d. The research described an associative learning model.

27. Which noun is incorrectly capitalized in the following example?

    Bern's Theory of Self-Perception suggests that a woman will like a stranger more after she dances with him.

    a. Theory
    b. Self
    c. Perception
    d. Bern's
    e. All of the above are incorrect except d.

28. Edit the following for correct use of abbreviations:

    Three kinds of scene identification tasks were given to the police officers: a murder scene, a robbery scene, and an assault scene. The identification tasks were given in either an MS-RS-AS or AS-RS-MS sequence.

    a. Define the abbreviations earlier by putting them within parentheses following the terms they abbreviated.
    b. Use no abbreviations because they are not known by most readers.
    c. Make no change because the connection between terms and abbreviations is obvious.
    d. Make no change because the writer used standard abbreviations.

29. Which abbreviations are used only in parentheses?

    a. vs., kg, i.e.
    b. i.e., cf., viz.
    c. e.g., etc., min
    d. none of the above.
    e. all of the above.

30. Identify the error in the following quotation:

    Confusing this issue is the overlapping nature of roles in palliative care, whereby "medical needs are met by those in the medical disciplines; nonmedical needs may be addressed by anyone on the team" (Csikai & Chaitin, 2006).

    a. There are no errors.
    b. The quote should be in block form.
    c. The entire sentence should be in quotation marks.
    d. The page number needs to be cited.

31. Any direct, short quotation (fewer than 400 words) of text from an APA journal or book must

    a. be accompanied by a reference citation.
    b. include a page number.
    c. be used only with the permission of the copyright owner.
    d. be footnoted if copyrighted.
    e. Answers a and b are correct.

32. When a work has more than two authors and fewer than six authors, cite

    a. all of the authors every time the reference occurs in text.

    b. all of the authors the first time the reference occurs in text; use the surname of the first author followed by *et al.* in subsequent citations.

    c. the surname of the first author followed by *et al.* every time the reference occurs in text.

    d. none of the above.

33. When a reference source is cited in the text,

    a. each author's surname must be cited every time a reference occurs in the text when there are two authors of a single work.

    b. every author's surname is used only the first time a reference is made when a work has more than two and fewer than six authors.

    c. only the first author's surname is used followed by *et al.* every time the reference is made when a work has six or more authors.

    d. All of the above are correct.

    e. Only b and c are correct.

34. Edit the following for the citation of references in text:

    Several studies have attempted to explain the construct of temperament (Derryberry & Reed, 2005a, 2005b, in-press-a; Rothbart, 2003a, 2003b).

    a. leave as is

    b. Several studies have attempted to explain the construct of temperament (Derryberry & Reed, 2005a, b, in-press-a; Rothbart, 2003a, b).

    c. Several studies have attempted to explain the construct of temperament (Derryberry & Reed, 2005a; Derryberry & Reed, 2005b; Derryberry & Reed, in-press-a; Rothbart, 2003a; Rothbart, 2003b).

    d. Several studies have attempted to explain the construct of temperament (Rothbart, 2003a, 2003b; Derryberry & Reed, 2005a, 2005b, in-press-a).

35. Edit the following for the citation of a specific part of a reference in text:

    Lock (1999, chap. 3), an anthropologist, also developed the idea that the meaning of illness is a crucial issue in the understanding of health and illness.

    a. leave as is

    b. Lock (1999, ch. 3), an anthropologist, also developed the idea that the meaning of illness is a crucial issue in the understanding of health and illness.

    c. Lock (1999, chapter 3), an anthropologist, also developed the idea that the meaning of illness is a crucial issue in the understanding of health and illness.

    d. Lock (1999, Chapter 3), an anthropologist, also developed the idea that the meaning of illness is a crucial issue in the understanding of health and illness.

36. The reference list at the end of a journal article

    a. includes personal communications, such as letters, memoranda, and informal electronic communications.
    b. provides the information necessary to identify and retrieve each source.
    c. includes only references that document the article and provide recoverable data.
    d. b and c.
    e. all of the above.

37. Edit the following for ordering the references in a reference list. Choose the sequence of numbers that indicates the correct order of the four references. (Note: The numbers are not part of APA Style but are used here for brevity.)

    1. Allport, G. W. (1930–1967). Correspondence. Gordon W. Allport Papers (HUG 4118.10), Harvard University Archives, Cambridge, MA.
    2. Allport, G. W. (1979). *The nature of prejudice* (25th anniversary ed.). Cambridge, MA: Addison-Wesley. (Original work published 1954)
    3. Allport, G. W. (2001). Introduction. In S. Akhilananda, *Hindu psychology: Its meaning for the West* (pp. ix–x). London, England: Routledge. (Original work published 1948)
    4. Allport, G. W., & Ross, M. J. (1967). Personal religious orientation and prejudice. *Journal of Personality and Social Psychology, 5*, 432–443.

    a. leave as is (i.e., 1, 2, 3, 4)
    b. 3, 2, 1, 4
    c. 4, 2, 3, 1
    d. 1, 3, 2, 4

38. Edit the following for the application of APA reference style:

    Marshall-Pescini, S., & Whiten, A. (2008). Social learning of nut-cracking behavior in East African sanctuary-living chimpanzees (*Pan troglodytes schweinfurthii*) [Supplemental material]. *Journal of Comparative Psychology, Vol. 122*, 186–194. doi:10.1037/0735-7036.122.2.186

    a. leave as is
    b. Marshall-Pescini, S., & Whiten, A. (2008). Social learning of nut-cracking behavior in East African sanctuary-living chimpanzees (*Pan troglodytes schweinfurthii*) [Supplemental material]. *Journal of Comparative Psychology, 122*, 186–194. doi: 10.1037/0735-7036.122.2.186
    c. Marshall-Pescini, S., & Whiten, A. (2008). Social learning of nut-cracking behavior in East African sanctuary-living chimpanzees (*Pan troglodytes schweinfurthii*)—Supplemental material. *Journal of Comparative Psychology,* 122, 186–194. doi: 10.1037/0735-7036.122.2.186
    d. Marshall-Pescini, S., & Whiten, A. (2008). Social learning of nut-cracking behavior in East African sanctuary-living chimpanzees (*Pan troglodytes schweinfurthii*) [Supplemental material]. *Journal of Comparative Psychology,* 122, 186–194. Retrieved from doi. 10.1037/0735-7036.122.2.186

39. Edit the following for the application of APA reference style:

Bronfenbrenner, U. (1970). *Two worlds of childhood: U.S. and U.S.S.R.* New York, NY: Russell Sage
   Foundation.

   a. leave as is
   b. Bronfenbrenner, U. *Two worlds of childhood: U.S. and U.S.S.R.* New York, NY: Russell Sage
      Foundation. (1970).
   c. Bronfenbrenner, U. (1970). "Two worlds of childhood: U.S. and U.S.S.R." New York, NY: Russell
      Sage Foundation.
   d. Bronfenbrenner, U. (1970). *Two Worlds of Childhood: U.S. and U.S.S.R.* New York, NY: Russell
      Sage Foundation.

40. A uniform, serif typeface

   a. should be used for all text, with the exception of figures.
   b. helps the publisher estimate the article length.
   c. improves readability.
   d. all of the above.

41. Edit the following by selecting the correct spacing:

Naturalistic Observation of the Duration and Distribution
of Sleep Across the Life Span

   Although individual differences within each age group are certainly recognized, our
society has general notions about the sleep patterns—duration and distribution—of people
at different ages.

   a. leave as is
   b.

Naturalistic Observation of the Duration and Distribution

of Sleep Across the Life Span

   Although individual differences within each age group are certainly recognized, our
society has general notions about the sleep patterns—duration and distribution—of people
at different ages.

   c.

Naturalistic Observation of the Duration and Distribution
of Sleep Across the Life Span

   Although individual differences within each age group are certainly recognized, our
society has general notions about the sleep patterns—duration and distribution—of people
at different ages.

   d.

Naturalistic Observation of the Duration and Distribution
of Sleep Across the Life Span

   Although individual differences within each age group are certainly recognized, our
society has general notions about the sleep patterns—duration and distribution—of people
at different ages.

42. Edit the following for numbering of an abstract page:

Running head: PROCRASTINATION   1

   a. leave as is

   b. Change the page number 1 to the number 2.

   c. The page number is correct, but it should not be typed flush with the right margin.

   d. The page number is correct, but the short title should not appear on the abstract page.

TERM PAPER MASTERY TEST 3
ANSWER SHEET AND FEEDBACK REPORT

Question Number	Answer	APA Codes	Question Number	Answer	APA Codes
1		2.01–2.08	22		4.01–4.11
2		2.01–2.08	23		4.01–4.11
3		2.11	24		4.01–4.11
4		3.01–3.03	25		4.12–4.13
5		3.02–3.03	26		4.14–4.20
6		3.02–3.03	27		4.14–4.20
7		3.05–3.06	28		4.22–4.30
8		3.05–3.06	29		4.22–4.30
9		3.08–3.09	30		6.03–6.10
10		3.10–3.11	31		6.03–6.10
11		3.12–3.17	32		6.11–6.21
12		3.12–3.17	33		6.11–6.21
13		3.18–3.19	34		6.11–6.21
14		3.20–3.23	35		6.11–6.21
15		3.20–3.23	36		6.22–6.25
16		3.20–3.23	37		6.22–6.25
17		4.01–4.11	38		6.27–6.32, 7.01
18		4.01–4.11	39		6.27–6.32, 7.02
19		4.01–4.11	40		8.03
20		4.01–4.11	41		8.03
21		4.01–4.11	42		8.03

TERM PAPER MASTERY TEST 3
ANSWER KEY

Question Number	Answer	APA Codes	Question Number	Answer	APA Codes
1	a	2.01–2.08	22	a	4.01–4.11
2	d	2.01–2.08	23	b	4.01–4.11
3	c	2.11	24	a	4.01–4.11
4	b	3.01–3.03	25	d	4.12–4.13
5	a	3.02–3.03	26	a	4.14–4.20
6	a	3.02–3.03	27	e	4.14–4.20
7	a	3.05–3.06	28	a	4.22–4.30
8	d	3.05–3.06	29	b	4.22–4.30
9	e	3.08–3.09	30	d	6.03–6.10
10	d	3.10–3.11	31	e	6.03–6.10
11	c	3.12–3.17	32	b	6.11–6.21
12	c	3.12–3.17	33	d	6.11–6.21
13	b	3.18–3.19	34	a	6.11–6.21
14	b	3.20–3.23	35	d	6.11–6.21
15	c	3.20–3.23	36	d	6.22–6.25
16	c	3.20–3.23	37	a	6.22–6.25
17	a	4.01–4.11	38	b	6.27–6.32, 7.01
18	c	4.01–4.11	39	a	6.27–6.32, 7.02
19	d	4.01–4.11	40	d	8.03
20	a	4.01–4.11	41	d	8.03
21	a	4.01–4.11	42	b	8.03

TERM PAPER MASTERY TEST 4

1. Headings are important in scientific writing because they

    a. satisfy the requirements of APA style.
    b. establish the hierarchy of sections via format or appearance.
    c. fulfill a tradition in scientific writing.
    d. are used in place of paragraph indentation.
    e. All of the above are correct.

2. In articles in which one level of heading is sufficient, use

    a. a flush left, boldface, uppercase and lowercase heading (Level 2).
    b. a centered, boldface, uppercase and lowercase heading (Level 1).
    c. any type (level) of heading.
    d. none of the above.

3. Readers will better understand your ideas if you aim for continuity by

    a. using punctuation to show relationships between ideas.
    b. using transitional words such as time links (e.g., *then* or *next*) or cause–effect links (e.g., *therefore* or *consequently*).
    c. using contrast links (*however* or *whereas*).
    d. using all of the above.
    e. using only a and b.

4. Synonyms should be used

    a. with care because they may suggest subtle differences.
    b. as much as possible to make the manuscript interesting.
    c. whenever the same word is mentioned three or more times in one paragraph.
    d. only in the conclusion.

5. Colloquial expressions such as *the wind in his sails died* or approximations of quantity such as *the lion's share of*

    a. reduce word precision and clarity.
    b. add warmth to dull scientific prose.
    c. have a place even in serious scientific writing.
    d. can be used to enhance communication.
    e. are more acceptable in written than in oral communication.

6. Choose the best strategy for improving your writing style:

   a. Write from an outline.

   b. Put aside the first draft, then reread it after a delay.

   c. Ask a colleague to critique the first draft for you.

   d. Begin writing close to a deadline to enhance your motivation.

   e. Any of the above except d can be used, but the strategy must match your personality and work habits.

7. Edit the following for the use of nonsexist language:

   They predicted that men would be selected more frequently as partners for the cognitive tasks and that females would be chosen more frequently for the interpersonal tasks.

   a. leave as is

   b. They predicted that males would be selected more frequently as partners for the cognitive tasks and that nonmales would be chosen more frequently for the interpersonal tasks.

   c. They predicted that men would be selected more frequently as partners for the cognitive tasks and that women would be chosen more frequently for the interpersonal tasks.

   d. They predicted that guys would be selected more frequently as partners for the cognitive tasks and that girls would be chosen more frequently for the interpersonal tasks.

8. Edit the following for avoiding ethnic bias:

   Participation in ethnic celebrations was compared for Oriental immigrants and their first-, second-, and third-generation counterparts of the same cohort.

   a. leave as is

   b. Participation in ethnic celebrations was compared for immigrants from Oriental countries and their first-, second-, and third-generation counterparts of the same cohort.

   c. Participation in ethnic celebrations was compared for Oriental immigrants and first-, second-, and third-generation Orientals of the same cohort.

   d. Participation in ethnic celebrations was compared for Asian immigrants and for first-, second-, and third-generation Asian Americans of the same cohort.

9. Which of the following sentences is an example of correct agreement between subject and verb?

   a. The percentage of correct responses increase with practice.

   b. The data indicate that Brenda was correct.

   c. The phenomena occurs every 100 years.

   d. Neither the participants nor the confederate were in the classroom.

10. Edit the following for the placement of modifiers:

    The victims reported to trained volunteers still experiencing anxiety.

    a. leave as is
    b. The victims reported to trained volunteers, still experiencing anxiety.
    c The victims, still experiencing anxiety, reported to trained volunteers.
    d. The victims, reported to trained volunteers, still experiencing anxiety.

11. Which of the following sentences is incorrect according to the preferred style stated in the APA *Publication Manual?*

    a. While these findings are unusual, they are not unique.
    b. Although these findings are unusual, they are not unique.
    c. These findings are unusual, but they are not unique.
    d. All of the above are incorrect.

12. Edit the following for sentence structure:

    Interviewees are often instructed to dress conservatively, to pay attention to their nonverbal communications, and that they should ask a few job-related questions of the interviewer.

    a. leave as is
    b. Interviewees are often instructed to dress conservatively, to pay attention to their nonverbal communications, and to ask a few job-related questions of the interviewer.
    c. Interviewees are often instructed to dress conservatively, pay attention to their nonverbal communications, and that they should be prepared to ask a few job-related questions of the interviewer.
    d. Interviewees are often instructed to dress conservatively and pay attention to their nonverbal communications, and that they should ask a few job-related questions of the interviewer.

13. Edit the following for punctuation:

    According to Piaget, the four stages of intellectual development are the sensorimotor stage, the preoperational stage, the concrete-operational stage, and the formal-operational stage.

    a. leave as is
    b. According to Piaget, the four stages of intellectual development are the sensorimotor stage, the preoperational stage, the concrete-operational stage and the formal-operational stage.
    c. According to Piaget, the four stages of intellectual development are the sensorimotor stage; the preoperational stage; the concrete-operational stage; and the formal-operational stage.
    d. According to Piaget, the four stages of intellectual development are the sensorimotor stage— the preoperational stage—the concrete-operational stage—and the formal-operational stage.

14. Use a comma

    a. before *and* and *or* in a series of three or more items.
    b. between the two parts of a compound predicate.
    c. to separate two independent clauses joined by a conjunction.
    d. in all of the above instances.
    e. in instances a and c above.

15. Edit the following for punctuation:

    From shortest to longest wavelength, the colors of the visible spectrum appear in the following order: blue-purple, blue, blue-green, green, yellow-green, yellow, orange, and red.

    a. leave as is
    b. From shortest to longest wavelength, the colors of the visible spectrum appear in the following order—blue-purple, blue, blue-green, green, yellow-green, yellow, orange, and red.
    c. From shortest to longest wavelength, the colors of the visible spectrum appear in the following order: Blue-purple, blue, blue-green, green, yellow-green, yellow, orange, and red.
    d. From shortest to longest wavelength, the colors of the visible spectrum appear in the following order . . . blue-purple, blue, blue-green, green, yellow-green, yellow, orange, and red.

16. The em dash is used

    a. to indicate a sudden interruption in the continuity of a sentence.
    b. in APA articles only with permission of the manuscript editor.
    c. frequently in APA articles in the statistical section.
    d. by Type A psychologists.

17. Edit the following for punctuation:

    Kazdin's (2008) article, *Evidence-Based Treatments and Delivery of Psychological Services: Shifting Our Emphases to Increase Impact,* discusses evidence-based treatments as currently studied in relation to an overarching goal of interventions, namely, to reduce the burden of mental illness and the full range of social, emotional, and behavioral problems leading to impairment.

    a. leave as is
    b. Kazdin's (2008) article titled Evidence-Based Treatments and Delivery of Psychological Services: Shifting Our Emphases to Increase Impact, discusses evidence-based treatments as currently studied in relation to an overarching goal of interventions, namely, to reduce the burden of mental illness and the full range of social, emotional, and behavioral problems leading to impairment.
    c. Kazdin's (2008) article, 'Evidence-Based Treatments and Delivery of Psychological Services: Shifting Our Emphases to Increase Impact,' discusses evidence-based treatments as currently studied in relation to an overarching goal of interventions, namely, to reduce the burden of mental illness and the full range of social, emotional, and behavioral problems leading to impairment.
    d. Kazdin's (2008) article, "Evidence-Based Treatments and Delivery of Psychological Services: Shifting Our Emphases to Increase Impact," discusses evidence-based treatments as currently studied in relation to an overarching goal of our interventions, namely, to reduce the burden of mental illness and the full range of social, emotional, and behavioral problems leading to impairment.

18. Use double quotation marks

   a. every time an invented expression is used.

   b. only the first time an invented expression is introduced.

   c. to introduce a technical or key term.

   d. Answers b and c are correct.

19. Edit the following for punctuation:

Individuals with Type A personalities are more likely to develop coronary heart disease, CHD, than are those with Type B personalities.

   a. leave as is

   b. Individuals with Type A personalities are more likely to develop coronary heart disease, "CHD," than are those with Type B personalities.

   c. Individuals with Type A personalities are more likely to develop coronary heart disease—CHD—than are those with Type B personalities.

   d. Individuals with Type A personalities are more likely to develop coronary heart disease (CHD) than are those with Type B personalities.

20. One space should follow

   a. colons used in the text.

   b. all punctuation marks at the end of sentences.

   c. periods that separate parts of a reference.

   d. a and c are correct.

   e. none of the above.

21. Edit the following for spacing and punctuation:

When the applicant's ethnic origin was stated explicitly, ethnic origin did affect selection (see Table 1,) but when ethnic origin was not stated explicitly, it did not affect selection (see Table 2) (The interviewers represented a variety of ethnic origins).

   a. leave as is

   b. When the applicant's ethnic origin was stated explicitly, ethnic origin did affect selection, (see Table 1), but when ethnic origin was not stated explicitly, it did not affect selection, (see Table 2). (The interviewers represented a variety of ethnic origins.).

   c. When the applicant's ethnic origin was stated explicitly, ethnic origin did affect selection (see Table 1), but when ethnic origin was not stated explicitly it did not affect selection (see Table 2). (The interviewers represented a variety of ethnic origins.)

   d. When the applicant's ethnic origin was stated explicitly, ethnic origin did affect selection, (see Table 1), but when ethnic origin was not stated explicitly, it did not affect selection, (see Table 2). (The interviewers represented a variety of ethnic origins).

22. Regarding spelling,

    a. the standard spelling reference is the most recent edition of *Merriam-Webster's Collegiate Dictionary*.
    b. APA accepts all the spelling choices listed in popular English dictionaries.
    c. APA has no standard and leaves the matter up to the individual journal editors.
    d. spelling of psychological terms should conform to the *APA Dictionary of Psychology*.
    e. both a and d are correct.

23. Which of the following words with a prefix require a hyphen?

    a. compounds in which the base word is an abbreviation (e.g., pre-UCS)
    b. *self* compounds (e.g., self-esteem)
    c. words that could be misunderstood or misread (e.g., un-ionized)
    d. all of the above
    e. none of the above

24. From the alternatives below, select the one that correctly uses capitalization:

    a. few significant differences were found.
    b. However, one important observation was made: Participatory followers do not like to be led by authoritarian leaders.
    c. Authoritarian followers behaved in a curious way: they acted in a participatory manner with participatory leaders.
    d. these results were reported by Skutley and Jackson (2009).

25. In the following example, which abbreviation should be spelled out when it is first introduced?

    After the depressed clients received ECT treatments, changes in central nervous system activity were assessed with an EEG and effects on sleep were measured by observing REM periods.

    a. EEG
    b. ECT
    c. REM
    d. all of the above
    e. any that do not appear in the latest edition of *Merriam-Webster's Collegiate Dictionary*

26. Latin abbreviations, except *et al.,* should

    a. be spelled out each time they are used.
    b. not be used.
    c. be used only in parenthetical material.
    d. be spelled out the first time they are used.

27. Edit the following for a quotation of a source:

McDowell and Clarke (2009) found that "in terms of the provision-of-opportunity pathway, parents play a direct role in creating social contact opportunities for infants and young children, but this role diminishes in frequency and form as the child reaches adolescence."

    a. leave as is

    b. The quote should be in block form.

    c. A page number should be cited.

    d. Quotation marks are not necessary.

28. From the examples below, identify the correct form of citation:

    a. According to McMahon (p. 94), math ability is acquired.

    b. McVay and Kane's (2009) findings support the notion that variation in conscious thoughts predict (if not cause) some variation in task performance.

    c. In a study completed last year, Scarano found that androgynous women respond to self-worth dilemmas differently than do stereotypic women.

    d. Csikai concluded that a coordinated team approach to end-of-life decision making may "possibly lead to increased and earlier referral to hospice" (Conclusion section).

29. Edit the following for the citation of a reference in text:

Thus, the relationship between acculturation and ethnic-minority health behavior varies by ethnic group, by health behavior, by gender, and by the two- and three-way interactions of these variables (Landrine & Klonoff, 2004). Such complex data seem largely unintelligible and consequently remain largely peripheral to behavioral-health interventions (Landrine & Klonoff).

    a. leave as is

    b. Thus, the relationship between acculturation and ethnic-minority health behavior varies by ethnic group, by health behavior, by gender, and by the two- and three-way interactions of these variables (Landrine and Klonoff, 2004). Such complex data seem largely unintelligible and consequently remain largely peripheral to behavioral-health interventions (Landrine and Klonoff, 2004).

    c. Thus, the relationship between acculturation and ethnic-minority health behavior varies by ethnic group, by health behavior, by gender, and by the two- and three-way interactions of these variables (Landrine & Klonoff, 2004). Such complex data seem largely unintelligible and consequently remain largely peripheral to behavioral-health interventions (Landrine & Klonoff, 2004).

    d. Thus, the relationship between acculturation and ethnic-minority health behavior varies by ethnic group, by health behavior, by gender, and by the two- and three-way interactions of these variables (Landrine & Klonoff: 2004). Such complex data seem largely unintelligible and consequently remain largely peripheral to behavioral-health interventions (Landrine & Klonoff: 2004).

30. When a work has two authors, cite

    a. only one name every time the reference occurs in text.
    b. both names the first time the reference occurs in text and only one thereafter.
    c. both names every time the reference occurs in text.
    d. None of the above is correct.

31. Edit the following for the citation of references for the first mention of sources in text:

    This diversity, along with the heavily bicultural context of the South Florida area, makes Miami a fertile background in which to conduct research on acculturation (cf. Coatsworth, Maldonado-Molina, Pantin, & Szapocznik, 2005; Schwartz, Pantin, Sullivan, Prado, & Szapocznik, 2006; Sullivan et al., 2007).

    a. leave as is
    b. This diversity, along with the heavily bicultural context of the South Florida area, makes Miami a fertile background in which to conduct research on acculturation (cf., Schwartz, Pantin, Sullivan, Prado, & Szapocznik, 2006; Sullivan et al., 2007; Coatsworth, Maldonado-Molina, Pantin, & Szapocznik, 2005).
    c. This diversity, along with the heavily bicultural context of the South Florida area, makes Miami a fertile background in which to conduct research on acculturation (cf. Coatsworth et al., 2005; Schwartz, Pantin, Sullivan, Prado, & Szapocznik, 2006; Sullivan, Schwartz, Prado, Pantin, Huang, & Szapocznik, 2007).
    d. This diversity, along with the heavily bicultural context of the South Florida area, makes Miami a fertile background in which to conduct research on acculturation (cf. Sullivan et al., 2007; Schwartz, Pantin, Sullivan, Prado, & Szapocznik, 2006; Coatsworth, Maldonado-Molina, Pantin, & Szapocznik, 2005).

32. Edit the following for the citation of a specific part of a reference in text:

    To help raise public awareness, we can encourage industry groups to "develop media awards for positive portrayals of girls as strong, competent, and nonsexualized" (American Psychological Association, 2007).

    a. leave as is
    b. To help raise public awareness, we can encourage industry groups to "develop media awards for positive portrayals of girls as strong, competent, and nonsexualized" (American Psychological Association, http://www.apa.org/pi/wpo/sexualizationrep.pdf).
    c. To help raise public awareness, we can encourage industry groups to "develop media awards for positive portrayals of girls as strong, competent, and nonsexualized" (American Psychological Association, 2007, p. 45).
    d. To help raise public awareness, we can encourage industry groups to "develop media awards for positive portrayals of girls as strong, competent, and nonsexualized (p. 45)" (American Psychological Association, 2007).

33. Reference entries

    a. may consist of the author's name only, if the bibliography is totally complete.
    b. may contain only the author's name and title of publication, if the bibliography is totally complete.
    c. should be complete and correct.
    d. should be updated periodically if they contain URLs.
    e. c and d are correct

34. Edit the following for ordering the references in a reference list. Choose the sequence of numbers that indicates the correct order of the four references. (Note: The numbers are not part of APA Style but are used here for brevity.)

    1. McKenzie, B., & Over, R. (1983). Young infants fail to imitate facial and manual gestures. *Infant Behavior and Development, 6,* 85–96.
    2. Martin, G. B., & Clark, R. D. (1982). Distress crying in neonates: Species and peer specificity. *Developmental Psychology, 18,* 3–9.
    3. Maurer, D. (2005). Neonatal synesthesia: A reevaluation. In C. K. Mondloch & L. C. Robertson (Eds.), *Synesthesia: Perspectives from cognitive neuroscience* (pp. 193–213). New York, NY: Oxford University Press.
    4. Meltzoff, A. N. (2007). The "like me" framework for recognizing and becoming an intentional agent. *Acta Psychologica, 124,* 26–43.

    a. leave as is (i.e., 1, 2, 3, 4)
    b. 3, 4, 2, 1
    c. 3, 2, 4, 1
    d. 2 ,3, 1, 4

35. Edit the following for the application of APA reference style:

    Von Ledebur, S. C. (2007). Optimizing knowledge transfer by new employees in companies. *Knowledge Management Research & Practice* (Advance publication). doi:10.1057/palgrave .kmrp.8500141

    a. leave as is
    b. Von Ledebur, S. C. (2007). Optimizing knowledge transfer by new employees in companies. *Knowledge Management Research & Practice.* Advance online publication. doi:10.1057 /palgrave.kmrp.8500141
    c. Von Ledebur, S. C. (2007). Optimizing knowledge transfer by new employees in companies. *Knowledge Management Research & Practice.* Retrieved from advance online publication. doi:10.1057/palgrave.kmrp.8500141
    d. Von Ledebur, S. C. (2007). Optimizing knowledge transfer by new employees in companies. *Knowledge Management Research & Practice* [Advance online publication]. doi:10.1057 /palgrave.kmrp.8500141
    e. Von Ledebur, S. C. (2007). Optimizing knowledge transfer by new employees in companies. *Knowledge Management Research & Practice.* Advance Online Publication. DOI:10.1057 /palgrave.kmrp.8500141

36. Edit the following for the application of APA reference style:

Marshall-Pescini, S., & Whiten, A. (2008). Social learning of nut-cracking behavior in East African sanctuary-living chimpanzees (*Pan troglodytes schweinfurthii*) (Supplemental material). *Journal of Comparative Psychology, 122,* 186–194. doi:10.1037/0735-7036.122.2.186

   a. leave as is

   b. Marshall-Pescini, S., & Whiten, A. (2008). Social learning of nut-cracking behavior in East African sanctuary-living chimpanzees (*Pan troglodytes schweinfurthii*) [Supplemental material]. *Journal of Comparative Psychology, 122,* 186–194. doi:10.1037/0735 -7036.122.2.186

   c. Marshall-Pescini, S., & Whiten, A. (2008). Social learning of nut-cracking behavior in East African sanctuary-living chimpanzees (*Pan troglodytes schweinfurthii*): Supplemental material. *Journal of Comparative Psychology, 122,* 186–194. doi:10.1037/0735 -7036.122.2.186

   d. Marshall-Pescini, S., & Whiten, A. (2008). Social learning of nut-cracking behavior in East African sanctuary-living chimpanzees (*Pan troglodytes schweinfurthii*) [*Supplemental material*]. *Journal of Comparative Psychology, 122,* 186–194. doi:10.1037/0735 -7036.122.2.186

37. Edit the following for the application of APA reference style:

Haybron, D. M. (2008). Philosophy and the science of subjective well-being. In Eid, M. & Larsen, R. J. (Eds.), *The science of subjective well-being* (pp. 17–43). New York, NY: Guilford Press.

   a. leave as is

   b. Haybron, D. M. (2008). *Philosophy and the science of subjective well-being.* In M. Eid & R. J. Larsen (Eds.), *The science of subjective well-being* (pp. 17–43). New York, NY: Guilford Press.

   c. Haybron, D. M. (2008). "Philosophy and the science of subjective well-being." In M. Eid & R. J. Larsen (Eds.), The science of subjective well-being (pp. 17–43). New York, NY: Guilford Press.

   d. Haybron, D. M. (2008). Philosophy and the science of subjective well-being. In M. Eid & R. J. Larsen (Eds.), *The science of subjective well-being* (pp. 17–43). New York, NY: Guilford Press.

38. Edit the following for the application of APA reference style:

Thomas, N. (Ed.). (2002). *Perspectives on the community college: A journey of discovery* [Monograph]. Retrieved from http://eric.ed.gov/

   a. leave as is

   b. Thomas, N. (Ed.). (2002). Perspectives on the community college: A journey of discovery [Monograph]. Retrieved from http://eric.ed.gov/

   c. Thomas, N. (Ed.). (2002). *Perspectives on the community college: A journey of discovery* [Monograph]. No publisher or DOI available.

   d. Thomas, N. (Ed.). (2002). Perspectives on the community college: A journey of discovery. Monograph. Retrieved from http://eric.ed.gov/

39. Use a typeface that

    a. is uniform.
    b. enhances readability.
    c. allows the publisher to estimate article length.
    d. all of the above.

40. Edit the following by selecting the correct spacing arrangement:

Method

Participants and Procedure

    This study was part of a larger project designed to explore civic attitudes and behaviors among diverse youth. Recruited for participation were 304 students from four high schools in the Northeast between 2000 and 2002.

a. leave as is

b.
Method

Participants and Procedure

    This study was part of a larger project designed to explore civic attitudes and behaviors among diverse youth. Recruited for participation were 304 students from four high schools in the Northeast between 2000 and 2002.

c.
Method

Participants and Procedure

    This study was part of a larger project designed to explore civic attitudes and behaviors among diverse youth. Recruited for participation were 304 students from four high schools in the Northeast between 2000 and 2002.

d.
Method

Participants and Procedure

    This study was part of a larger project designed to explore civic attitudes and behaviors among diverse youth. Recruited for participation were 304 students from four high schools in the Northeast between 2000 and 2002.

41. Concerning page numbers,

    a. number your pages consecutively starting with the title page.
    b. place the numbers in the center of each page at the top margin.
    c. if a page is inserted after numbering is complete, number the inserted page with an a (e.g., 6a).
    d. pages used for figures are not numbered.
    e. a and d are correct.

42. When typing a reference list,

    a. begin it after the last word of the Discussion section on the same page.
    b. single-space each reference but double-space in between references.
    c. double-space all reference entries.
    d. indent all lines of each reference except the first line at least 0.5 in (1.27 cm).
    e. c and d are correct.

TERM PAPER MASTERY TEST 4
ANSWER SHEET AND FEEDBACK REPORT

Question Number	Answer	APA Codes	Question Number	Answer	APA Codes
1	_____	3.01–3.04	22	_____	4.12–4.13
2	_____	3.02–3.03	23	_____	4.12–4.13
3	_____	3.05–3.06	24	_____	4.14–4.20
4	_____	3.05–3.06	25	_____	4.22–4.30
5	_____	3.07–3.11	26	_____	4.22–4.30
6	_____	3.07–3.11	27	_____	6.03–6.10
7	_____	3.12–3.17	28	_____	6.11–6.21
8	_____	3.12–3.17	29	_____	6.11–6.21
9	_____	3.18–3.19	30	_____	6.11–6.21
10	_____	3.20–3.23	31	_____	6.11–6.21
11	_____	3.20–3.23	32	_____	6.11–6.21
12	_____	3.20–3.23	33	_____	6.22–6.31
13	_____	4.01–4.11	34	_____	6.22–6.31
14	_____	4.01–4.11	35	_____	6.22–6.32, 7.01
15	_____	4.01–4.11	36	_____	6.22–6.32, 7.01
16	_____	4.01–4.11	37	_____	6.22–6.32, 7.02
17	_____	4.01–4.11	38	_____	6.22–6.32, 7.02
18	_____	4.01–4.11	39	_____	8.03
19	_____	4.01–4.11	40	_____	8.03
20	_____	4.01–4.11	41	_____	8.03
21	_____	4.01–4.11	42	_____	8.03

TERM PAPER MASTERY TEST 4
ANSWER KEY

Question Number	Answer	APA Codes	Question Number	Answer	APA Codes
1	b	3.01–3.04	22	e	4.12–4.13
2	b	3.02–3.03	23	d	4.12–4.13
3	d	3.05–3.06	24	b	4.14–4.20
4	a	3.05–3.06	25	e	4.22–4.30
5	a	3.07–3.11	26	c	4.22–4.30
6	e	3.07–3.11	27	c	6.03–6.10
7	c	3.12–3.17	28	b	6.11–6.21
8	d	3.12–3.17	29	c	6.11–6.21
9	b	3.18–3.19	30	c	6.11–6.21
10	c	3.20–3.23	31	a	6.11–6.21
11	a	3.20–3.23	32	c	6.11–6.21
12	b	3.20–3.23	33	e	6.22–6.31
13	a	4.01–4.11	34	d	6.22–6.31
14	e	4.01–4.11	35	b	6.22–6.31, 7.01
15	a	4.01–4.11	36	b	6.22–6.31, 7.01
16	a	4.01–4.11	37	d	6.22–6.32, 7.02
17	d	4.01–4.11	38	a	6.22–6.32, 7.02
18	b	4.01–4.11	39	d	8.03
19	d	4.01–4.11	40	d	8.03
20	d	4.01–4.11	41	e	8.03
21	c	4.01–4.11	42	e	8.03

RESEARCH REPORT MASTERY TEST 1

1. A report of an empirical study usually includes an introduction and sections called Method, _____, and Discussion.

   a. Results
   b. Bibliography
   c. Statement of the Problem
   d. Conclusion

2. The abstract of an article should be

   a. a brief, comprehensive summary of the contents of the article.
   b. about 75 to 100 words long.
   c. an evaluation of the research report.
   d. all of the above.

3. The introduction section of a research report should

   a. include a thorough historical review of the literature.
   b. define all of the terms that would be unintelligible to a reader with no previous exposure to the field.
   c. present the importance of the problem to be explored and specific hypotheses and objectives.
   d. be clearly labeled.

4. When animals are the subjects in a study, it is not usually necessary to report

   a. the name and location of the supplier.
   b. genus, species, and strain number.
   c. their age, sex, weight, and physiological condition.
   d. the cost of maintaining them.

5. Results are sometimes difficult to read and understand; therefore, it is useful to

   a. summarize the collected data and the analysis performed on those data relevant to the discourse that is to follow.
   b. introduce the reader to statistical theory before you report the results of even basic statistical analyses.
   c. let the statistics drive the logic of your Results section, not the logic you developed in your introduction (i.e., your hypotheses).
   d. report raw data, descriptive statistics, and the results of inferential analyses.

6. Speculation is permitted in the Discussion section if it is

   a. faithful to the intuition of the authors.
   b. related closely and logically to empirical data or theory.
   c. expressed verbosely and eloquently.
   d. none of the above.

7. In a paper that integrates several experiments, you should

   a. not combine the discussion with the description of results.
   b. have only one Results section for all of the experiments.
   c. make it at least twice as long as a one-experiment study.
   d. include a comprehensive general discussion of all of the work.

8. Choose the correct format for the use of three levels of headings:

   a.   **Experiment 2**
      Method
            Participants.
   b.   **METHOD**
                                               Procedure
      Pretraining Period.
   c.   **Method**
      Procedure
            Participants.
   d.   **Method**
      Procedure
      Pretraining period.

9. Past tense is usually appropriate for describing

   a. previous experiments.
   b. the literature review.
   c. a procedure if the discussion is of past events.
   d. all of the above.

10. Which of the following examples represents correct hyphenation?

    a. *t*-test results
    b. pro-Freudian
    c. 2-, 3-, and 10-min trials
    d. all of the above

11. Edit the following for capitalization:

On Day 2 of Experiment 3, the students read Chapter 2 of their textbook, which described Eriksonian Life Span Theory and Life History Theory.

   a. leave as is
   b. *Day* and *Experiment* do not need to be capitalized.
   c. *Chapter* does not require capitalization.
   d. *Life Span Theory* and *Life History Theory* should not be capitalized.

12. Capitalize

   a. the word *factor* when it is followed by a number (e.g., Factor 6).
   b. nouns that precede a variable.
   c. names of conditions or groups in an experiment.
   d. all of the above.
   e. none of the above.

13. In general, use abbreviations

   a. if the reader is more familiar with the abbreviation than with the complete word or words being used.
   b. for all units of time.
   c. if considerable space can be saved and repetition avoided.
   d. Answers a and c of the above are correct.
   e. All of the above are correct.

14. Edit the following for the expression of numbers:

The participants were tested on items from 10 seven-point scales, and results included 2 two-way interactions.

   a. leave as is
   b. The participants were tested on items from ten 7-point scales, and results included two 2-way interactions.
   c. The participants were tested on items from ten seven-point scales, and results included two two-way interactions.
   d. The participants were tested on items from ten 7-point scales, and results included 2 two-way interactions.

15. Edit the following for the expression of numbers:

Procedural errors occurred while 2 rats in the drug condition and 3 rats in the placebo condition were being tested.

   a. leave as is
   b. Procedural errors occurred while 2.0 rats in the drug condition and 3.0 rats in the placebo condition were being tested.
   c. Procedural errors occurred while two rats in the drug condition and three rats in the placebo condition were being tested.
   d. Procedural errors occurred while two (2) rats in the drug condition and three (3) rats in the placebo condition were being tested.

16. Edit the following for the expression of numbers:

The 3-dimensional conceptualization allows for 8 possible dyadic relationships.

   a. leave as is
   b. The 3-dimensional conceptualization allows for eight possible dyadic relationships.
   c. The three-dimensional conceptualization allows for eight possible dyadic relationships.
   d. The three-dimensional conceptualization allows for 8 possible dyadic relationships.

17. Edit the following for the expression of numbers:

There were twenty 6-year-olds, eighteen 10-year-olds, and twenty-four 14-year-olds.

   a. leave as is
   b. There were 20 6-year-olds, 18 10-year-olds, and 24 14-year-olds.
   c. There were 20 six-year-olds, 18 ten-year-olds, and 24 fourteen-year-olds.
   d. There were twenty six-year-olds, eighteen 10-year-olds, and twenty-four 14-year-olds.

18. Edit the following for the expression of ordinal numbers:

The 6th and 12th graders in each of the treatment conditions returned for a 5th session in which the performance measures were taken.

   a. leave as is
   b. The sixth and 12th graders in each of the treatment conditions returned for a fifth session in which the performance measures were taken.
   c. The sixth and twelfth graders in each of the treatment conditions returned for a fifth session in which the performance measures were taken.
   d. The 6th and 12th graders in each of the treatment conditions returned for a fifth session in which the performance measures were taken.

19. When using decimal numbers,

    a. use a zero before the decimal point with numbers that are less than 1 when the statistic can exceed 1 (e.g., 0.23 cm, Cohen's $d = 0.70$, 0.48 s).
    b. never use a zero before the decimal point (.05).
    c. check with the editor of each specific APA journal.
    d. use a zero before a decimal fraction when the statistic cannot be greater than 1.

20. Edit the following for the presentation of numbers:

    In comparison with girls, boys were rated as having higher levels of externalizing symptoms at first grade, $t(1,364) = 2.00$, $p < .01$, $d = 0.11$.

    a. leave as is
    b. In comparison with girls, boys were rated as having higher levels of externalizing symptoms at first grade, $t(1364) = 2.00$, $p < .01$, $d = 0.11$.
    c. In comparison with girls, boys were rated as having higher levels of externalizing symptoms at first grade, $t(1.364K) = 2.00$, $p < .01$, $d = 0.11$.

21. Physical measurements should be expressed in

    a. metric units.
    b. traditional nonmetric units.
    c. units of the original measurement.
    d. physical units.

22. Which of the following is correctly expressed?

    a. 13 cms
    b. 313 cm.
    c. 31 cm
    d. 313 cms.

23. Edit the following for the typing of statistical copy:

    The one-degree-of-freedom contrast of primary interest (the mean difference between Conditions 1 and 2) was also statistically significant at the specified .05 level, $t(177) = 3.51$, $p < .001$, $d = 0.65$, 95% CI (0.35, 0.95).

    a. leave as is
    b. The one-degree-of-freedom contrast of primary interest (the mean difference between Conditions 1 and 2) was also statistically significant at the specified .05 level, $t(177) = 3.51$, $p<.001$, $d=0.65$, 95% CI [0.35, 0.95].
    c. The one-degree-of-freedom contrast of primary interest (the mean difference between Conditions 1 and 2) was also statistically significant at the specified .05 level, $t(177) = 3.51$, $p < .001$, $d = 0.65$, 95% CI [0.35, 0.95].
    d. The one-degree-of-freedom contrast of primary interest (the mean difference between Conditions 1 and 2) was also statistically significant at the specified .05 level, $t(177) = 3.51$, $p < .001$, $d = 0.65$, 95% CI [0.35,0.95].

24. Edit the following for the citation of a statistic in text:

    A *t* test for related means was used to compare the number of targets found by birds in the experimental group with the number found by their yoked partners.

    a. leave as is

    b. A *t* test for related means (Grimm & Yarnold, 2000) was used to compare the number of targets found by birds in the experimental group with the number found by their yoked partners.

    c. A *t* test for related means (see any standard statistics reference work) was used to compare the number of targets found by birds in the experimental group with the number found by their yoked partners.

25. Edit the following for the presentation of a formula:

    We used a *t* test to compare the frequencies of heterosexual intercourse per month by heterosexual and bisexual men.

    a. leave as is

    b. We used a *t* test (t = difference between means/standard error of difference between means) to compare the frequencies of heterosexual intercourse per month by heterosexual and bisexual men.

    c. We used a t test [$t = (M_H - M_B)$/standard error of difference between means] to compare the frequencies of heterosexual intercourse per month by heterosexual and bisexual men.

    d. We used a *t* test [$(M_H - M_B)/(SE_{M_H-M_B})$] to compare the frequencies of heterosexual intercourse per month by heterosexual and bisexual men.

26. When presenting an inferential statistic in text, give

    a. sample sizes.

    b. cell means.

    c. standard deviations.

    d. all of the above.

    e. none of the above.

27. Edit the following for the use of statistical symbols:

    We first conducted a pilot study to determine the % of participants who could complete the task with different time limits.

    a. leave as is

    b. We first conducted a pilot study to determine the percentage of participants who could complete the task with different time limits.

    c. We first conducted a pilot study to determine the % age of participants who could complete the task with different time limits.

    d. We first conducted a pilot study to determine the percentage (%) of participants who could complete the task with different time limits.

28. Which of the following should be used to designate the number of members in a part of a total sample?

    a. N

    b. n

    c. n

    d. N

29. Choose the correct format for presenting a confidence interval:

    a. $M = 30.5$ cm, 99% CI [18.0, 43.0] cm

    b. $M = 30.5$ cm, 99% CI (18.0, 43.0)

    c. $M = 30.5$ cm, 99% CI (18.0, 43.0) cm

    d. $M = 30.5$ cm, 99% CI [18.0, 43.0]

30. Edit the table below for tabular presentation:

Table 6

Mean Imagined Scores of Students Reporting an Out-of-Body Experience

Condition	Imaginal scores
Visual	7.1
Auditory	4.0

    a. Means should be carried out to two decimal places.

    b. No standard deviations are given.

    c. Results consisting of only two means should be presented in the text, not in a table.

    d. b and c

31. Tables should be

    a. integral to the text but understandable in isolation.

    b. referred to but not duplicated in the text.

    c. referred to in text by their numbers.

    d. all of the above.

32. Every table should have a title that is

    a. brief.

    b. clear.

    c. explanatory.

    d. all of the above.

33. Which of the following abbreviations need not be explained in table headings or table notes?

    a. abbreviations of technical terms
    b. standard abbreviations for nontechnical terms
    c. group names
    d. none of the above

34. A specific note to a table

    a. refers to a particular column or individual entry.
    b. is indicated by a superscript uppercase letter.
    c. is placed within the body of the table.
    d. does none of the above.

35. When checking whether data are effectively presented in your table, what question should you *not* ask yourself?

    a. Should this table be vertically displayed?
    b. Is the table necessary?
    c. Does every column have a heading?
    d. Are confidence intervals reported for all major point estimates?
    e. all of the above

36. What factors weigh against using a figure?

    a. It duplicates elements of the paper.
    b. It complements text and reduces lengthy discussions.
    c. It cannot be produced in a way that captures essential information features without visually distracting detail.
    d. Answers a and c are correct.
    e. Answers a and b are correct.

37. What kind of figure generally displays nonquantitative information such as the flow of subjects through a process?

    a. photograph
    b. chart
    c. map
    d. drawing
    e. graph

38. Select the figure caption that does not explain its figure effectively:

    a. *Figure 1.* Videocamera effects.
    b. *Figure 4.* Varimax rotation of factors.
    c. *Figure 2.* Outpatient and inpatient contrasts.
    d. all of the above.

39. Which of the following is essential in presenting electrophysiological, radiological, and other genetic data?

    a. clear and complete labeling
    b. limiting the number of different shadings
    c. type style
    d. all of the above

40. Which part of a research report should not always begin on a new page?

    a. abstract
    b. References
    c. Method
    d. a and b

41. The title page includes the title,

    a. author byline and abstract.
    b. author byline, institutional affiliation, running head, and the page number 1.
    c. author byline, institutional affiliation, running head, the page number 1, and author note.
    d. author byline, institutional affiliation, and abstract.

42. Choose the correct statement about the placing of a table in a manuscript:

    a. Type the table in full exactly in the place in the text where it should be printed.
    b. Type the table on the back of the page that first refers to it.
    c. Try to type all of the tables on the same page.
    d. Type each table on a separate page.

RESEARCH REPORT MASTERY TEST 1
ANSWER SHEET AND FEEDBACK REPORT

Question Number	Answer	APA Codes	Question Number	Answer	APA Codes
1	_____	1.01–1.06	22	_____	4.39–4.40
2	_____	2.01–2.04	23	_____	4.41–4.49
3	_____	2.05–2.06	24	_____	4.41–4.49
4	_____	2.05–2.06	25	_____	4.41–4.49
5	_____	2.07–2.11	26	_____	4.41–4.49
6	_____	2.07–2.11	27	_____	4.41–4.49
7	_____	2.07–2.11	28	_____	4.41–4.49
8	_____	3.02–3.03	29	_____	4.41–4.49
9	_____	3.05–3.06	30	_____	5.07–5.19
10	_____	4.12–4.13	31	_____	5.07–5.19
11	_____	4.14–4.20	32	_____	5.07–5.19
12	_____	4.14–4.20	33	_____	5.07–5.19
13	_____	4.22–4.30	34	_____	5.07–5.19
14	_____	4.31–4.38	35	_____	5.19
15	_____	4.31–4.38	36	_____	5.20–5.30
16	_____	4.31–4.38	37	_____	5.20–5.30
17	_____	4.31–4.38	38	_____	5.23–5.24
18	_____	4.31–4.38	39	_____	5.26–5.30
19	_____	4.31–4.38	40	_____	8.03
20	_____	4.31–4.38	41	_____	8.03
21	_____	4.39–4.40	42	_____	8.03

RESEARCH REPORT MASTERY TEST 1
ANSWER KEY

Question Number	Answer	APA Codes	Question Number	Answer	APA Codes
1	a	1.01–1.06	22	c	4.39–4.40
2	a	2.01–2.04	23	c	4.41–4.49
3	c	2.05–2.06	24	a	4.41–4.49
4	d	2.05–2.06	25	a	4.41–4.49
5	a	2.07–2.11	26	d	4.41–4.49
6	b	2.07–2.11	27	b	4.41–4.49
7	d	2.07–2.11	28	b	4.41–4.49
8	d	3.02–3.03	29	d	4.41–4.49
9	d	3.05–3.06	30	d	5.07–5.19
10	d	4.12–4.13	31	d	5.07–5.19
11	d	4.14–4.20	32	d	5.07–5.19
12	a	4.14–4.20	33	b	5.07–5.19
13	d	4.22–4.30	34	a	5.07–5.19
14	d	4.31–4.38	35	a	5.19
15	c	4.31–4.38	36	d	5.20–5.30
16	c	4.31–4.38	37	b	5.20–5.30
17	a	4.31–4.38	38	d	5.23–5.24
18	b	4.31–4.38	39	a	5.26–5.30
19	a	4.31–4.38	40	c	8.03
20	b	4.31–4.38	41	c	8.03
21	a	4.39–4.40	42	d	8.03

RESEARCH REPORT MASTERY TEST 2

1. When writing a report of original research, the sections should reflect the

    a. order of importance.
    b. relation to each other.
    c. stages of the research process.
    d. none of the above.

2. The abstract of a report of an empirical study should describe

    a. the problem, participants, essential features of the study method, basic findings, and conclusions.
    b. raw data statements with conclusions.
    c. conclusions not found in the text of the report.
    d. *F* values, degrees of freedom, and probability levels.

3. Examples of supplemental materials that are included in online supplemental archives are

    a. lengthy computer code.
    b. detailed description of a complex piece of equipment.
    c. audio or video clips.
    d. a and c.

4. Before writing the introduction section, consider the following questions:

    a. How do hypotheses and research design relate to one another?
    b. What are the theoretical and practical implications of the study?
    c. What statistical tests were used?
    d. all of the above.
    e. a and b.

5. When describing participants in your research, you should

    a. give specific demographic characteristics such as age; sex; ethnic and/or racial group; level of education; and socioeconomic, generation, or immigrant status.
    b. describe the procedures for selecting participants, including sampling method.
    c. report whether the participants were provided incentives used to increase compliance.
    d. do all of the above.

6. When reporting inferential statistical tests, include the

    a. obtained magnitude or value of the test statistic.

    b. degrees of freedom.

    c. exact p value.

    d. all of the above.

7. For experimental and quasi-experimental designs, always include in the Results section

    a. a description of the flow of participants through the study.

    b. the total number of participants recruited into the study and the number of participants assigned to each group.

    c. the number of participants who did not complete the experiment or who crossed over to other conditions, and explain why.

    d. all of the above.

    e. a and c.

8. The Discussion section is a part of the report in which you can

    a. discuss theory independent of your results.

    b. interpret your results and discuss their implications.

    c. discuss relevant related literature.

    d. reformulate and repeat points already made.

9. In a paper that integrates several experiments, you should

    a. not try to relate the experiments to each other.

    b. have only one Results section for all of the experiments.

    c. include a comprehensive general discussion of all the work.

    d. make it at least twice as long as a one-experiment study.

10. Edit the following by selecting the correct arrangement of headings:

Method

Subjects

Procedure

Results

Discussion

  a. leave as is

  b.   **Method**

Subjects.

Procedure.

Results

Discussion

  c.   **Method**

Subjects

Procedure

Results

Discussion

  d.   *Method*

Subjects

Procedure

Results

Discussion

11. Consistency of verb tense helps to smooth expression. Select the preferred match of paper section with verb tense from the choices below:

  a. conclusion: present tense
  b. literature review: present tense
  c. Results: past tense
  d. Method: past tense
  e. all of the above except b

12. Which of the following examples represents correct hyphenation?

  a. *t*-test results
  b. results from *t* tests
  c. 2-, 3-, and 10-min trials
  d. all of the above

13. Which of the following examples demonstrates correct use of capitalization?

    a. Trial 3 and Item 4
    b. trial *n* and item *x*
    c. Chapter 4
    d. Table 2 and Figure 3
    e. all of the above.

14. Edit the following for capitalization of statistical and mathematical copy:

    A 2 × 2 × 3 (Sex of Participant × Sex of Target × Activity Profile) analysis of variance was performed on the attractiveness scores.

    a. leave as is
    b. A 2 × 2 × 3 (sex of participant × sex of target × activity profile) analysis of variance was performed on the attractiveness scores.
    c. A 2 (Sex of Participant) × 2 (Sex of Target) × 3 (Activity Profile) analysis of variance was performed on the attractiveness scores.
    d. A 2 (Sex of participant) × 2 (Sex of target) × 3 (Activity profile) analysis of variance was performed on the attractiveness scores.

15. Edit the following for capitalization of names of variables, factors, or effects:

    In light of the fact that both Baseline and Intervention Effect factors are qualified by gender, a full presentation of the moderated findings follows.

    a. leave as is
    b. The words *Baseline* and *Intervention Effect* should not be capitalized.
    c. The word *Factors* should be capitalized.

16. Abbreviations appearing in several figures or tables

    a. must be explained in the figure caption or table note for every figure or table in which they are used.
    b. must be explained in the figure caption or table note of only the first figure or table in which they are used.
    c. should be explained only in the text.
    d. need not be explained.

17. Edit the following for the expression of numbers:

    Study 1 showed that 3 times as many students studied abroad in the current year than did in the past 6 years.

    a. leave as is
    b. Study 1 showed that three times as many students studied abroad in the current year than did in the past 6 years.
    c. Study 1 showed that three times as many students studied abroad in the current year than did in the past six years.

18. Edit the following for the expression of numbers:

    The survey had a sampling error of four %.

    a. leave as is
    b. The survey had a sampling error of four percent.
    c. The survey had a sampling error of 4%.
    d. The survey had a sampling error of 4 percent.

19. Edit the following for the expression of numbers:

    To test the program, we sought schools which at least one fourth of the students did not finish the year above grade level on the criterion measure.

    a. leave as is
    b. To test the program, we sought schools in which at least 1/4 of the students did not finish the year above grade on the criterion measure.
    c. To test the program, we sought schools in which at least 1/4th of the students did not finish the year above grade level on the criterion measure.
    d. To test the program, we sought schools in which at least one-fourth of the students did not finish the year above grade level on the criterion measure.

20. Edit the following for the expression of numbers:

    Each client was asked to describe his or her actual and ideal selves on 16 5-point rating scales.

    a. leave as is
    b. Each client was asked to describe his or her actual and ideal selves on sixteen five-point rating scales.
    c. Each client was asked to describe his or her actual and ideal selves on sixteen 5-point rating scales.
    d. Each client was asked to describe his or her actual and ideal selves on 16 five-point rating scales.

21. Edit the following for the expression of decimal fractions:

The dots appeared simultaneously on the screen, .5 cm apart.

a. leave as is

b. The dots appeared simultaneously on the screen, 0.5 cm apart.

c. The dots appeared simultaneously on the screen, .50 cm apart.

22. Edit the following for the expression and punctuation of numbers:

A content analysis was performed on 1,480 episodes of soap operas that had been televised in the preceding 5 years.

a. leave as is

b. A content analysis was performed on 1480 episodes of soap operas that had been televised in the preceding 5 years.

c. A content analysis was performed on 1,480 episodes of soap operas that had been televised in the preceding five years.

d. A content analysis was performed on 1480 episodes of soap operas that had been televised in the preceding five years.

23. Experimenters who use instruments that record measurements in nonmetric units

a. should report the measurement as recorded.

b. may report the nonmetric units but must also report the SI (metric) equivalents.

c. can report either the nonmetric units or the SI (metric) equivalents.

d. None of the above is correct.

24. Spell out the metric unit

a. when the unit does not appear with a numeric value.

b. when the unit appears with a numeric value.

c. in table headings.

d. None of the above is correct.

25. Edit the following for citing the source of a statistic in text:

A one-way analysis of variance (see any standard statistics text) was used to assess the effect of drug dosage.

a. leave as is

b. A one-way analysis of variance was used to assess the effect of drug dosage.

c. A one-way analysis of variance (Grimm & Yarnold, 2000) was used to assess the effect of drug dosage.

26. Include formulas for

    a. new or rare statistics or mathematical expressions.
    b. a statistical or mathematical expression essential to a paper.
    c. all statistics and mathematical expressions.
    d. a and b.
    e. none of the above.

27. Edit the following for the presentation of statistics:

    High-school GPA statistically predicted college mathematics performance, $R^2 = .12$, $F(1, 148) = 20.18$, $p < .001$, 95% CI [.02, .22].

    a. leave as is
    b. High-school GPA statistically predicted college mathematics performance, $R^2 = .12$, $F(df = 1, 148) = 20.18$, $p < .001$, 95% CI [.02, .22].
    c. High-school GPA statistically predicted college mathematics performance, $R^2 = .12$, $F(1, 148) = 20.18$, $p < 0.001$, 95% CI (.02, .22).
    d. High-school GPA statistically predicted college mathematics performance, $R^2 = .12$, $F(1/48) = 20.18$, $p < .001$, 95% CI [.02, .22].

28. Edit the following for the presentation of statistics:

    The volunteers who appeared for the orientation session (sample size = 120) were then randomly assigned to one of the three conditions.

    a. leave as is
    b. The volunteers who appeared for the orientation session (N = 120) were then randomly assigned to one of the three conditions.
    c. The volunteers who appeared for the orientation session (N = 120) were then randomly assigned to one of the three conditions.
    d. The volunteers who appeared for the orientation session (n = 120) were then randomly assigned to one of the three conditions.

29. A table should be used

    a. whenever numbers are involved.
    b. when an article is more than five pages.
    c. when it supplements rather than duplicates text.
    d. for all of the above.

30. Identify tabular presentation error(s) in the following:

Table 3

Estimated Distance (cm) for Letter and Digit Stimuli

Condition	M (SD)	95% CI	
		LL	UL
Letters	14.5 (28.6)	5.4	23.6
Digits	31.8 (33.2)	21.2	42.4

  a. Table 3 should be Table III.

  b. CI, *LL,* and *UL* need to be defined in a table note.

  c. Centimeters should be spelled out in the table title.

  d. b and c

31. For all tables within one paper, use

  a. the same terminology.

  b. similar formats.

  c. the same title.

  d. a and b.

32. A table title should be

  a. brief but explanatory.

  b. clear and reflect basic content of the table.

  c. detailed about all independent and dependent variables.

  d. a and b are correct.

33. The left-hand column of a table (the *stub)* has a heading (the *stubhead)* that usually describes the

  a. elements in that column.

  b. dependent variables.

  c. independent variables.

  d. data.

  e. a and c.

34. When reporting confidence intervals in a table, you can

  a. use brackets as in text.

  b. use the same confidence level throughout the paper.

  c. give upper and lower limits in separate columns.

  d. all of the above.

35. The word *figure* refers to

    a. maps.
    b. graphs and charts.
    c. drawings.
    d. all of the above.

36. A figure is not necessary if it

    a. augments text.
    b. duplicates text.
    c. eliminates lengthy discussion from the text.
    d. does none of the above.

37. A figure legend should be positioned

    a. within the figure.
    b. to the left of the figure.
    c. below the figure.
    d. above the figure.

38. Figure captions

    a. serve as the explanation and as the title of the figure.
    b. should describe the contents of the figure in a brief sentence or phrase.
    c. should include explanations of units of measurement, symbols, and abbreviations not included in the legend.
    d. all of the above.

39. Which of the following is the correct ordering of manuscript sections in a research report?

    a. title page, abstract, introduction
    b. Method, Results, Discussion
    c. References, figures, tables
    d. a and b

40. A running head to be used in a research report should be

    a. centered at the bottom of the title page in all uppercase letters.
    b. flush left at the top of the title page in all uppercase letters.
    c. centered at the bottom of the title page in uppercase and lowercase letters.
    d. flush right at the bottom of the title page in all uppercase and lowercase letters.

RESEARCH REPORT MASTERY TEST 2
ANSWER SHEET AND FEEDBACK REPORT

Question Number	Answer	APA Codes	Question Number	Answer	APA Codes
1	_____	1.01–1.06	21	_____	4.31–4.38
2	_____	2.01–2.04	22	_____	4.31–4.38
3	_____	2.01–2.13	23	_____	4.39–4.40
4	_____	2.05–2.06	24	_____	4.39–4.40
5	_____	2.05–2.06	25	_____	4.41–4.47
6	_____	2.07–2.11	26	_____	4.41–4.47
7	_____	2.07–2.11	27	_____	4.41–4.47
8	_____	2.07–2.11	28	_____	4.41–4.47
9	_____	2.07–2.11	29	_____	5.07–5.19
10	_____	3.02–3.03	30	_____	5.07–5.19
11	_____	3.05–3.06	31	_____	5.07–5.19
12	_____	4.12–4.13	32	_____	5.07–5.19
13	_____	4.14–4.20	33	_____	5.07–5.19
14	_____	4.14–4.20	34	_____	5.07–5.19
15	_____	4.14–4.20	35	_____	5.20–5.30
16	_____	4.22–4.30	36	_____	5.20–5.30
17	_____	4.31–4.38	37	_____	5.20–5.30
18	_____	4.31–4.38	38	_____	5.20–5.23
19	_____	4.31–4.38	39	_____	8.03
20	_____	4.31–4.38	40	_____	8.03

RESEARCH REPORT MASTERY TEST 2
ANSWER KEY

Question Number	Answer	APA Codes	Question Number	Answer	APA Codes
1	c	1.01–1.06	21	b	4.31–4.38
2	a	2.01–2.04	22	a	4.31–4.38
3	d	2.01–2.13	23	b	4.39–4.40
4	e	2.05–2.06	24	a	4.39–4.40
5	d	2.05–2.06	25	b	4.41–4.47
6	d	2.07–2.11	26	d	4.41–4.47
7	d	2.07–2.11	27	a	4.41–4.47
8	b	2.07–2.11	28	c	4.41–4.47
9	c	2.07–2.11	29	c	5.07–5.19
10	c	3.02–3.03	30	b	5.07–5.19
11	e	3.05–3.06	31	d	5.07–5.19
12	d	4.12–4.13	32	d	5.07–5.19
13	e	4.14–4.20	33	e	5.07–5.19
14	a	4.14–4.20	34	d	5.07–5.19
15	a	4.14–4.20	35	d	5.20–5.30
16	a	4.22–4.30	36	b	5.20–5.30
17	a	4.31–4.38	37	a	5.20–5.30
18	c	4.31–4.38	38	d	5.20–5.23
19	a	4.31–4.38	39	d	8.03
20	c	4.31–4.38	40	b	8.03

RESEARCH REPORT MASTERY TEST 3

1. Journal article reporting standards were developed to

   a. make it easier to generalize across fields.
   b. provide a degree of comprehensiveness in the information routinely included in reports of empirical investigations.
   c. help decision makers in policy and practice understand how research was conducted and what was found.
   d. allow techniques of meta-analysis to proceed more efficiently.
   e. all of the above.

2. A research report usually includes an introduction and sections called _____, Results, and Discussion.

   a. Method
   b. Bibliography
   c. Statement of the Problem
   d. Hypotheses

3. An abstract of a literature review or meta-analysis should describe

   a. the problem or relation(s) under investigation.
   b. type(s) of participants included in primary studies.
   c. main results, including most important effect sizes and any important moderators of these effect sizes.
   d. all of the above.
   e. a and b.

4. When citing references in the introduction,

   a. include an exhaustive historical account.
   b. cite select studies pertinent to the issue under investigation.
   c. refer the reader to reviews if they are available.
   d. stick to print sources rather than electronic sources.
   e. b and c.

5. The Method section should be described in enough detail to

   a. permit a reader to evaluate the plausibility of your hypotheses.
   b. permit an experienced investigator to replicate your study.
   c. allow a perfect duplication of your investigation.
   d. allow an editor to judge the external validity of your study.

6. In the Results section, you should

    a. summarize collected data.

    b. discuss the analytic treatment of data.

    c. discuss the implications of the findings.

    d. do all of the above.

    e. a and b.

7. The Discussion section generally includes

    a. a statement of support or nonsupport of all original hypotheses.

    b. a discussion of similarities and differences between your results and the results of others.

    c. an interpretation of the results that takes into account sources of potential bias.

    d. does all of the above.

    e. b and c.

8. Edit the following by selecting the correct arrangement of headings:

Results

    Pretraining Phase

        Accuracy.

    a. leave as is

    b. **RESULTS**

    Pretraining Phase

        Accuracy.

    c. **Results**

    Pretraining Phase

        Accuracy.

    d. **Results**

    Pretraining Phase

        Accuracy.

9. Consistency of verb tense helps to ensure smooth expression. Select the preferred match of section with verb tense from the following choices:

    a. conclusion: present tense

    b. literature review: present tense

    c. Results: past tense

    d. Method: past tense

    e. a, c, and d

10. The present tense is usually appropriate when you are

    a. presenting past research.
    b. describing the demographic details of the subjects.
    c. discussing implications of the results and presenting conclusions.
    d. describing the results.
    e. The present tense is never used.

11. Identify the example with incorrect use of capitalization:

    a. The conclusion is obvious: forgiveness is not granted to the stronger partner in an inequitable relationship.
    b. The Method section of the article described the Asian sample, which included 30 Chinese and 45 Vietnamese persons.
    c. The article referred to the associate learning model.
    d. The items were taken from the Depression scale of the Minnesota Multiphasic Personality Inventory—2 (Butcher, Dahlstrom, Graham, Tellegen, & Kaemmer, 1989).

12. Edit the following for capitalization of experimental conditions:

    The Sex-education and No-sex-education groups were then asked to view a film on the ethics of physical intimacy.

    a. leave as is
    b. The names of experimental conditions or groups should not be capitalized.
    c. All nouns following hyphens should be capitalized.
    d. The word *groups* also should be capitalized.

13. Capitalize

    a. the word *factor* when it is followed by a number (e.g., Factor 6).
    b. effects or variables that do not appear with multiplication signs.
    c. nouns that precede a variable.
    d. all of the above.
    e. none of the above.

14. The abbreviations S, E, and O (for subject, experimenter, and observer, respectively)

    a. are treated the same as other abbreviations in the text.
    b. are not used in APA articles.
    c. should be used only in table notes and figure captions.
    d. None of the above is correct.

15. Edit the following for the expression of numbers and scientific abbreviations:

The stimulus presentations were separated by a masking field that lasted for 2 ms.

   a. leave as is
   b. The stimulus presentations were separated by a masking field that lasted for two milliseconds.
   c. The stimulus presentations were separated by a masking field that lasted for 2 mss.

16. Edit the following for the expression of numbers:

Each critical word was preceded by zero, one, two, or three priming words in the list.

   a. leave as is
   b. Each critical word was preceded by zero, 1, 2, or 3 priming words in the list.
   c. Each critical word was preceded by 0, 1, 2, or 3 priming words in the list.
   d. Each critical word was preceded by zero (0), one (1), two (2), or three (3) priming words in the list.

17. Edit the following for the expression of numbers:

Each participant evaluated each of the 12 social portraits on each of 6 dimensions.

   a. leave as is
   b. Each participant evaluated each of the twelve social portraits on each of six dimensions.
   c. Each participant evaluated each of the 12 social portraits on each of six dimensions.
   d. Each participant evaluated each of the twelve social portraits on each of 6 dimensions.

18. Edit the following for the expression of numbers:

There were 20 4-person teams in each leadership-style condition.

   a. leave as is
   b. There were twenty four-person teams in each leadership-style condition.
   c. There were 20 four-person teams in each leadership-style condition.
   d. There were twenty 4-person teams in each leadership-style condition.

19. Edit the following for the expression of decimal fractions:

The correlation between scores on the two measures of job satisfaction was .84.

   a. leave as is
   b. The correlation between scores on the two measures of job satisfaction was 0.84.
   c. The correlation between scores on the two measures of job satisfaction was 84×10^{-2}.
   d. The correlation between scores on the two measures of job satisfaction was .8400.

20. Edit the following for the expression of numbers:

    Experiment I was a normative study to determine the reactions of hospital staff members to different diseases and illnesses.

    a. leave as is
    b. Experiment One was a normative study to determine the reactions of hospital staff members to different diseases and illnesses.
    c. Experiment 1 was a normative study to determine the reactions of hospital staff members to different diseases and illnesses.
    d. Experiment one was a normative study to determine the reactions of hospital staff members to different diseases and illnesses.

21. Edit the following for the expression of numbers:

    The tones were presented at 6,000 Hz for varying durations.

    a. leave as is
    b. The tones were presented at 6000 Hz for varying durations.
    c. The tones were presented at 6×10^3 Hz for varying durations.

22. The APA policy on the use of metric units in writing states that

    a. due to the complex nature of the metric system, it should be used only for publication in international journals.
    b. the metric system is used in journals if possible; when not possible, nonmetric units must also be accompanied by their equivalents (in parentheses) in the International System of Units.
    c. either system, metric or nonmetric, is acceptable.
    d. the use of nonmetric units is completely unacceptable.

23. When you include statistics from another source in a research report, cite the reference

    a. for less common statistics.
    b. for statistics used in a controversial way.
    c. when the statistic itself is the focus of an article.
    d. all of the above.

24. Edit the following for citing the source of a statistic in text:

    A chi-square test (Grimm & Yarnold, 2000) was used to compare the preference distributions for girls and boys.

    a. leave as is
    b. A chi-square test (see any standard statistics text) was used to compare the preference distributions for girls and boys.
    c. A chi-square test was used to compare the preference distributions for girls and boys.

25. Edit the following for the presentation of statistics:

The one-degree-of-freedom contrast of primary interest (the mean difference between Conditions 1 and 2) was also statistically significant at the specified .05 level, $t(df = 177) = 3.51, p < .001, d = 0.65$, 95% CI [0.35, 0.95].

   a. leave as is

   b. The one-degree-of-freedom contrast of primary interest (the mean difference between Conditions 1 and 2) was also statistically significant at the specified .05 level, $t_{177} = 3.51, p < .001, d = 0.65$, 95% CI [0.35, 0.95].

   c. The one-degree-of-freedom contrast of primary interest (the mean difference between Conditions 1 and 2) was also statistically significant at the specified .05 level, $t(177) = 3.51, p < .001, d = 0.65$, 95% CI [0.35, 0.95].

   d. The one-degree-of-freedom contrast of primary interest (the mean difference between Conditions 1 and 2) was also statistically significant at the specified .05 level, $t = 3.51, p < .001, d = 0.65$, 95% CI [0.35, 0.95].

26. Edit the following for the presentation of statistics:

High-school GPA statistically predicted college mathematics performance, $R^2 = .12, F(1, 148) = 20.18, p < .001$, 95% CI (.02, .22).

   a. leave as is

   b. High-school GPA statistically predicted college mathematics performance, $R^2 = .12, F(1, 148) = 20.18, p < .001$, 95% CI [$LL = .02, UL = .22$].

   c. High-school GPA statistically predicted college mathematics performance, $R^2 = .12, F(1, 148) = 20.18, p < .001$, 95% CI [.02, .22].

   d. High-school GPA statistically predicted college mathematics performance, $R^2 = .12, F(1, 148) = 20.18, p < .001$, 95% CI [.02; .22].

27. Edit the following for the presentation of statistics:

The applicants in the support condition ($n = 18$) were given a training course in resume writing and interview techniques.

   a. leave as is

   b. The applicants in the support condition (n = 18) were given a training course in resume writing and interview techniques.

   c. The applicants in the support condition ($N = 18$) were given a training course in resume writing and interview techniques.

   d. The applicants in the support condition (sample size = 18) were given a training course in resume writing and interview techniques.

28. Edit the following for typing statistical and mathematical copy:

The four-subtest battery added to this prediction, $R^2 = .21$, $\Delta R^2 = .09$, $F(4, 144) = 3.56$, p = .004, 95% CI [.10, .32].

   a. leave as is

   b. The four-subtest battery added to this prediction, $R^2 = .21$, $\Delta R^2 = .09$, $F(4, 144) = 3.56$, $p = .004$, 95% CI [.10, .32].

   c. The four-subtest battery added to this prediction, $R^2 = .21$, delta$R^2 = .09$, $F(4,144) = 3.56$, $p = .004$, 95% CI [.10,.32].

   d. The four-subtest battery added to this prediction, $R^2 = .21$, $\Delta R^2 = .09$, $F(4, 144)=3.56$, $p=.004$, 95% CI [.10, .32].

29. Tables should be used for

   a. any data relevant to the article.

   b. important data directly related to the content of the article.

   c. any data presented in the text.

   d. all of the above.

30. Tables should be an integral part of the text yet designed to be understood in isolation. To accomplish this end,

   a. use extensive footnotes (one third of a page).

   b. explain all but the most common statistical abbreviations.

   c. cite the table in the text by saying "in the above table."

   d. put tables in an appendix.

   e. do all of the above.

31. For all tables within one paper, use

   a. the same terminology.

   b. similar formats.

   c. similar titles.

   d. a and b.

32. The left-hand column of a table (the *stub*) usually lists

   a. mean values.

   b. the major independent variables.

   c. decked heads.

   d. none of the above.

33. The body of a table

    a. always contains data that are rounded off to the number of decimal places the precision of measurement justifies.
    b. contains columns of data even if those data can be easily calculated from other columns.
    c. contains words or numerical data.
    d. does all of the above.
    e. a and c.

34. When reporting confidence intervals in a table,

    a. use brackets as in text.
    b. use parentheses.
    c. give upper and lower limits in separate columns.
    d. do not state the confidence level.
    e. a and c.

35. Which of the following is the correct order of notes in a table?

    a. specific, probability, general
    b. general, specific, probability
    c. general, probability, specific
    d. none of the above.

36. When inserting rules in tables,

    a. limit the use of rules.
    b. use horizontal and vertical rules to separate rows and columns throughout.
    c. you may substitute appropriately positioned white spaces for rules.
    d. a and c.
    e. all of the above.

37. Which type of figure typically displays the relationship between two quantitative indices?

    a. maps
    b. graphs
    c. charts
    d. all of the above

38. A good figure caption

    a. describes the figure in detail no matter how lengthy it becomes.
    b. should refer the reader to a place in the text for explanation of the figure.
    c. is concise but explanatory.
    d. does none of the above.

39. What kind of lettering should be used in a figure?

    a. serif typeface
    b. simple, sans serif typeface
    c. boldface 16-point type
    d. boldface 6-point type
    e. a and c

40. Which of the following is the correct ordering of manuscript sections in a research report?

    a. Method, Results, tables, Discussion
    b. References, tables, figures
    c. author notes, figures, figure captions, tables
    d. none of the above

RESEARCH REPORT MASTERY TEST 3
ANSWER SHEET AND FEEDBACK REPORT

Question Number	Answer	APA Codes	Question Number	Answer	APA Codes
1		2.01–2.08	21		4.31–4.38
2		2.01–2.08	22		4.39–4.40
3		2.01–2.08	23		4.41–4.47
4		2.01–2.08	24		4.41–4.47
5		2.06–2.07	25		4.41–4.47
6		2.06–2.07	26		4.41–4.47
7		2.07–2.08	27		4.41–4.47
8		3.02–3.03	28		4.41–4.47
9		3.05–3.09	29		5.07–5.19
10		3.05–3.09	30		5.07–5.19
11		4.14–4.20	31		5.07–5.19
12		4.14–4.20	32		5.07–5.19
13		4.14–4.20	33		5.07–5.19
14		4.22–4.30	34		5.14–5.16
15		4.31–4.38	35		5.14–5.16
16		4.31–4.38	36		5.17
17		4.31–4.38	37		5.20–5.24
18		4.31–4.38	38		5.20–5.30
19		4.31–4.38	39		5.20–5.30
20		4.31–4.38	40		8.03

RESEARCH REPORT MASTERY TEST 3
ANSWER KEY

Question Number	Answer	APA Codes	Question Number	Answer	APA Codes
1	e	2.01–2.08	21	b	4.31–4.38
2	a	2.01–2.08	22	b	4.39–4.40
3	d	2.01–2.08	23	d	4.41–4.47
4	e	2.01–2.08	24	c	4.41–4.47
5	b	2.06–2.07	25	c	4.41–4.47
6	e	2.06–2.07	26	c	4.41–4.47
7	d	2.07–2.08	27	a	4.41–4.47
8	d	3.02–3.03	28	b	4.41–4.47
9	e	3.05–3.09	29	b	5.07–5.19
10	c	3.05–3.09	30	b	5.07–5.19
11	a	4.14–4.20	31	d	5.07–5.19
12	b	4.14–4.20	32	b	5.07–5.19
13	a	4.14–4.20	33	e	5.07–5.19
14	b	4.22–4.30	34	e	5.14–5.16
15	a	4.31–4.38	35	b	5.14–5.16
16	c	4.31–4.38	36	d	5.17
17	c	4.31–4.38	37	b	5.20–5.24
18	c	4.31–4.38	38	c	5.20–5.30
19	a	4.31–4.38	39	b	5.20–5.30
20	c	4.31–4.38	40	b	8.03

RESEARCH REPORT MASTERY TEST 4

1. Which of the following must identify the variables or theoretical issues under investigation and the relationship between them?

    a. the first sentence of the introduction section
    b. the conclusion of the Discussion section
    c. the title of the report
    d. the first table that is cited

2. The abstract should be formatted as

    a. a single paragraph in block format.
    b. one or more paragraphs with the first line indented.
    c. a single paragraph with the first line indented.
    d. more than one paragraph with space between paragraphs.

3. A good abstract

    a. needs to be dense with information.
    b. should include information that does not appear in the body of the manuscript.
    c. should be written in the present tense.
    d. all of the above.

4. Before writing the introduction, questions to bear in mind include the following:

    a. Why is this problem important?
    b. How does the study relate to previous work in the area?
    c. What are the theoretical and practical implications of the study?
    d. How do the study's hypotheses and research design relate to one another?
    e. all of the above

5. The subsections of the Method section generally include

    a. introduction, procedures, and design.
    b. procedures, tests, and participants.
    c. participants, apparatus, and procedure.
    d. none of the above.

6. In the Method section, the procedures section often includes descriptions of

    a. sampling procedures and sample size and precision.
    b. experimental manipulations or interventions used and how they were delivered.
    c. a summary of the collected data and analysis performed on that data.
    d. all of the above
    e. a and b.

7. An analysis of variance on your 2×2 design has revealed two main effects without an inter-action effect (fewer errors were made with easy tasks, and 6-month-olds did better than 1-month-olds in all tasks). In planning your Results section, the best alternative from among the possibilities is to include

    a. no figure.
    b. one figure to show the main effect of age.
    c. a simple table showing the main effect means.
    d. both a table and a figure.

8. The Discussion section should begin with

    a. a statement regarding implications for future research.
    b. a statement of the support or nonsupport of your original hypothesis.
    c. a reformulation of the important points of the paper.
    d. an analysis of the flaws in your study.

9. In the Discussion section, an interpretation of the results should take into account

    a. sources of potential bias and other threats to internal validity.
    b. the imprecision of measures.
    c. the overall number of tests or overlap among tests.
    d. other limitations or weaknesses of the study.
    e. all of the above.

10. On the basis of verb tense, in which part of a report is the following text segment likely to appear?

    College students judged time differently than did college faculty. Faculty were more accurate in judging the amount of time required to do academic tasks.

    a. Method
    b. hypotheses
    c. Results
    d. conclusion

11. Informal verb use such as *the participant felt that,* colloquial expressions such as *write up,* or approximations of quantity such as *quite a large part*

    a. have a place in serious scientific writing.
    b. add warmth to dull scientific prose.
    c. reduce word precision and clarity.
    d. can be used to enhance communication.
    e. are more acceptable in written than in oral communication.

12. In table headings and figure captions,

    a. capitalize only the first word and proper nouns.
    b. capitalize all major words.
    c. do not capitalize any words.
    d. capitalization will depend on the message you wish to convey.

13. Edit the following for the capitalization of names of experimental conditions:

    Participants in the tobacco-chewing therapy condition and in the no-therapy control condition then each received two wads of chewing tobacco.

    a. leave as is
    b. The names of experimental conditions should always be capitalized.
    c. The names of treatments such as *two wads* should be capitalized.
    d. Because *chewing tobacco* is a commercial term, it should be capitalized.

14. Which of the following should not be italicized?

    a. *a priori*
    b. 1973, *26,* 46–77
    c. *F*(I, 53) = 10.03
    d. *Journal of Experimental Psychology*

15. The abbreviations S, E, and O (for subject, experimenter, and observer, respectively)

    a. should always be used in articles.
    b. should be used only in journals that deal with physiological aspects of psychology.
    c. should be used only in the Method section.
    d. are not used in APA articles.

16. The general rule on expressing numbers is

    a. use words to express all numbers.
    b. use numerals to express all numbers.
    c. use numerals to express numbers 10 and above and words to express numbers below 10.
    d. use numerals to express numbers in tables and graphs and words to express numbers in the text.

17. Edit the following for the expression of numbers:

    The number of times the client used *I* in each therapy sessions is shown in Figure Two.

    a. leave as is
    b. The number of times the client used *I* in each therapy session is shown in Figure II.
    c. The number of times the client used *I* in each therapy session is shown in Figure 2.
    d. The number of times the client used *I* in each therapy session is shown in Figure two.

18. Edit the following for the expression of numbers:

The investigation compared the effectiveness of 3 methods for disseminating health information in 8 locations in the local community.

a. leave as is

b. The investigation compared the effectiveness of three methods for disseminating health information in 8 locations in the local community.

c. The investigation compared the effectiveness of three methods for disseminating health information in eight locations in the local community.

d. The investigation compared the effectiveness of 3 methods for disseminating health information in eight locations in the local community.

19. Edit the following for the expression of numbers:

Sixty percent of the victims' closest relatives, but only twenty-eight percent of the victims themselves, showed signs of anxiety and stress on the delayed tests.

a. leave as is

b. Sixty percent of the victims' closest relatives, but only 28% of the victims themselves, showed signs of anxiety and stress on the delayed tests.

c. 60% of the victims' closest relatives, but only 28% of the victims themselves, showed signs of anxiety and stress on the delayed tests.

d. Sixty percent (60%) of the victims' closest relatives, but only 28% of the victims themselves, showed signs of anxiety and stress on the delayed tests.

20. Edit the following for the expression of ordinal numbers:

The sequence of events changed on the fourth trial.

a. leave as is

b. The sequence of events changed on the 4th trial.

c. The sequence of events changed on the IVth trial.

21. Edit the following for the expression of decimal fractions:

The four-subtest battery added to this prediction, $R^2 = .21$, $\Delta R^2 = .09$, $F(4, 144) = 3.56$, $p = 0.004$, 95% CI [.10, .32].

a. leave as is

b. The four-subtest battery added to this prediction, $R^2 = .21$, $\Delta R^2 = .09$, $F(4, 144) = 3.56$, $p = .004$, 95% CI [.10, .32].

c. The four-subtest battery added to this prediction, $R^2 = .21$, $\Delta R^2 = .09$, $F(4, 144) = 3.56$, $p = .0040$, 95% CI [.10, .32].

22. Edit the following for the expression of numbers:

    The differential treatments were implemented on Trial 2.

    a. leave as is
    b. The differential treatments were implemented on Trial II.
    c. The differential treatments were implemented on Trial Two.
    d. The differential treatments were implemented on trial two.

23. Edit the following for the punctuation of numbers:

    We counted the number of times that incumbent and nonincumbent candidates referred to themselves and their opposition in a total of 1663 speeches during the 1984 and the 1988 political campaigns.

    a. leave as is
    b. We counted the number of times that incumbent and nonincumbent candidates referred to themselves and their opposition in a total of 1,663 speeches during the 1,984 and the 1,988 political campaigns.
    c. We counted the number of times that incumbent and nonincumbent candidates referred to themselves and their opposition in a total of 1,663 speeches during the 1984 and the 1988 political campaigns.

24. The APA policy on the use of metric units in writing states that

    a. because of the complex nature of the metric system, it should be used only for publication in international journals.
    b. the metric system is used in journals if possible; when not possible, nonmetric units must also be accompanied by their equivalents (in parentheses) in the International System of Units.
    c. either system, metric or nonmetric, is acceptable.
    d. the use of nonmetric units is completely unacceptable.

25. Formulas for statistics should be given

    a. at all times.
    b. for common statistics and for a statistic that is used only once in the article.
    c. for a statistic not yet widely known or for one that is the focus of the article.
    d. None of the above is correct.

26. Edit the following for the presentation of formulas:

    The participants were divided into high and low self-monitors by a median split (Mdn = 50th percentile).

    a. leave as is
    b. The participants were divided into high and low self-monitors by a median split (Mdn = 50th %ile).
    c. The participants were divided into high and low self-monitors by a median split [Mdn = (n + 1)/2].
    d. The participants were divided into high and low self-monitors by a median split.

27. Which of the following is the correct way to present a statistic in text?

    a. $t = 3.51(177)$, $p < .001$, $d = 0.65$, 95% CI [0.35, 0.95]
    b. $t = 3.51(177)$, $p < .001$, $d = 0.65$, 95% CI [0.35, 0.95]
    c. $t(177) = 3.51$, $p < .001$, $d = 0.65$, 95% CI [0.35, 0.95]
    d. any of the above
    e. none of the above

28. Edit the following for the presentation of statistics:

    The means for the no-treatment, placebo, and drug conditions were 8.8, 7.2, and 4.6, respectively.

    a. leave as is
    b. The means for the three conditions were 8.8, 7.2, and 4.6.
    c. The means for the three conditions were 8.8, 7.2, and 4.6, respectively.

29. Edit the following for the expression of statistical terms:

    The Ms for the alcohol and no-alcohol conditions were 18.4 and 13.6, respectively.

    a. leave as is
    b. The means for the alcohol and no-alcohol conditions were 18.4 and 13.6, respectively.
    c. The MEANS for the alcohol and no-alcohol conditions were 18.4 and 13.6, respectively.
    d. The $\overline{Xs}$ for the alcohol and no-alcohol conditions were 18.4 and 13.6, respectively.

30. Edit the following for typing statistical and mathematical copy:

    High school GPA statistically predicted college mathematics performance, $R^2 = .12$, $F(1, 148) = 20.18$, $p < .001$, 95% Confidence Interval [.02, .22].

    a. leave as is
    b. High-school GPA statistically predicted college mathematics performance, $R^2 = .12$, $F(1, 148) = 20.18$, $p < .001$, 95% CI [.02, .22].
    c. High-school GPA statistically predicted college mathematics performance, $R^2 = .12$, $F(1, 148) = 20.18$, $p < .001$, 95% CI [.02,.22].
    d. High-school GPA statistically predicted college mathematics performance, $R^2 = .12$, $F(1,148) = 20.18$, $p < .001$, 95% CI [.02, .22].

31. In scientific writing, the dominant function of graphical displays is

    a. decoration.
    b. communication.
    c. storage.
    d. calculation.
    e. exploration.

32. Design your graphical display with the reader in mind by

    a. placing items that are to be compared next to each other.
    b. placing labels so that they clearly abut the elements they are labeling.
    c. using fonts large enough to be read without magnification.
    d. all of the above.

33. Tables should be numbered in the order

    a. in which they are first mentioned in the text.
    b. that seems most logical to the author.
    c. that seems most logical to an editor.
    d. any of the above

34. From the following examples, select the correct way to refer to a figure in text:

    a. see the figure above.
    b. see the figure on page 14.
    c. see Figure 2.
    d. see Figure 2 above on page 14.

35. A table should be used

    a. whenever data analyses are involved.
    b. when an article is more than 1,200 words long.
    c. when it compresses data and allows relationships to be seen that are not readily seen in text.
    d. all of the above

36. Tables should be an integral part of the text yet should be readable alone. To accomplish this end,

    a. use extensive footnotes (one third of a page).
    b. explain all but the most common statistical abbreviations in the table title or table notes.
    c. cite the table in the text by saying "in the above table."
    d. put tables in an appendix.
    e. all of the above

37. Table numbers and titles should be typed

    a. centered in uppercase and lowercase letters.
    b. single-spaced at the top of the table.
    c. flush left in uppercase and lowercase letters.
    d. a and b

38. The column spanner of a table

    a. is a thick line used to mark the top of the table.
    b. is used exclusively to list the dependent variables.
    c. is used to identify the entries in the vertical columns in the body of the table.
    d. should be no more than 20 characters wide.

39. The body of a table

    a. always contains data rounded off to the nearest tenth.
    b. contains columns of data even if those data can be easily calculated from other columns.
    c. contains words or numerical data.
    d. does all of the above.

40. Table notes

    a. are placed below the bottom rule of a table.
    b. explain table data or provide additional information.
    c. acknowledge the source of a reprinted table.
    d. do all of the above.
    e. do none of the above.

41. A probability note to a table

    a. includes an explanation of abbreviations.
    b. begins with a superscript lowercase letter *a*.
    c. indicates how asterisks and other symbols are used in a table to indicate *p* values.
    d. a and b

42. A good figure

    a. conveys only essential facts.
    b. is easy to understand.
    c. is prepared in the same style as similar figures in the same article.
    d. is all of the above.

43. A figure caption

    a. functions as the title of the figure.
    b. does not need to include abbreviations and symbols defined in the text.
    c. includes acknowledgments that a figure is reproduced from another source.
    d. is all of the above.
    e. a and c

44. Which of the following should be placed on a separate page of a manuscript?

    a. the abstract
    b. appendices
    c. figure captions
    d. all of the above
    e. a and b

**RESEARCH REPORT MASTERY TEST 4
ANSWER SHEET AND FEEDBACK REPORT**

Question Number	Answer	APA Codes	Question Number	Answer	APA Codes
1		2.01–2.03	23		4.37–4.38
2		2.01–2.04	24		4.39–4.40
3		2.04–2.05	25		4.41–4.49
4		2.05–2.06	26		4.41–4.49
5		2.06–2.11	27		4.41–4.49
6		2.06–2.11	28		4.41–4.49
7		2.06–2.11	29		4.41–4.49
8		2.06–2.11	30		4.41–4.49
9		2.06–2.11	31		5.01–5.06
10		3.05–3.06	32		5.01–5.06
11		3.07–3.10	33		5.01–5.06
12		4.14–4.20	34		5.01–5.06
13		4.14–4.20	35		5.07–5.19
14		4.21	36		5.07–5.19
15		4.22–4.30	37		5.07–5.19
16		4.31–4.38	38		5.07–5.19
17		4.31–4.38	39		5.07–5.19
18		4.31–4.38	40		5.07–5.19
19		4.31–4.38	41		5.07–5.19
20		4.31–4.38	42		5.20–5.30
21		4.31–4.38	43		5.20–5.30
22		4.31–4.38	44		8.03

RESEARCH REPORT MASTERY TEST 4
ANSWER KEY

Question Number	Answer	APA Codes	Question Number	Answer	APA Codes
1	c	2.01–2.03	23	c	4.37–4.38
2	a	2.01–2.04	24	b	4.39–4.40
3	a	2.04–2.05	25	c	4.41–4.49
4	e	2.05–2.06	26	d	4.41–4.49
5	c	2.06–2.11	27	e	4.41–4.49
6	e	2.06–2.11	28	a	4.41–4.49
7	a	2.06–2.11	29	b	4.41–4.49
8	b	2.06–2.11	30	b	4.41–4.49
9	e	2.06–2.11	31	b	5.01–5.06
10	c	3.05–3.06	32	d	5.01–5.06
11	c	3.07–3.10	33	a	5.01–5.06
12	a	4.14–4.20	34	c	5.01–5.06
13	a	4.14–4.20	35	c	5.07–5.19
14	a	4.21	36	b	5.07–5.19
15	d	4.22–4.30	37	c	5.07–5.19
16	c	4.31–4.38	38	c	5.07–5.19
17	c	4.31–4.38	39	c	5.07–5.19
18	c	4.31–4.38	40	d	5.07–5.19
19	b	4.31–4.38	41	c	5.07–5.19
20	a	4.31–4.38	42	d	5.20–5.30
21	b	4.31–4.38	43	e	5.20–5.30
22	a	4.31–4.38	44	e	8.03

The Master Test Files

TERM PAPER MASTER TEST FILE

In contrast to empirical studies or theoretical articles, literature reviews

a. define and clarify a problem.
b. summarize previous investigations.
c. identify relations, contradictions, or inconsistencies in the literature.
d. suggest steps for future research.
e. do all of the above.

APA CODES: 1.01–1.06
answer: e
TP-FAMILIARIZATION

Edit the following for typing a title page:

THE SLEEPER EFFECT IN PERSUASION:
A META-ANALYTIC REVIEW

G. Tarcan Kumkale and Dolores Albarracín
University of Florida

a. leave as is

b.

The Sleeper Effect in Persuasion:
A Meta-Analytic Review

G. Tarcan Kumkale and Dolores Albarracín
University of Florida

c.

The Sleeper Effect in Persuasion:
A Meta-Analytic Review

G. Tarcan Kumkale & Dolores Albarracín
University of Florida

117

d.

The Sleeper Effect in Persuasion:
A Meta-Analytic Review

G. Tarcan Kumkale
University of Florida

Dolores Albarracín
University of Florida

APA CODES: 2.01–2.02
answer: b
TP-PRACTICE

A manuscript title should

   a. use abbreviations wherever possible.
   b. contain at least 30 words.
   c. be fully explanatory when standing alone.
   d. begin with the words *A Study of.*

APA CODES: 2.01–2.05
answer: c
TP-PRACTICE

In an introduction, controversial issues may be discussed when relevant; however, an author must

   a. present both sides of the issue.
   b. develop sound ad hominem arguments.
   c. cite authorities out of context.
   d. disguise his or her bias.
   e. do none of the above.

APA CODES: 2.01–2.05
answer: a
TP-MASTERY 1

The introduction of a manuscript

   a. discusses the importance of the problem and why it needs research.
   b. describes in detail how the study was conducted.
   c. describes the sample adequately.
   d. includes information essential to comprehend and replicate the study.

APA CODES: 2.01–2.08
answer: a
TP-MASTERY 3

In the Results section of a manuscript,

   a. report the data in sufficient detail to justify your conclusions.
   b. include a clear statement of support or nonsupport for your original hypotheses.
   c. provide dates defining the periods of recruitment and follow-up and the primary sources of the potential subjects, where appropriate.
   d. a and c are correct.

APA CODES: 2.01–2.08
answer: d
TP-MASTERY 3

A good title should

   a. include terms such as *A Study of* or *An Experimental Investigation of.*
   b. include abbreviations to keep it concise.
   c. be fully explanatory when standing alone.
   d. b and c.

APA CODES: 2.01–2.11
answer: c
TP-MASTERY 2

When listing an author of a paper, it is incorrect to

a. give titles (PhD or OFM).
b. spell out the middle name.
c. use informal names (Marty Seligman).
d. do all of the above.

APA CODES: 2.02–2.03
answer: d
TP-FAMILIARIZATION

Edit the following for the typing of a reference list:

1.	Employee Benefit Research Institute. (1992, February). *Sources of health insurance and characteristics of the uninsured* (Issue Brief No. 123). Washington, DC: Author.

2.	Kaiser Commission on Medicaid and the Uninsured. (2007, January). *Health coverage for low-income children: Fact sheet* (Publication No. 2144-05). Washington, DC: Kaiser Family Foundation.

a. leave as is

b. 1. Employee Benefit Research Institute. (1992, February). *Sources of health insurance and characteristics of the uninsured* (Issue Brief No. 123). Washington, DC: Author.

	2. Kaiser Commission on Medicaid and the Uninsured (2007, January). *Health coverage for low-income children: Fact sheet* (Publication No. 2144-05). Washington, DC: Kaiser Family Foundation.

c. Employee Benefit Research Institute. (1992, February). *Sources of health insurance and characteristics of the uninsured* (Issue Brief No. 123). Washington, DC: Author.

	Kaiser Commission on Medicaid and the Uninsured (2007, January). *Health coverage for low-income children: Fact sheet* (Publication No. 2144-05). Washington, DC: Kaiser Family Foundation.

d. 1. Employee Benefit Research Institute. (1992, February). *Sources of health insurance and characteristics of the uninsured* (Issue Brief No. 123). Washington, DC: Author.

	2. Kaiser Commission on Medicaid and the Uninsured (2007, January). *Health coverage for low-income children: Fact sheet* (Publication No. 2144-05). Washington, DC: Kaiser Family Foundation.

APA CODE: 2.11
answer: c
TP-MASTERY 2

Edit the following for the format of a reference list:

REFERENCES

Baron, J. B., & Sternberg, R. J. (1987). *Teaching thinking skills: Theory and practice.* San Francisco, CA: Freeman.

Nickerson, R. S., Perkins, D. N., & Smith, E. E. (1985). *The teaching of thinking.* Hillsdale, NJ: Erlbaum.

a. leave as is

b.   References

    Baron, I. B., & Sternberg, R. J. (1987). *Teaching thinking skills: Theory and practice.* San Francisco, CA: Freeman.

    Nickerson, R. S., Perkins, D. N., & Smith, E. E. (1985). *The teaching of thinking.* Hillsdale, NJ: Erlbaum.

c.   References

Baron, J. B., & Sternberg, R. I. (1987). *Teaching thinking skills: Theory and practice.* San Francisco, CA: Freeman.

Nickerson, R. S., Perkins, D. N., & Smith, E. E. (1985). *The teaching of thinking.* Hillsdale, NJ: Erlbaum.

d.   *References*

Baron, J. B., & Sternberg, R. J. (1987). *Teaching thinking skills: Theory and practice.* San Francisco, CA: Freeman.

Nickerson, R. S., Perkins, D. N., & Smith, E. E. (1985). *The teaching of thinking.* Hillsdale, NJ: Erlbaum.

APA CODE: 2.11
answer: c
TP-MASTERY 3

Which characteristic of a manuscript helps readers anticipate key points and track the development of an argument in a study?

    a. voice

    b. verb tense

    c. hypotheses

    d. headings

    e. all of the above

APA CODES: 3.01–3.03
answer: d
TP-PRACTICE

Before you begin to write, you should consider

    a. statistical analyses.

    b. length and structure of your paper.

    c. the hypotheses.

    d. all of the above.

APA CODES: 3.01–3.03
answer: b
TP-MASTERY 3

If a paper you have written is too long, shorten it by stating points clearly, confining discussion to the specific problem under investigation, writing in the active voice, and

   a. deleting or combining data displays.
   b. using more figures.
   c. developing new theories.
   d. repeating the major points.
   e. Do none of the above.

APA CODES: 3.01–3.03
answer: a
TP-MASTERY 1

Edit the following two levels of headings:

Amphibian Phobias
Fear of Forest Newts

   a. leave as is
   b.

Amphibian Phobias

Fear of Forest Newts

   c.

AMPHIBIAN PHOBIAS

Fear of Forest Newts

   d.

Amphibian Phobias

Fear of Forest Newts

APA CODES: 3.02–3.03
answer: d
TP-PRACTICE

Headings are important in scientific writing because they

   a. satisfy the requirements of APA style.
   b. establish the hierarchy of sections via format or appearance.
   c. fulfill a tradition in scientific writing.
   d. are used in place of paragraph indentation.
   e. All of the above are correct.

APA CODES: 3.02–3.03
answer: b
TP-MASTERY 4

It is important that headings convey to the reader

   a. a sense of style.
   b. the hierarchy of sections via format or appearance.
   c. the relative importance of the parts of the paper.
   d. b and c.
   e. all of the above.

APA CODES: 3.02–3.03
answer: d
TP-MASTERY 2

Articles in APA journals use

    a. centered, boldface, upper and lowercase headings only.

    b. centered, italicized, upper and lowercase headings only.

    c. centered, boldface upper and lowercase headings and flush left upper and lowercase headings only.

    d. a and c.

    e. as many as five levels of headings.

APA CODES: 3.02–3.03
answer: e
TP-MASTERY 2

A heading that is flush left

    a. should be boldface and typed in uppercase and lowercase letters.

    b. should be italicized.

    c. may be typed in all uppercase letters or all lowercase letters depending on the heading's level.

    d. must end with a period.

APA CODES: 3.02–3.03
answer: a
TP-MASTERY 3

Level 5 headings (indented, boldface, italicized lowercase paragraph headings ending with a period) are used

    a. only when the article requires five levels of headings.

    b. in short articles where one level of heading is sufficient.

    c. after any other type of heading in single-experiment papers.

    d. only in multiexperiment papers.

APA CODES: 3.02–3.03
answer: a
TP-MASTERY 3

In articles in which one level of heading is sufficient, use

    a. a flush left, boldface, uppercase and lowercase heading (Level 2).

    b. a centered, boldface, uppercase and lowercase heading (Level 1).

    c. any type (level) of heading.

    d. none of the above.

APA CODES: 3.02–3.03
answer: b
TP-MASTERY 4

The headings of a manuscript should

    a. reveal the logical organization of the paper to the reader.

    b. be at the same level for topics of equal importance.

    c. not be labeled with numbers or letters.

    d. do all of the above.

APA CODES: 3.02–3.04
answer: d
TP-FAMILIARIZATION

Which example is correct for an article in which four levels of heading are required?

a.

A History of Psychology

    Early Laboratories
        Harvard laboratories.
        James's basement.

b.

A History of Psychology
Early Laboratories

    Harvard Laboratories
        James's basement.

c.

A HISTORY OF PSYCHOLOGY

    Early Laboratories
        Harvard Laboratories
        James's basement.

d.

A HISTORY OF PSYCHOLOGY

    Early Laboratories
        Harvard laboratories.
        James's basement.

APA CODES: 3.02–3.03
answer: a
TP-FAMILIARIZATION

Edit the following by selecting the correct format:

Scenario and settings. The same action scenario was described in the context of eight different settings, designed to represent the eight physical–social conditions of the experiment.

a. leave as is
b. **Scenario and settings:** The same action scenario was described in the context of eight different settings, designed to represent the eight physical–social conditions of the experiment.
c.   **Scenario and settings.** The same action scenario was described in the context of eight different settings, designed to represent the eight physical–social conditions of the experiment.
d.   **Scenario and Settings.** The same action scenario was described in the context of eight different settings, designed to represent the eight physical–social conditions of the experiment.

APA CODES: 3.02–3.03
answer: c
TP-MASTERY 1

Within a paragraph or sentence, identify elements in a series by

a. Arabic numerals in parentheses.
b. Arabic numerals underlined.
c. lowercase letters in parentheses.
d. lowercase letters followed by a colon.

APA CODES: 3.02–3.04
answer: c
TP-MASTERY 1

Edit the following for the presentation of a series:

The participants were divided into three groups: (1) experts, who had completed at least four courses in computer programming; (2) intermediates, who had completed one course in computer programming and (3) novices, who had no experience in computer programming.

a. leave as is

b. The participants were divided into three groups: (a) experts, who had completed at least four courses in computer programming, (b) intermediates, who had completed one course in computer programming, and (c) novices, who had no experience in computer programming,

c. The participants were divided into three groups: a) experts, who had completed at least four courses in computer programming, b) intermediates, who had completed one course in computer programming, and c) novices, who had no experience in computer programming.

d. The participants were divided into three groups: (a) experts, who had completed at least four courses in computer programming; (b) intermediates, who had completed one course in computer programming; and (c) novices, who had no experience in computer programming.

APA CODE: 3.04
answer: d
TP-PRACTICE

Edit the following for the presentation of a series:

The researchers attempted to determine the relation between the age of the mother at the child's birth and (1) the child's intellectual development, (2) the child's social development, and (3) the mother's personal adjustment.

a. leave as is

b. The researchers attempted to determine the relation between the age of the mother at the child's birth and (a) the child's intellectual development, (b) the child's social development, and (c) the mother's personal adjustment.

c. The researchers attempted to determine the relation between the age of the mother at the child's birth and a) the child's intellectual development, b) the child's social development, and c) the mother's personal adjustment.

d. The researchers attempted to determine the relation between the age of the mother at the child's birth and (A) the child's intellectual development, (B) the child's social development, and (C) the mother's personal adjustment.

APA CODE: 3.04
answer: b
TP-FAMILIARIZATION

In casual conversation the word *since* is synonymous with _____, but in scientific writing it should be used only in its temporal meaning.

a. *however*

b. *because*

c. *after*

d. all of the above

APA CODES: 3.05, 3.22
answer: b
TP-FAMILIARIZATION

Continuity in the presentation of ideas can be achieved through

a. the use of only one type of punctuation.
b. the use of transitional words.
c. the use of the full range of punctuation to cue the reader to the pauses, inflections, subordination, and pacing normally heard in speech.
d. all of the above.
e. b and c.

APA CODES: 3.05–3.06
answer: e
TP-PRACTICE

Report your conclusions in

a. the past tense.
b. the past perfect tense.
c. the present tense.
d. any of the above.

APA CODES: 3.05–3.06
answer: c
TP-MASTERY 1

A finished report should possess

a. no recognizable theme or logical structure.
b. disconnected but logical subsections.
c. continuity in words, concepts, and thematic presentation.
d. inferential statistical tests of the data.

APA CODES: 3.05–3.06
answer: c
TP-MASTERY 2

You can check your writing for smoothness of expression by

a. looking for sudden shifts in topic, tense, or person.
b. having a colleague search the paper for abrupt transitions.
c. reading the paper aloud.
d. doing all of the above.
e. doing a and b.

APA CODES: 3.05–3.06
answer: d
TP-MASTERY 2

In scientific writing, continuity

a. is achieved partly by proper use of punctuation marks and transitional words.
b. is improved by avoiding the use of pronouns.
c. is enhanced by using many commas.
d. is not really necessary.

APA CODES: 3.05–3.06
answer: a
TP-MASTERY 3

Verb tense should

a. be varied to keep the reader's interest.
b. never change.
c. always be the past or past perfect.
d. be consistent within a section of a paper such as the Results.

APA CODES: 3.05–3.06
answer: d
TP-MASTERY 3

Which of the following sentences contains the preferable use of verb tense and voice?

a. The same results have been shown by Komarraju (2008).
b. Komarraju (2008) shows the same results.
c. Komarraju (2008) showed the same results.
d. Komarraju (2008) had shown the same results.

APA CODES: 3.05–3.06
answer: c
TP-FAMILIARIZATION

Readers will better understand your ideas if you aim for continuity by

a. using punctuation to show relationships between ideas.
b. using transitional words such as time links (e.g., *then* or *next*) or cause–effect links (e.g., *therefore* or *consequently*).
c. using contrast links (*however* or *whereas*).
d. using all of the above.
e. using only a and b.

APA CODES: 3.05–3.06
answer: d
TP-MASTERY 4

Synonyms should be used

a. with care because they may suggest subtle differences.
b. as much as possible to make the manuscript interesting.
c. whenever the same word is mentioned three or more times in one paragraph.
d. only in the conclusion.

APA CODES: 3.05–3.06
answer: a
TP-MASTERY 4

Redundancy, wordiness, jargon, evasiveness, and circumlocution contribute to

a. poor economy of expression.
b. clear scientific writing.
c. smoothness of expression.
d. erudite precision.
e. a more readable, less pompous style of writing.

APA CODES: 3.07–3.11
answer: a
TP-MASTERY 2

The best person to select to critique your manuscript is

a. your spouse or another person whom you know very well.
b. a colleague who is very familiar with your work.
c. a colleague who does not follow your work closely.
d. a stranger off the street.

APA CODES: 3.07–3.11
answer: c
TP-MASTERY 2

Colloquial expressions such as *the wind in his sails died* or approximations of quantity such as *the lion's share of*

a. reduce word precision and clarity.
b. add warmth to dull scientific prose.
c. have a place even in serious scientific writing.
d. can be used to enhance communication.
e. are more acceptable in written than in oral communication.

APA CODES: 3.07–3.11
answer: a
TP-MASTERY 4

Choose the best strategy for improving your writing style:

a. Write from an outline.

b. Put aside the first draft, then reread it after a delay.

c. Ask a colleague to critique the first draft for you.

d. Begin writing close to a deadline to enhance your motivation.

e. Any of the above except d can be used, but the strategy must match your personality and work habits.

APA CODES: 3.07–3.11
answer: e
TP-MASTERY 4

Good economy of expression may be achieved through using

a. short words.

b. short sentences.

c. direct, simple declarative sentences.

d. short paragraphs.

e. all of the above.

APA CODE: 3.08
answer: e
TP-FAMILIARIZATION

Which of the following phrases is redundant?

a. a total of 68 respondents

b. has been previously found

c. in close proximity

d. all of the above

e. none of the above

APA CODES: 3.08–3.09
answer: d
TP-PRACTICE

Which of the following should be used in scientific writing?

a. rhyming

b. poetic expressions

c. sexist language

d. none of the above

APA CODES: 3.08–3.09
answer: d
TP-PRACTICE

A writer must be careful when using the pronouns *this, that, these,* and *those.* The writer can eliminate or reduce the vagueness of these pronouns by

a. using them to modify a noun (e.g., this frenulum, that hypothalamus, these electrodes, those mice).

b. using them frequently.

c. clarifying what is being referred to for the reader.

e. a and c

APA CODES: 3.08–3.09
answer: e
TP-MASTERY 3

Which of the following phrases is an example of economical writing?

a. absolutely essential

b. four groups saw

c. one and the same

d. the reason is because

APA CODES: 3.08–3.11
answer: b
TP-MASTERY 1

Identify problems with clarity in the following sentences:

We read instructions to the students. This was done to reduce experimenter bias.

a. Both sentences are expressed clearly.
b. The first sentence is clear, but the second starts with *this,* a vague reference pronoun, and is in the passive voice.
c. The first sentence uses a first-person pronoun.
d. Instructions should be read to subjects, not students.
e. Both sentences are unclear.

APA CODES: 3.08–3.11
answer: b
TP-MASTERY 1

The phrase "the experiment demonstrated" is an example of which of the following writing errors?

a. ambiguity
b. redundancy
c. anthropomorphism
d. none of the above

APA CODE: 3.09
answer: c
TP-FAMILIARIZATION

Colloquial expressions such as *write up,* approximations of quantity such as *quite* a *large part,* and informal or imprecise use of verbs such as *the client felt that*

a. diffuse meaning and weaken statements.
b. add warmth to dull scientific prose.
c. have a place even in serious scientific writing.
d. can be used to enhance communication.
e. are more acceptable in written as compared with oral communication.

APA CODES: 3.09–3.11
answer: a
TP-PRACTICE

Which of the following is a good strategy for improving writing style?

a. Revise the first draft after a delay.
b. Use an outline.
c. Ask a colleague to review and critique the draft.
d. Do all of the above.

APA CODES: 3.10–3.11
answer: d
TP-MASTERY 3

Edit the following for the use of nonsexist language:

The data in Table 2 are the proportion of male participants who selected the competitive action over the cooperative one on each trial and, similarly, the proportion of female participants who were willing to act aggressively on each trial.

a. leave as is
b. The data in Table 2 are the proportion of male and female participants who selected the competitive action over the cooperative one on each trial.
c. The data in Table 2 are the proportion of male participants who selected the competitive action over the cooperative one on each trial and the proportion of female participants who were willing to act aggressively on each trial.
d. The data in Table 2 are the proportion of males who selected the competitive action over the cooperative one on each trial and, similarly, the proportion of females who were willing to act in typically male fashion (aggressively) on each trial.

APA CODES: 3.12–3.17
answer: a
TP-PRACTICE

In choosing nouns referring to ethnic groups, one should use

a. the preferred designation within a particular group.
b. the standard terms of the media.
c. anthropological terms.
d. none of the above.

APA CODES: 3.12–3.17
answer: a
TP-PRACTICE

Edit the following for avoiding gender bias:

It has been suggested that the major factor giving man a performance advantage over other primates on many cognitive tasks is that the tasks have been selected and administered by other men.

a. leave as is
b. It has been suggested that the major factor giving the species of man a performance advantage over other primates on many cognitive tasks is that the tasks have been selected and administered by men of the same species.
c. It has been suggested that the major factor giving human beings a performance advantage over other primates on many cognitive tasks is that the tasks have been selected and administered by other human beings.
d. It has been suggested that the major factor giving human beings (men or women) a performance advantage over other primates on many cognitive tasks is that the tasks have been selected and administered by other \human beings.

APA CODES: 3.12–3.17
answer: c
TP-FAMILIARIZATION

Edit the following for the use of nonsexist language:

The researcher must avoid letting biases and expectations influence his interpretation of the results.

a. leave as is

b. The researcher must avoid letting biases and expectations influence the interpretation of the results.

c. Researchers must avoid letting biases and expectations influence their interpretation of the results.

d. Both b and c are correct.

APA CODES: 3.12–3.17
answer: d
TP-MASTERY 1

Edit the following for the use of nonsexist language:

In the informational intervention, a nurse met briefly with her patient so that she could assess his recent risk behavior and stage-of-change for taking an HIV test.

a. leave as is

b. In the informational intervention, a nurse met briefly with his patient so that he could assess her recent risk behavior and stage-of-change for taking an HIV test.

c. In the informational intervention, a nurse met briefly with her patient so that she could assess his or her recent risk behavior and stage-of-change for taking an HIV test.

d. In the informational intervention, a nurse met briefly with the patient to assess his or her recent risk behavior and stage-of-change for taking an HIV test.

APA CODES: 3.12–3.17
answer: d
TP-MASTERY 2

Edit the following for the use of nonsexist language:

Before an experienced web developer attempts a particular solution, he tries to relate the problem structure to other problems he has solved successfully.

a. leave as is

b. Before an experienced web developer attempts a particular solution, he/she tries to relate the problem structure to other problems he/she has solved successfully.

c. Before experienced web developers attempt a particular solution, they try to relate the problem structure to other problems they have solved successfully.

d. none of the above

APA CODES: 3.12–3.17
answer: c
TP-MASTERY 3

Edit the following for the use of nonsexist language:

They predicted that men would be selected more frequently as partners for the cognitive tasks and that females would be chosen more frequently for the interpersonal tasks.

a. leave as is
b. They predicted that males would be selected more frequently as partners for the cognitive tasks and that nonmales would be chosen more frequently for the interpersonal tasks.
c. They predicted that men would be selected more frequently as partners for the cognitive tasks and that women would be chosen more frequently for the interpersonal tasks.
d. They predicted that guys would be selected more frequently as partners for the cognitive tasks and that girls would be chosen more frequently for the interpersonal tasks.

APA CODES: 3.12–3.17
answer: c
TP-MASTERY 4

Edit the following for avoiding bias in racial and ethnic identity:

Because of their cultural deprivation, children in Third World countries have fewer opportunities to develop our moral values.

a. leave as is
b. Because of cultural differences, children in Third World countries may develop moral values different from those of children in Western countries.
c. Because of their cultural deprivation, children in Third World countries may not develop higher moral values.
d. Because of their cultural experiences, children in Third World countries have fewer opportunities to develop our moral values.

APA CODES: 3.12–3.17
answer: b
TP-FAMILIARIZATION

Edit the following for language that avoids sexual orientation bias:

In the past few years, 26 states have changed their constitutions to restrict marriage to one man and one woman. There has been little research on the psychological effects of this political process on homosexual individuals.

a. leave as is
b. In the past few years, 26 states have changed their constitutions to restrict marriage to one man and one woman. There has been little research on the psychological effects of this political process on gay individuals.
c. In the past few years, 26 states have changed their constitutions to restrict marriage to one man and one woman. There has been little research on the psychological effects of this political process on gay men, lesbian women, and bisexual and transgender individuals.
d. In the past few years, 26 states have changed their constitutions to restrict marriage to one man and one woman. There has been little research on the psychological effects of this political process on deviant individuals.

APA CODES: 3.12–3.17
answer: c
TP-MASTERY 1

Edit the following for avoiding ethnic bias:

The sample of 400 undergraduates included 250 Black students (125 women and 125 men) and 150 Asian students (75 women and 75 men).

a. leave as is

b. The sample of 400 undergraduates included 250 Negro students (125 women and 125 men) and 150 Asian students (75 women and 75 men).

c. The sample of 400 undergraduates included 250 African American students (125 women and 125 men) and 150 Oriental students (75 women and 75 men).

d. The sample of 400 undergraduates included 250 Black students (125 women and 125 men) and 150 Oriental students (75 women and 75 men).

APA CODES: 3.12–3.17
answer: a
TP-MASTERY 2

Edit the following for avoiding ethnic bias:

Similarly, in community-based studies of diagnosed psychiatric disorders, uncultured migrant Mexican farmworkers, when compared with native-born Mexican Americans and with non-Hispanic White Americans, exhibited the lowest rates of psychiatric disorder (Alderete, Vega, Kolody, & Aguilar-Gaxiola, 2000).

a. leave as is

b. Similarly, in community-based studies of diagnosed psychiatric disorders, low-acculturated migrant Mexican farmworkers, when compared with native-born Mexican Americans and with the non-Hispanic White majority, exhibited the lowest rates of psychiatric disorder (Alderete, Vega, Kolody, & Aguilar-Gaxiola, 2000).

c. Similarly, in community-based studies of diagnosed psychiatric disorders, low-acculturated migrant Mexican farmworkers, when compared with native-born Mexican Americans and with non-Hispanic White Americans, exhibited the lowest rates of psychiatric disorder (Alderete, Vega, Kolody, & Aguilar-Gaxiola, 2000).

d. Similarly, in community-based studies of diagnosed psychiatric disorders, low-acculturated migrant Mexican farmworkers, when compared with the more sophisticated native-born Mexican Americans and with non-Hispanic normal White Americans, exhibited the lowest rates of psychiatric disorder (Alderete, Vega, Kolody, & Aguilar-Gaxiola, 2000).

APA CODES: 3.12–3.17
answer: c
TP-MASTERY 3

Edit the following for avoiding ethnic bias:

Participation in ethnic celebrations was compared for Oriental immigrants and their first-, second-, and third-generation counterparts of the same cohort.

a. leave as is
b. Participation in ethnic celebrations was compared for immigrants from Oriental countries and their first-, second-, and third-generation counterparts of the same cohort.
c. Participation in ethnic celebrations was compared for Oriental immigrants and first-, second-, and third-generation Orientals of the same cohort.
d. Participation in ethnic celebrations was compared for Asian immigrants and for first-, second-, and third-generation Asian Americans of the same cohort.

APA CODES: 3.12–3.17
answer: d
TP-MASTERY 4

Edit the following for verb tense:

After completing the preliminary battery of rating scales, each worker watched one of the six videotapes of a problem-solving session.

a. leave as is
b. After completing the preliminary battery of rating scales, each worker would watch one of the six videotapes of a problem-solving session.
c. After completing the preliminary battery of rating scales, each worker had watched one of the six videotapes of a problem-solving session.
d. After completing the preliminary battery of rating scales, each worker was watching one of the six videotapes of a problem-solving session.

APA CODES: 3.18–3.19
answer: a
TP-MASTERY 1

Edit the following for verb tense:

If the experiment was not designed this way, the results could not be interpreted properly.

a. leave as is
b. If the experiment was not being designed this way, the results could not be interpreted properly.
c. If the experiment was not designed this way, the results have not been interpreted properly.
d. If the experiment were not designed this way, the results could not be interpreted properly.

APA CODES: 3.18–3.19
answer: d
TP-MASTERY 2

Edit the following for grammar:

The six stimulus were presented to each participant simultaneously.

a. leave as is

b. The six stimuli were presented to each participant simultaneously.

c. The six stimuli was presented to each participant simultaneously.

d. The six stimuluses were presented to each participant simultaneously.

APA CODES: 3.18–3.19
answer: b
TP-MASTERY 3

Which of the following sentences is an example of correct agreement between subject and verb?

a. The percentage of correct responses increase with practice.

b. The data indicate that Brenda was correct.

c. The phenomena occurs every 100 years.

d. Neither the participants nor the confederate were in the classroom.

APA CODES: 3.18–3.19
answer: b
TP-MASTERY 4

Edit the following for the placement of the modifier *only:*

Although the authors reported the data for the mild and extreme patients in the placebo condition, they only reported the data for the extreme patients in the treatment condition.

a. leave as is

b. Although the authors reported the data for the mild and extreme patients in the placebo condition, they reported only the data for the extreme patients in the treatment condition.

c. Although the authors reported the data for the mild and extreme patients in the placebo condition, they reported the data for only the extreme patients in the treatment condition.

d. Although the authors reported the data for the mild and extreme patients in the placebo condition, they reported the data for the extreme patients only in the treatment condition.

APA CODES: 3.18–3.21
answer: c
TP-FAMILIARIZATION

Which of the following sentences is an example of correct agreement between the pronoun and its antecedent?

a. The instructions that were included in the experiment were complex.

b. Neither the highest scorer nor the lowest scorer had any doubt about their competence.

c. The group improved their scores 30%.

d. All of the above are correct.

e. None of the above is correct.

APA CODES: 3.18–3.23
answer: b
TP-FAMILIARIZATION

Edit the following for verb tense:

Wrightsman (2006) would demonstrate the same effect.

a. leave as is

b. Wrightsman (2006) demonstrated the same effect.

c. Wrightsman (2006) demonstrate the same effect.

d. The same effect was demonstrated by Wrightsman (2006).

APA CODES: 3.18–3.23
answer: b
TP-PRACTICE

Edit the following for the use of subordinate conjunctions:

Since left-handers constitute a minority of the population, there are less likely to be appropriate models for them to watch

a. leave as is

b. Because left-handers constitute a minority of the population, there are less likely to be appropriate models for them to watch.

c. Although left-handers constitute a minority of the population, there are less likely to be appropriate models for them to watch.

d. While left-handers constitute a minority of the population, there are less likely to be appropriate models for them to watch.

APA CODES: 3.20–3.23
answer: a
TP-FAMILIARIZATION

Edit the following for sentence structure:

Erikson's psychosocial theory emphasizes not only developmental stages but also the role of the ego.

a. leave as is

b. Erikson's psychosocial theory not only emphasizes developmental stages but also the role of the ego.

c. Erikson's psychosocial theory emphasizes not only developmental stages but also the role of the ego, as well.

d. Erikson's psychosocial theory emphasizes not only developmental stages but neither the role of the ego.

APA CODES: 3.20–3.23
answer: a
TP-FAMILIARIZATION

Which of the following sentences is grammatically correct?

a. Name the participant whom you found scored above the median.

b. The instructions that were included in the experiment were complex.

c. We had nothing to do with them being the winners.

d. None of the above is correct.

APA CODES: 3.20–3.23
answer: b
TP-PRACTICE

Edit the following for the placement of modifiers:

To manipulate ego-involvement, the respondents were given different average scores for their norm group.

a. leave as is
b. To manipulate ego-involvement, we gave the respondents different average scores for their norm group.
c. Manipulating ego-involvement, the respondents were given different average scores for their norm group.
d. The respondents were given different average scores for their norm group to manipulate ego-involvement.

APA CODES: 3.20–3.23
answer: b
TP-PRACTICE

Edit the following for the use of subordinate conjunctions:

While the argument is purely philosophical, the conclusion can also yield an empirical hypothesis, amenable to empirical investigation.

a. leave as is
b. The argument is purely philosophical, but the conclusion can also yield an empirical hypothesis, amenable to empirical investigation.
c. Since the argument is purely philosophical, the conclusion can also yield an empirical hypothesis, amenable to empirical investigation.
d. Both a and b are correct.

APA CODES: 3.20–3.23
answer: b
TP-PRACTICE

Edit the following for the use of pronouns:

The students that were assigned to the delay condition were asked to return at the same time in 3 days.

a. leave as is
b. The students who were assigned to the delay condition were asked to return at the same time in 3 days.
c. The students whom were assigned to the delay condition were asked to return at the same time in 3 days.
d. The students which were assigned to the delay condition were asked to return at the same time in 3 days.

APA CODES: 3.20–3.23
answer: b
TP-MASTERY 1

Edit the following for the choice and placement of modifiers:

Hopefully, the different types of music will induce different levels of arousal in the listeners.

a. leave as is
b. The different types of music will, hopefully, induce different levels of arousal in the listeners.
c. Hopefully the different types of music will induce different levels of arousal in the listeners.
d. We hope that the different types of music will induce different levels of arousal in the listeners.

APA CODES: 3.20–3.23
answer: d
TP-MASTERY 1

Edit the following for the use of relative pronouns:

The pictorial feedback: which was interpreted more rapidly than the verbal feedback: was remembered better.

a. leave as is
b. The pictorial feedback which was interpreted more rapidly than the verbal feedback was remembered better.
c. The pictorial feedback, which was interpreted more rapidly than the verbal feedback was remembered better.
d. The pictorial feedback that was interpreted more rapidly than the verbal feedback was remembered better.

APA CODES: 3.20–3.23
answer: d
TP-MASTERY 1

Edit the following for the use of pronouns:

The volunteer whom the confederate selected had to use nonverbal gestures to convey the emotion to the other volunteers.

a. leave as is
b. The volunteer that the confederate selected had to use nonverbal gestures to convey the emotion to the other volunteers.
c. The volunteer who the confederate selected had to use nonverbal gestures to convey the emotion to the other volunteers.
d. The volunteer which the confederate selected had to use nonverbal gestures to convey the emotion to the other volunteers.

APA CODES: 3.20–3.23
answer: a
TP-MASTERY 2

Misplaced modifiers can be avoided by

a. placing adjectives and adverbs at the end of sentences wherever possible.
b. placing adjectives and adverbs as close as possible to the words that they modify.
c. using the word *only* for clarification.
d. writing in the passive voice.

APA CODES: 3.20–3.23
answer: b
TP-MASTERY 2

Edit the following for sentence structure:

We recorded the difference between the performance of subjects who completed the first task and the second task.

a. leave as is
b. We recorded the difference between the performance of subjects who completed the first task and those who completed the second task.
c. We recorded the difference between both the performance of subjects who completed the first task as well as those who completed the second task.
d. We recorded the difference between the performance of subjects who completed the first task and the performance of those who completed the second task.

APA CODES: 3.20–3.23
answer: d
TP-MASTERY 2

Edit the following for the use of pronouns:

The team achieved a 38% improvement in their scores after undergoing imagery training.

a. leave as is

b. The team achieved a 38% improvement in its scores after undergoing imagery training.

c. The team achieved a 38% improvement in each of their scores after undergoing imagery training.

d. The team achieved a 38% improvement in scores after undergoing imagery training.

APA CODES: 3.20–3.23
answer: b
TP-MASTERY 3

Which of the following sentences illustrates the correct use of the word *while* in scientific writing?

a. Skutley (2003) found that participants performed well, while Jackson (2006) found that participants did poorly.

b. While these findings are unusual, they are not unique.

c. Skutley found that participants performed well while listening to music.

d. All of the above are correct.

APA CODES: 3.20–3.23
answer: c
TP-MASTERY 3

Edit the following for sentence structure:

Successful problem solvers were both more adept at representing the problem and using heuristics.

a. leave as is

b. Successful problem solvers were both more adept at representing the problem as well as using heuristics.

c. Successful problem solvers were more adept both at representing the problem and at using heuristics.

d. Successful problem solvers were more adept at both representing the problem and at using heuristics.

APA CODES: 3.20–3.23
answer: c
TP-MASTERY 3

Edit the following for the placement of modifiers:

The victims reported to trained volunteers still experiencing anxiety.

a. leave as is

b. The victims reported to trained volunteers, still experiencing anxiety.

c The victims, still experiencing anxiety, reported to trained volunteers.

d. The victims, reported to trained volunteers, still experiencing anxiety.

APA CODES: 3.20–3.23
answer: c
TP-MASTERY 4

Which of the following sentences is incorrect according to the preferred style stated in the APA *Publication Manual?*

a. While these findings are unusual, they are not unique.

b. Although these findings are unusual, they are not unique.

c. These findings are unusual, but they are not unique.

d. All of the above are incorrect.

APA CODES: 3.20–3.23
answer: a
TP-MASTERY 4

Edit the following for sentence structure:

Interviewees are often instructed to dress conservatively, to pay attention to their nonverbal communications, and that they should ask a few job-related questions of the interviewer.

a. leave as is

b. Interviewees are often instructed to dress conservatively, to pay attention to their nonverbal communications, and to ask a few job-related questions of the interviewer.

c. Interviewees are often instructed to dress conservatively, pay attention to their nonverbal communications, and that they should be prepared to ask a few job-related questions of the interviewer.

d. Interviewees are often instructed to dress conservatively and pay attention to their nonverbal communications, and that they should ask a few job-related questions of the interviewer.

APA CODES: 3.20–3.23
answer: b
TP-MASTERY 4

Edit the following for punctuation:

The participants were introduced to each of the trainers, but they were not allowed to choose their own trainer.

a. leave as is

b. The participants were introduced to each of the trainers but they were not allowed to choose their own trainer.

c. The participants were introduced to each of the trainers; but they were not allowed to choose their own trainer.

d. The participants were introduced to each of the trainers. But they were not allowed to choose their own trainer.

APA CODES: 4.01–4.05
answer: a
TP-MASTERY 1

In most cases, space once after all of the following punctuation marks except

a. periods in a reference citation.

b. internal periods in abbreviations.

c. periods ending a sentence.

d. colons.

APA CODES: 4.01–4.05
answer: c
TP-PRACTICE

One space should follow

a. semicolons.

b. colons in two-part titles.

c. periods in the initials of personal names.

d. all of the above.

e. none of the above.

APA CODES: 4.01–4.05
answer: d
TP-FAMILIARIZATION

Edit the following for punctuation:

The James–Lange theory of emotion states that our emotional experience is caused by our awareness of our bodily reaction to some stimulus: Schachter and Singer (1962) proposed that a cognitive evaluation mediates between the bodily reaction and the subjective emotion.

a. leave as is

b. The James–Lange theory of emotion states that our emotional experience is caused by our awareness of our bodily reaction to some stimulus. Schachter and Singer (1962) proposed that a cognitive evaluation mediates between the bodily reaction and the subjective emotion.

c. The James–Lange theory of emotion states that our emotional experience is caused by our awareness of our bodily reaction to some stimulus—Schachter and Singer (1962) proposed that a cognitive evaluation mediates between the bodily reaction and the subjective emotion.

d. The James–Lange theory of emotion states that our emotional experience is caused by our awareness of our bodily reaction to some stimulus. And Schachter and Singer (1962) proposed that a cognitive evaluation mediates between the bodily reaction and the subjective emotion.

APA CODES: 4.01–4.11
answer: b
TP-FAMILIARIZATION

Which of the following phrases is correctly punctuated?

a. the study, by Wenzel Brown and Beck (2008)

b. the study by Wenzel, Brown, and Beck (2008)

c. the study by Wenzel, Brown, and Beck, (2008)

d. the study by Wenzel, Brown and Beck (2008)

e. the study by Wenzel Brown and Beck (2008)

APA CODES: 4.01–4.11
answer: b
TP-FAMILIARIZATION

Edit the following for the punctuation of a reference entry:

VandenBos, G. R. (Ed.) (2007). *APA dictionary of psychology.* Washington, DC, American Psychological Association.

a. leave as is

b. VandenBos, G. R. (Ed.). (2007). *APA dictionary of psychology.* Washington, DC: American Psychological Association.

c. VandenBos, G. R. (Ed.). (2007). *APA dictionary of psychology,* Washington, DC: American Psychological Association.

d. VandenBos, G. R. (Ed.). (2007). *APA dictionary of psychology.* Washington DC: American Psychological Association.

APA CODES: 4.01–4.11
answer: b
TP-FAMILIARIZATION

When is the em dash used?

a. to extend a thought

b. instead of commas to set off restrictive clauses

c. never in APA articles

d. to indicate a sudden interruption in the continuity of a sentence

APA CODES: 4.01–4.11
answer: d
TP-FAMILIARIZATION

Edit the following for the correct way to report verbatim instructions:

The participants were instructed to COMPLETE EACH SENTENCE BASED ON YOUR OWN FEELINGS AT THIS MOMENT.

a. leave as is

b. The participants were instructed to *complete each sentence based on your own feelings at this moment.*

c. The participants were instructed to "complete each sentence based on your own feelings at this moment."

d. The participants were instructed to 'complete each sentence based on your own feelings at this moment.'

APA CODES: 4.01–4.11
answer: c
TP-FAMILIARIZATION

When quoting long sections of material (e.g., verbatim instructions to participants of more than 40 (words),

a. set the quote off with double quotation marks.

b. indent and use a block format without any quotation marks.

c. use a single quotation at the beginning and the end of the quotation.

d. use double quotation marks and single-spacing.

APA CODES: 4.01–4.11
answer: b
TP-FAMILIARIZATION

Edit the following for the punctuation of a series:

Theories of work motivation that emphasize the cognitive effects of information include *a* expectancy theory, *b* equity theory, and *c* goal-setting theory.

a. leave as is

b. Theories of work motivation that emphasize the cognitive effects of information include (a) expectancy theory, (b) equity theory, and (c) goal-setting theory.

c. Theories of work motivation that emphasize the cognitive effects of information include a) expectancy theory, b) equity theory, and c) goal-setting theory.

d. Theories of work motivation that emphasize the cognitive effects of information include: a. expectancy theory, b. equity theory, and c. goal-setting theory.

APA CODES: 4.01–4.11
answer: b
TP-FAMILIARIZATION

Edit the following for punctuation:

The confederate always sat to the experimenter's immediate left and the experimenter began the discussion by asking the confederate to evaluate the therapist's degree of empathy.

a. leave as is

b. The confederate always sat to the experimenter's immediate left; and the experimenter began the discussion by asking the confederate to evaluate the therapist's degree of empathy.

c. The confederate always sat to the experimenter's immediate left, the experimenter began the discussion by asking the confederate to evaluate the therapist's degree of empathy.

d. The confederate always sat to the experimenter's immediate left. The experimenter began the discussion by asking the confederate to evaluate the therapist's degree of empathy.

APA CODES: 4.01–4.11
answer: d
TP-PRACTICE

Use a semicolon

    a. to set off a nonessential or nonrestrictive clause.

    b. to separate two independent clauses that are not joined by a conjunction.

    c. in references between place of publication and publisher.

    d. to do all of the above.

APA CODES: 4.01–4.11
answer: b
TP-PRACTICE

Edit the following for the punctuation of ratios:

Moving from the lowest subordinate level of the organization to the highest executive level, the ratios of men to women were 1.2 to 1, 2 to 1, 6 to 1, and 14 to 1, respectively.

    a. leave as is

    b. Moving from the lowest subordinate level of the organization to the highest executive level, the ratios of men/women were 1.2/1, 2/1, 6/1, and 14/1, respectively.

    c. Moving from the lowest subordinate level of the organization to the highest executive level, the ratios of men:women were 1.2:1, 2:1, 6:1, and 14:1, respectively.

    d. Moving from the lowest subordinate level of the organization to the highest executive level, the ratios of men-women were 1.2-1, 2-1, 6-1, and 14-1, respectively.

APA CODES: 4.01–4.11
answer: c
TP-PRACTICE

Edit the following for punctuation:

The children: none of whom had previously heard the story: listened as a master storyteller told the story.

    a. leave as is

    b. The children; none of whom had previously heard the story; listened as a master storyteller told the story.

    c. The children . . . none of whom had previously heard the story . . . listened as a master storyteller told the story.

    d. The children—none of whom had previously heard the story—listened as a master storyteller told the story.

APA CODES: 4.01–4.11
answer: d
TP-PRACTICE

Punctuation is used incorrectly in which example?

    a. The results were significant (see Figure 5).

    b. Walker and Wang, 2009, reported results similar to those of Ho and Card (2001).

    c. Rats that have sustained bilateral excitotoxic lesions of the ventral hippocampus as neonates develop behavioral abnormalities as adults (Powell et al., 2006).

    d. "When sea turtles were studied, the effect was not seen" (p. 276).

APA CODES: 4.01–4.11
answer: b
TP-PRACTICE

THE MASTER TEST FILES 143

Edit the following for quotation from a source:

According to Diamond (2008), "the mind and brain often tend to work at a relatively gross level and only with effort (often in the form of inhibition) work more selectively, even in adults" [p. 4].

a. leave as is

b. According to Diamond (2008), "the mind and brain often tend to work at a relatively gross level and only with effort (often in the form of inhibition) work more selectively, even in adults" p. 4.

c. According to Diamond (2008), "the mind and brain often tend to work at a relatively gross level and only with effort (often in the form of inhibition) work more selectively, even in adults (p. 4)."

d. According to Diamond (2008), "the mind and brain often tend to work at a relatively gross level and only with effort (often in the form of inhibition) work more selectively, even in adults" (p. 4).

APA CODES: 4.01–4.11
answer: d
TP-PRACTICE

End a complete declarative sentence with a

a. prepositional clause followed by a question mark.

b. semicolon.

c. period.

d. comma.

APA CODES: 4.01–4.11
answer: c
TP-MASTERY 1

What punctuation should follow *volunteers* in the example below?

The participants in the first study were unpaid volunteers those in the second study were paid for their participation.

a. comma

b. colon

c. dash

d. semicolon

APA CODES: 4.01–4.11
answer: d
TP-MASTERY 1

Edit the following for punctuation:

They have agreed on the outcome . . . informed participants perform better than do uninformed participants.

a. leave as is

b. They have agreed on the outcome: Informed participants perform better than do uninformed participants.

c. They have agreed on the outcome: informed participants perform better than do uninformed participants.

d. They have agreed on the outcome; Informed participants perform better than do uninformed participants.

APA CODES: 4.01–4.11
answer: b
TP-MASTERY 1

Edit the following for punctuation:

The book—that the client selected to read aloud—was given to the client as a reward for completing the task.

   a. leave as is

   b. The book that the client selected to read aloud was given to the client as a reward for completing the task.

   c. The book, that the client selected to read aloud, was given to the client as a reward for completing the task.

   d. The book (that the client selected to read aloud) was given to the client as a reward for completing the task.

APA CODES: 4.01–4.11
answer: b
TP-MASTERY 1

Put no space after

   a. the colon in ratios.

   b. periods in the initials of personal names.

   c. periods that separate parts of a reference.

   d. all of the above.

   e. none of the above.

APA CODES: 4.01–4.11
answer: a
TP-MASTERY 1

Edit the following for highlighted key terms:

Among the most common types of synesthesia is *colored grapheme synesthesia,* in which black letters and digits induce colored percepts, and *time–space synesthesia,* in which units of time (weekdays, months, digits) are laid out regularly in space (e.g., Simner et al., 2006).

   a. leave as is

   b. Among the most common types of synesthesia is "colored grapheme synesthesia," in which black letters and digits induce colored percepts, and "time–space synesthesia," in which units of time (weekdays, months, digits) are laid out regularly in space (e.g., Simner et al., 2006).

   c. Among the most common types of synesthesia is 'colored grapheme synesthesia,' in which black letters and digits induce colored percepts, and 'time–space synesthesia,' in which units of time (weekdays, months, digits) are laid out regularly in space (e.g., Simner et al., 2006).

   d. Among the most common types of synesthesia is COLORED GRAPHEME SYNESTHESIA, in which black letters and digits induce colored percepts, and TIME–SPACE SYNESTHESIA, in which units of time (weekdays, months, digits) are laid out regularly in space (e.g., Simner et al., 2006).

APA CODES: 4.01–4.11
answer: a
TP-MASTERY 1

Edit the following for punctuation:

Culture change refers to leaving one's indigenous cultural context to spend increasing time in an alternative (e.g., White majority) one—*acculturation* refers to the extent to which those who do so retain their indigenous culture versus adopt the White-majority host culture as a result (Chun, Organista, & Marin, 2003; B. Kim & Abreu, 2001).

a. leave as is

b. *Culture change* refers to leaving one's indigenous cultural context to spend increasing time in an alternative (e.g., White majority) one: *acculturation* refers to the extent to which those who do so retain their indigenous culture versus adopt the White-majority host culture as a result (Chun, Organista, & Marin, 2003; B. Kim & Abreu, 2001).

c. *Culture change* refers to leaving one's indigenous cultural context to spend increasing time in an alternative (e.g., White majority) one; *acculturation* refers to the extent to which those who do so retain their indigenous culture versus adopt the White-majority host culture as a result (Chun, Organista, & Marin, 2003; B. Kim & Abreu, 2001).

d. *Culture change* refers to leaving one's indigenous cultural context to spend increasing time in an alternative (e.g., White majority) one, *acculturation* refers to the extent to which those who do so retain their indigenous culture versus adopt the White-majority host culture as a result (Chun, Organista, & Marin, 2003; B. Kim & Abreu, 2001).

APA CODES: 4.01–4.11
answer: c
TP-MASTERY 2

Edit the following for punctuation:

Damage to the left temporal cortex may impair language comprehension; whereas damage to the left frontal cortex may impair language production.

a. leave as is

b. Damage to the left temporal cortex may impair language comprehension. Whereas damage to the left frontal cortex may impair language production.

c. Damage to the left temporal cortex may impair language comprehension, whereas damage to the left frontal cortex may impair language production.

d. Damage to the left temporal cortex may impair language comprehension— whereas damage to the left frontal cortex may impair language production.

APA CODES: 4.01–4.11
answer: c
TP-MASTERY 2

Edit the following for punctuation:

These two participants, one from the first group and one from the second, were tested separately.

a. leave as is

b. These two participants; one from the first group and one from the second; were tested separately.

c. These two participants—one from the first group and one from the second—were tested separately.

d. These two participants [one from the first group and one from the second] were tested separately.

APA CODES: 4.01–4.11
answer: c
TP-MASTERY 2

Which of the following examples is correctly punctuated?

a. They have agreed on the outcome, informed participants perform better than uninformed participants.

b. They have agreed on the outcome; Informed participants perform better than uninformed participants.

c. They have agreed on the outcome: Informed participants perform better than uninformed participants.

d. None of the above is correct.

APA CODES: 4.01–4.11
answer: c
TP-MASTERY 2

Edit the following for punctuation:

The stimuli were six songs—matched for length, complexity of melody, and familiarity of lyrics.

a. leave as is

b. The stimuli were six songs: matched for length, complexity of melody, and familiarity of lyrics.

c. The stimuli were six songs; matched for length, complexity of melody, and familiarity of lyrics.

d. The stimuli were six songs matched for length, complexity of melody, and familiarity of lyrics.

APA CODES: 4.01–4.11
answer: d
TP-MASTERY 2

Edit the following for the correct way to identify an ironic, coined, or invented expression:

Although we found null results for a Gene × Environment interaction with parental education at the favorable end of the inattention distribution, it is likely that our measure of good attention indicated only an absence of attention problems because it was based on ratings of inattention, not on ratings of good attention.

a. leave as is

b. Although we found null results for a Gene × Environment interaction with parental education at the favorable end of the inattention distribution, it is likely that our measure of GOOD attention indicated only an absence of attention problems because it was based on ratings of inattention, not on ratings of good attention.

c. Although we found null results for a Gene × Environment interaction with parental education at the favorable end of the inattention distribution, it is likely that our measure of *good* attention indicated only an absence of attention problems because it was based on ratings of inattention, not on ratings of good attention.

d. Although we found null results for a Gene × Environment interaction with parental education at the favorable end of the inattention distribution, it is likely that our measure of "good" attention indicated only an absence of attention problems because it was based on ratings of inattention, not on ratings of good attention.

APA CODES: 4.01–4.11
answer: d
TP-MASTERY 2

Edit the following for punctuation:

Scores were higher when participants were tested in the same environment as the one in which they learned (the effect of environmental similarity is reflected in the interaction between study environment and test environment).

a. leave as is

b. Scores were higher when participants were tested in the same environment as the one in which they learned. (The effect of environmental similarity is reflected in the interaction between study environment and test environment.)

c. Scores were higher when participants were tested in the same environment as the one in which they learned. (The effect of environmental similarity is reflected in the interaction between study environment and test environment).

d. Scores were higher when participants were tested in the same environment as the one in which they learned (The effect of environmental similarity is reflected in the interaction between study environment and test environment.).

APA CODES: 4.01–4.11
answer: b
TP-MASTERY 2

Edit the following for punctuation:

The heated blocks were replaced every 20 min, whereas the frozen blocks were replaced every 2 hr, and the floors were kept clean with a damp cloth (see Ward-Robinson & Honey, 2000, for further details).

a. leave as is

b. The heated blocks were replaced every 20 min, whereas the frozen blocks were replaced every 2 hr, and the floors were kept clean with a damp cloth (see Ward-Robinson & Honey (2000) for further details).

c. The heated blocks were replaced every 20 min, whereas the frozen blocks were replaced every 2 hr, and the floors were kept clean with a damp cloth (see Ward-Robinson & Honey [2000] for further details).

d. The heated blocks were replaced every 20 min, whereas the frozen blocks were replaced every 2 hr, and the floors were kept clean with a damp cloth [see Ward-Robinson & Honey (2000) for further details].

e. The heated blocks were replaced every 20 min, whereas the frozen blocks were replaced every 2 hr, and the floors were kept clean with a damp cloth (see Ward-Robinson & Honey [2000], for further details).

APA CODES: 4.01–4.11
answer: a
TP-MASTERY 2

Edit the following for punctuation:

Optimal-level theories of motivation follow a homeostatic model. Opponent-process theories were advanced to account for addiction and other phenomena.

a. leave as is

b. Optimal-level theories of motivation follow a homeostatic model, opponent-process theories were advanced to account for addiction and other phenomena.

c. Optimal-level theories of motivation follow a homeostatic model -- Opponent-process theories were advanced to account for addiction and other phenomena.

d. Optimal-level theories of motivation follow a homeostatic model; Opponent-process theories were advanced to account for addiction and other phenomena.

APA CODES: 4.01–4.11
answer: a
TP-MASTERY 3

Edit the following for correct punctuation:

The floor was covered with cedar shavings and paper was available for shredding and nest building.

a. The sentence is correct as it stands.
b. Put a semicolon after *shavings.*
c. Put a comma after *shavings.*
d. Put a comma after *floor.*

APA CODES: 4.01–4.11
answer: c
TP-MASTERY 3

Edit the following for punctuation:

Thus, the light status for the three trials in the four conditions was on, off, on: off, on, off: on, on, on: or off, off, off.

a. leave as is

b. Thus, the light status for the three trials in the four conditions was on, off, on, off, on, off, on, on, on, or off, off, off.

c. Thus, the light status for the three trials in the four conditions was on, off, and on, or off, on, and off, or on, on, and on, or off, off, and off.

d. Thus, the light status for the three trials in the four conditions was on, off, on; off, on, off; on, on, on; or off, off, off.

APA CODES: 4.01–4.11
answer: d
TP-MASTERY 3

Which sentence is correct?

a. The digits were shown in the following order: 3, 2, 4, 1.
b. The digits were shown in the following order, 3, 2, 4, 1.
c. The digits were shown in the following order; 3, 2, 4, 1.
d. The digits were shown in the following order--3, 2, 4, 1.

APA CODES: 4.01–4.11
answer: a
TP-MASTERY 3

Edit the following for punctuation:

The four participants—two in the vicarious condition, one in the direct condition, and one in the control condition—who recognized the confederate as a fellow student were excused from the second part of the experiment.

a. leave as is

b. The four participants, two in the vicarious condition, one in the direct condition, and one in the control condition, who recognized the confederate as a fellow student were excused from the second part of the experiment.

c. The four participants: two in the vicarious condition, one in the direct condition, and one in the control condition: who recognized the confederate as a fellow student were excused from the second part of the experiment.

d. The four participants . . . two in the vicarious condition, one in the direct condition, and one in the control condition . . . who recognized the confederate as a fellow student were excused from the second part of the experiment.

APA CODES: 4.01–4.11
answer: a
TP-MASTERY 3

When introducing slang or a coined expression, use

a. double quotation marks the first time the expression is used.

b. double quotation marks every time it is used.

c. dashes every time it is used.

d. single quotation marks the first time it is used.

APA CODES: 4.01–4.11
answer: a
TP-MASTERY 3

Edit the following for punctuation:

The length of utterances increases dramatically between the ages of 18 and 60 months. See Figure 1.

a. leave as is

b. The length of utterances increases dramatically between the ages of 18 and 60 months (see Figure 1).

c. The length of utterances increases dramatically between the ages of 18 and 60 months (see Figure 1.).

d. The length of utterances increases dramatically between the ages of 18 and 60 months, see Figure 1.

APA CODES: 4.01–4.11
answer: b
TP-MASTERY 3

Edit the following for spacing and punctuation:

Physical and psychological measures of the members of the medical emergency staff—nurses and doctors—were taken immediately and 48 hr after the crisis.

a. leave as is

b. Physical and psychological measures of the members of the medical emergency staff - nurses and doctors - were taken immediately and 48 hr after the crisis.

c. Physical and psychological measures of the members of the medical emergency staff-nurses and doctors-were taken immediately and 48 hr after the crisis.

d. Physical and psychological measures of the members of the medical emergency staff — nurses and doctors — were taken immediately and 48 hr after the crisis.

APA CODES: 4.01–4.11
answer: a
TP-MASTERY 3

Edit the following for punctuation:

According to Piaget, the four stages of intellectual development are the sensorimotor stage, the preoperational stage, the concrete-operational stage, and the formal-operational stage.

a. leave as is

b. According to Piaget, the four stages of intellectual development are the sensorimotor stage, the preoperational stage, the concrete-operational stage and the formal-operational stage.

c. According to Piaget, the four stages of intellectual development are the sensorimotor stage; the preoperational stage; the concrete-operational stage; and the formal-operational stage.

d. According to Piaget, the four stages of intellectual development are the sensorimotor stage—the preoperational stage—the concrete-operational stage—and the formal-operational stage.

APA CODES: 4.01–4.11
answer: a
TP-MASTERY 4

Use a comma

a. before *and* and *or* in a series of three or more items.

b. between the two parts of a compound predicate.

c. to separate two independent clauses joined by a conjunction.

d. in all of the above instances.

e. in instances a and c above.

APA CODES: 4.01–4.11
answer: e
TP-MASTERY 4

Edit the following for punctuation:

From shortest to longest wavelength, the colors of the visible spectrum appear in the following order: blue-purple, blue, blue-green, green, yellow-green, yellow, orange, and red.

a. leave as is

b. From shortest to longest wavelength, the colors of the visible spectrum appear in the following order—blue-purple, blue, blue-green, green, yellow-green, yellow, orange, and red.

c. From shortest to longest wavelength, the colors of the visible spectrum appear in the following order: Blue-purple, blue, blue-green, green, yellow-green, yellow, orange, and red.

d. From shortest to longest wavelength, the colors of the visible spectrum appear in the following order . . . blue-purple, blue, blue-green, green, yellow-green, yellow, orange, and red.

APA CODES: 4.01–4.11
answer: a
TP-MASTERY 4

The em dash is used

a. to indicate a sudden interruption in the continuity of a sentence.

b. in APA articles only with permission of the manuscript editor.

c. frequently in APA articles in the statistical section.

d. by Type A psychologists.

APA CODES: 4.01–4.11
answer: a
TP-MASTERY 4

Edit the following for punctuation:

Kazdin's (2008) article, *Evidence-Based Treatments and Delivery of Psychological Services: Shifting Our Emphases to Increase Impact,* discussed evidence-based treatments as currently studied in relation to an overarching goal of interventions, namely, to reduce the burden of mental illness and the full range of social, emotional, and behavioral problems leading to impairment.

 a. leave as is

 b. Kazdin's (2008) article titled Evidence-Based Treatments and Delivery of Psychological Services: Shifting Our Emphases to Increase Impact, discussed evidence-based treatments as currently studied in relation to an overarching goal of interventions, namely, to reduce the burden of mental illness and the full range of social, emotional, and behavioral problems leading to impairment.

 c. Kazdin's (2008) article, 'Evidence-Based Treatments and Delivery of Psychological Services: Shifting Our Emphases to Increase Impact,' discussed evidence-based treatments as currently studied in relation to an overarching goal of interventions, namely, to reduce the burden of mental illness and the full range of social, emotional, and behavioral problems leading to impairment.

 d. Kazdin's (2008) article, "Evidence-Based Treatments and Delivery of Psychological Services: Shifting Our Emphases to Increase Impact," discussed evidence-based treatments as currently studied in relation to an overarching goal of our interventions, namely, to reduce the burden of mental illness and the full range of social, emotional, and behavioral problems leading to impairment.

APA CODES: 4.01–4.11
answer: d
TP-MASTERY 4

Use double quotation marks

 a. every time an invented expression is used.
 b. only the first time an invented expression is introduced.
 c. to introduce a technical or key term.
 d. Answers b and c are correct.

APA CODES: 4.01–4.11
answer: b
TP-MASTERY 4

Edit the following for punctuation:

Individuals with Type A personalities are more likely to develop coronary heart disease, CHD, than are those with Type B personalities.

 a. leave as is

 b. Individuals with Type A personalities are more likely to develop coronary heart disease, "CHD," than are those with Type B personalities.

 c. Individuals with Type A personalities are more likely to develop coronary heart disease— CHD—than are those with Type B personalities.

 d. Individuals with Type A personalities are more likely to develop coronary heart disease (CHD) than are those with Type B personalities.

APA CODES: 4.01–4.11
answer: d
TP-MASTERY 4

One space should follow

a. colons used in the text.
b. all punctuation marks at the end of sentences.
c. periods that separate parts of a reference.
d. a and c are correct.
e. none of the above.

APA CODES: 4.01–4.11
answer: d
TP-MASTERY 4

Edit the following for spacing and punctuation:

When the applicant's ethnic origin was stated explicitly, ethnic origin did affect selection (see Table 1,) but when ethnic origin was not stated explicitly, it did not affect selection (see Table 2) (The interviewers represented a variety of ethnic origins).

a. leave as is

b. When the applicant's ethnic origin was stated explicitly, ethnic origin did affect selection, (see Table 1), but when ethnic origin was not stated explicitly, it did not affect selection, (see Table 2). (The interviewers represented a variety of ethnic origins.).

c. When the applicant's ethnic origin was stated explicitly, ethnic origin did affect selection (see Table 1), but when ethnic origin was not stated explicitly it did not affect selection (see Table 2). (The interviewers represented a variety of ethnic origins.)

d. When the applicant's ethnic origin was stated explicitly, ethnic origin did affect selection, (see Table 1), but when ethnic origin was not stated explicitly, it did not affect selection, (see Table 2). (The interviewers represented a variety of ethnic origins).

APA CODES: 4.01–4.11
answer: c
TP-MASTERY 4

Edit the following for the punctuation of a reference citation in text:

Basu and Jones, 2007, considered several models of legal regulation in cyberspace.

a. leave as is

b. Basu and Jones, in 2007, considered several models of legal regulation in cyberspace.

c. Basu and Jones [2007] considered several models of legal regulation in cyberspace.

d. Basu and Jones (2007) considered several models of legal regulation in cyberspace.

APA CODES: 4.01–4.11, 4.21
answer: d
TP-MASTERY 1

Edit the following for punctuation:

Clients on the waiting list who were assigned to the delayed-treatment condition (whose mean age and educational level did not differ from those assigned to the immediate-treatment condition (see Table 2)) were asked to return in 6 weeks.

a. leave as is
b. Clients on the waiting list who were assigned to the delayed-treatment condition [whose mean age and educational level did not differ from those assigned to the immediate-treatment condition (see Table 2)] were asked to return in 6 weeks.
c. Clients on the waiting list who were assigned to the delayed-treatment condition (whose mean age and educational level did not differ from those assigned to the immediate-treatment condition [see Table 2]) were asked to return in 6 weeks.
d. Clients on the waiting list who were assigned to the delayed-treatment condition (whose mean age and educational level did not differ from those assigned to the immediate-treatment condition; see Table 2) were asked to return in 6 weeks.

APA CODES: 4.01–4.11
answer: e
TP-MASTERY 1

Which of the following examples should not be hyphenated?

a. role-playing technique
b. super-ordinate variable
c. six-trial problem
d. high-anxiety group
e. all of the above

APA CODES: 4.12–4.13
answer: b
TP-FAMILIARIZATION

Which of the following examples needs a hyphen?

a. a posteriori test
b. Type II error
c. 12th grade students
d. unbiased

APA CODES: 4.12–4.13
answer: c
TP-PRACTICE

Of the following examples, which represents correct hyphenation?

a. randomly-assigned participants
b. higher-scoring students
c. self-report technique
d. all of the above

APA CODES: 4.12–4.13
answer: c
TP-MASTERY 1

Edit the following for the spacing of punctuation:

Some therapists select the method of treatment on a case–by–case basis.

a. leave as is
b. Some therapists select the method of treatment on a case by case basis.
c. Some therapists select the method of treatment on a case-by-case basis.
d. Some therapists select the method of treatment on a case - by - case basis.

APA CODES: 4.12–4.13
answer: c
TP-MASTERY 2

Which of the following words with a prefix require a hyphen?

a. compounds in which the base word is an abbreviation (e.g., pre-UCS)
b. *self* compounds (e.g., self-esteem)
c. words that could be misunderstood or misread (e.g., un-ionized)
d. all of the above
e. none of the above

APA CODES: 4.12–4.13
answer: d
TP-MASTERY 2

The standard spelling reference for APA journals is

a. the most recent edition of *Merriam-Webster's Collegiate Dictionary.*
b. the *British-American Speller.*
c. the *Random House Dictionary.*
d. *Merriam-Webster's Collegiate Dictionary* for standard spelling; *APA Dictionary of Psychology* for psychological terms.

APA CODES: 4.12–4.13
answer: d
TP-MASTERY 3

Regarding spelling,

a. the standard spelling reference is the most recent edition of *Merriam-Webster's Collegiate Dictionary.*
b. APA accepts all the spelling choices listed in popular English dictionaries.
c. APA has no standard and leaves the matter up to the individual journal editors.
d. spelling of psychological terms should conform to the *APA Dictionary of Psychology.*
e. Both a and d are correct.

APA CODES: 4.12–4.13
answer: e
TP-MASTERY 4

In titles of books and articles, initial letters are capitalized in

a. major words when titles appear in regular text.
b. words of four letters or more when titles appear in regular text.
c. the second word in a hyphenated compound when titles appear in regular text.
d. major words and words of four letters or more when titles appear in reference lists.
e. all of the above except d.

APA CODES: 4.14–4.20
answer: e
TP-FAMILIARIZATION

Which of the examples contains incorrect capitalization?

a. During Trial 5, Group B performed at criterion.
b. Column 5, Row 3
c. The animals ate Purina Lab Chow after tail-pinch administration.
d. In his book, *History of Psychology,* the author describes Small's first use of the white rat.

APA CODES: 4.14–4.20
answer: b
TP-PRACTICE

Do not capitalize

a. names of laws, theories, and hypotheses.
b. trade and brand names.
c. references to a specific department within a specific university.
d. all of the above.
e. b and c.

APA CODES: 4.14–4.20
answer: a
TP-MASTERY 1

Which of the following examples shows the wrong way to capitalize proper nouns?

a. All psychology departments are reviewing their instructional effectiveness.
b. Gardner (2004) has further suggested that a good story overcomes resistances.
c. Dolphins are pro-Skinnerian.
d. The study involved whether the presentation of information in preparation for cesarean delivery reduces physiologic reactivity during surgical intervention and enhances post-operative recovery.
e. None of the above is incorrect.

APA CODES: 4.14–4.20
answer: e
TP-MASTERY 2

Identify the example with incorrect use of capitalization:

a. The conclusion is obvious: forgiveness is not granted to the stronger partner in an inequitable relationship.
b. The students reviewed the criticism of the article, "Ultrasonic Vocalizations Are Elicited From Rat Pups."
c. Undergraduates were advised to take an introductory psychology course.
d. The research described an associative learning model.

APA CODES: 4.14–4.20
answer: a
TP-MASTERY 3

From the alternatives below, select the one that correctly uses capitalization:

a. few significant differences were found.
b. However, one important observation was made: Participatory followers do not like to be led by authoritarian leaders.
c. Authoritarian followers behaved in a curious way: they acted in a participatory manner with participatory leaders.
d. these results were reported by Skutley and Jackson (2009).

APA CODES: 4.14–4.20
answer: b
TP-MASTERY 4

Which noun is incorrectly capitalized in the following example?

Bern's Theory of Self-Perception suggests that a woman will like a stranger more after she dances with him.

a. Theory
b. Self
c. Perception
d. Bern's
e. All of the above are incorrect except d.

APA CODES: 4.14–4.20
answer: e
TP-MASTERY 3

From the following choices, select the sentence with the correct use of italics:

a. She published her results in the *Journal of Interpersonal Relations and Social Behavior.*

b. She published *her* results in the Journal of Interpersonal Relations and Social Behavior.

c. When the *participants* read the nonsense syllable gux, they had to soothe their fearful partners.

d. *Albino rabbits,* oryctolagus cuniculus, were given unconditional positive regard in both experimental groups.

APA CODES: 4.21
answer: a
TP-FAMILIARIZATION

Edit the following for the format for anchor points on a rating scale:

The respondents ranked each of the 30 characteristics on a scale ranging from "most like my mother" (1) to "most like my father" (5).

a. leave as is

b. The respondents ranked each of the 30 characteristics on a scale ranging from MOST LIKE MY MOTHER (1) to MOST LIKE MY FATHER (5).

c. The respondents ranked each of the 30 characteristics on a scale ranging from: most like my mother (1) to: most like my father (5).

d. The respondents ranked each of the 30 characteristics on a scale ranging from 1 (*most like my mother*) to 5 (*most like my father*).

APA CODES: 4.21
answer: d
TP-PRACTICE

Which word in the following sentence should be italicized?

Snails were much faster when allowed to bathe ad lib in the acetylcholine solution.

a. acetylcholine

b. ad lib

c. snails

d. bathe

e. none of the above

APA CODES: 4.21
answer: e
TP-PRACTICE

Edit the following for the use of abbreviations to describe a procedural sequence:

All the men read about (R), danced with (D), or smelled (S) potential romantic partners. The bachelor group received one of four romantic interest arousal sequences: RDS, SDR, RSD, or SRD.

a. leave as is

b. read about, danced with, smelled; smelled, danced with, read about; read about, smelled, danced with; or smelled, read about, danced with.

c. read, danced, smelled; smelled, danced, read; read, smelled, danced; or smelled, read, danced.

d. read about then danced with then smelled; smelled then danced with then read about; read about then smelled then danced with; or smelled then read about then danced with.

APA CODES: 4.22–4.29
answer: a
TP-MASTERY 2

Is the Latin abbreviation *i.e.* used incorrectly in the following example?

Some lonely individuals appear to be shy but are in fact isolated because of social rejection (i.e., are actively avoided and excluded by others).

a. The parentheses should be removed.
b. The Latin abbreviation *i.e.* should be *viz.*
c. The abbreviation *i.e.* should be spelled out as *that is.*
d. In the above example, *i.e.* is used correctly.

APA CODES: 4.22–4.29
answer: d
TP-MASTERY 2

Edit the following for use of abbreviations:

According to Pavlov (1927), the conditioned stimulus (CS) should be delivered about 1 s before the unconditioned stimulus (US).

a. leave as is
b. According to Pavlov (1927), the conditioned stimulus (CS) should be delivered about 1 second before the unconditioned stimulus (US).
c. According to Pavlov (1927), the conditioned stimulus (CS) should be delivered about 1 sec. before the unconditioned stimulus (US).
d. According to Pavlov (1927), the CS should be delivered about 1 s before the US.

APA CODES: 4.22–4.30
answer: a
TP-FAMILIARIZATION

Which Latin abbreviation is used incorrectly in the following example?

When management styles were compared (authoritarian vs. participatory), it was found that authoritarian managers, i.e., those who did not solicit or act on input from subordinates, did not do well in smaller organizations (e.g., corporations with fewer than 100 employees).

a. vs.
b. i.e.
c. e.g.
d. all of the above
e. none of the above

APA CODES: 4.22–4.30
answer: b
TP-PRACTICE

Select the alternative that corrects the error of abbreviation in the following sentence. (Assume that the abbreviations are being used for the first time in text.)

The TAT was given to all LH women after they watched 30 hours of TV commercials.

a. The Thematic Apperception Test (TAT) was given
b. to all left-handed (LH) women after
c. they watched 30 hr of
d. television (TV) commercials
e. a, b, and c

APA CODES: 4.22–4.30
answer: e
TP-MASTERY 1

Which Latin abbreviations are used correctly in the following example?

Not all traditional sex role expectancies (e.g., women may cry, men should not cry) transfer into all organizational cultures, i.e., an organization's social environment. Some organizations punish traditional sex role behavior in women but not in men in military organizations, heavy industries, etc.

a. e.g.
b. i.e.
c. etc.
d. all of the above
e. none of the above

APA CODES: 4.22–4.30
answer: a
TP-MASTERY 1

Edit the following for correct use of abbreviations:

Three kinds of scene identification tasks were given to the police officers: a murder scene, a robbery scene, and an assault scene. The identification tasks were given in either an MS-RS-AS or AS-RS-MS sequence.

a. Define the abbreviations earlier by putting them within parentheses following the terms they abbreviated.
b. Use no abbreviations because they are not known by most readers.
c. Make no change because the connection between terms and abbreviations is obvious.
d. Make no change because the writer used standard abbreviations.

APA CODES: 4.22–4.30
answer: a
TP-MASTERY 3

Which abbreviations are used only in parentheses?

a. vs., kg, i.e.
b. i.e., cf., viz.
c. e.g., etc., min
d. none of the above.
e. all of the above.

APA CODES: 4.22–4.30
answer: b
TP-MASTERY 3

In the following example, which abbreviation should be spelled out when it is first introduced?

After the depressed clients received ECT treatments, changes in central nervous system activity were assessed with an EEG and effects on sleep were measured by observing REM periods.

a. EEG
b. ECT
c. REM
d. all of the above
e. any that do not appear in the latest edition of *Merriam-Webster's Collegiate Dictionary*

APA CODES: 4.22–4.30
answer: e
TP-MASTERY 4

Latin abbreviations, except *et al.,* should

   a. be spelled out each time they are used.

   b. not be used.

   c. be used only in parenthetical material.

   d. be spelled out the first time they are used.

APA CODES: 4.22–4.30
answer: c
TP-MASTERY 4

Identify the error in the following quotation:

The author speculated that "negative exemplars within the self-concept are more confidently known than affirmative exemplars" (Brinthaup, 1983).

   a. The quotation is correctly cited.

   b. The quotation should be in block form.

   c. Quotation marks are not necessary.

   d. A page number should be cited.

APA CODES: 6.03–6.10
answer: d
TP-FAMILIARIZATION

Direct quotations

   a. must follow the wording, spelling, and interior punctuation of the original source even if incorrect. Errors in the original source are indicated with [*sic*].

   b. must follow the wording and interior punctuation of the original source, but any spelling errors should be corrected.

   c. should follow the original source but minor changes in wording, spelling, and interior punctuation are permissible.

   d. None of the above is correct.

APA CODES: 6.03–6.10
answer: a
TP-PRACTICE

When citing a direct quotation from a source, be sure to give

   a. the authors' names.

   b. the year of publication.

   c. the page number or other locator, such as paragraph number.

   d. all of the above.

   e. the authors' names and the year of publication.

APA CODES: 6.03–6.10
answer: d
TP-PRACTICE

When citing the source of a direct quotation that you found on the web,

   a. it is not necessary to give source information in text because it will be given in the reference list.

   b. in online material without pagination, the citation should include information to help readers locate the quotation, such as a paragraph number or heading followed by paragraph number.

   c. the citation is enclosed in parentheses after the final period of the quotation if the quoted passage is set off in a block and not put in quotation marks.

   d. b and c are correct.

APA CODES: 6.03–6.10
answer: d
TP-MASTERY 1

When quoting,

    a. provide the author's name in the text.

    b. provide the year in the text.

    c. provide the page citation in the text, or another locator such as paragraph number.

    d. include a complete reference in the reference list.

    e. do all of the above.

APA CODES: 6.03–6.10
answer: e
TP-MASTERY 2

At the end of a block quote,

    a. cite the quoted source in parentheses after the final punctuation mark.

    b. cite the quoted source in parentheses before the final punctuation mark.

    c. use a footnote with a superscript number and cite the quoted source in the footnote.

    d. insert closing quotation marks before the citation.

APA CODES: 6.03–6.10
answer: a
TP-MASTERY 2

Identify the error in the following quotation:

Confusing this issue is the overlapping nature of roles in palliative care, whereby "medical needs are met by those in the medical disciplines; nonmedical needs may be addressed by anyone on the team" (Csikai & Chaitin, 2006).

    a. There are no errors.

    b. The quote should be in block form.

    c. The entire sentence should be in quotation marks.

    d. The page number needs to be cited.

APA CODES: 6.03–6.10
answer: d
TP-MASTERY 3

Any direct, short quotation (fewer than 400 words) of text from an APA journal or book must

    a. be accompanied by a reference citation.

    b. include a page number.

    c. be used only with the permission of the copyright owner.

    d. be footnoted if copyrighted.

    e. Answers a and b are correct.

APA CODES: 6.03–6.10
answer: e
TP-MASTERY 3

Edit the following for a quotation of a source:

McDowell and Clarke (2009) found that "in terms of the provision-of-opportunity pathway, parents play a direct role in creating social contact opportunities for infants and young children, but this role diminishes in frequency and form as the child reaches adolescence."

a. leave as is
b. The quote should be in block form.
c. A page number should be cited.
d. Quotation marks are not necessary.

APA CODES: 6.03–6.10
answer: c
TP-MASTERY 4

Edit the following for the citation of a quotation in text:

It has been suggested that "therapists in dropout cases may have inadvertently validated parental negativity about the adolescent without adequately responding to the adolescent's needs or concerns" (Robbins et al., 2003: 541).

a. leave as is
b. It has been suggested that "therapists in the dropout cases may have inadvertently validated parental negativity about the adolescent without adequately responding to the adolescent's needs or concerns" (Robbins et al., 2003, p. 541).
c. It has been suggested that "therapists in the dropout cases may have inadvertently validated parental negativity about the adolescent without adequately responding to the adolescent's needs or concerns" (Robbins et al., second section).
d. It has been suggested that "therapists in the dropout cases may have inadvertently validated parental negativity about the adolescent without adequately responding to the adolescent's needs or concerns" (Robbins et al., PubMed, pp. 7–8).

APA CODES: 6.03–6.10
answer: b
TP-MASTERY 2

Edit the following for the citation of a reference in text:

Among epidemiological samples, Kessler (p. 67) found that early onset social anxiety disorder results in a more potent and severe course.

a. leave as is
b. Among epidemiological samples, Kessler (Kessler, 2003), found that early onset social anxiety disorder results in a more potent and severe course.
c. Among epidemiological samples, Kessler found that early onset social anxiety disorder results in a more potent and severe course
d. Among epidemiological samples, Kessler (2003) found that early onset social anxiety disorder results in a more potent and severe course.

APA CODES: 6.11–6.21
answer: d
TP-FAMILIARIZATION

Edit the following for the citation of a reference in text:

A low Factor of informant consensus (F_{ic}) value indicates that the informants disagree on the taxa to be used in the treatment within a category of illness (Schlage, Mabula, Mahunnah, & Heinrich, 2000; Owuor & Kisangau, 2006). Schlage and others (2000) used F_{ic} to evaluate the ethnobotanical importance of the medicinal plants of Washambaa in Tanzania.

a. leave as is

b. A low Factor of informant consensus (F_{ic}) value indicates that the informants disagree on the taxa to be used in the treatment within a category of illness (Schlage, Mabula, Mahunnah, Heinrich, 2000; Owuor & Kisangau, 2006). Schlage used F_{ic} to evaluate the ethnobotanical importance of the medicinal plants of Washambaa in Tanzania.

c. A low Factor of informant consensus (F_{ic}) value indicates that the informants disagree on the taxa to be used in the treatment within a category of illness (Owuor & Kisangau, 2006; Schlage, Mabula, Mahunnah, Heinrich, 2000). Schlage, Mabula, Mahunnah, and Heinrich used F_{ic} to evaluate the ethnobotanical importance of the medicinal plants of Washambaa in Tanzania.

d. A low Factor of informant consensus (F_{ic}) value indicates that the informants disagree on the taxa to be used in the treatment within a category of illness (Owuor & Kisangau, 2006; Schlage, Mabula, Mahunnah, & Heinrich, 2000). Schlage et al. (2000) used F_{ic} to evaluate the ethnobotanical importance of the medicinal plants of Washambaa in Tanzania.

APA CODES: 6.11–6.21
answer: d
TP-FAMILIARIZATION

When a publication has no author,

a. the text citation should list the author as Anonymous.
b. the text citation should use the publisher's name.
c. no citation is necessary.
d. none of the above is true.

APA CODES: 6.11–6.21
answer: d
TP-FAMILIARIZATION

Edit the following for the citation of references in text:

Several parameters for rehabilitation psychology research need to be established to improve evidence-based intervention and therapy in this field (Tate, Findley, Dijkers, Nobunaga, & Karunas, 1999; Tate, 2001; Tate, 2006). Personality changes may also occur later in life (Neugarten, 1973; Neugarten & Hagestad, 1976; Neugarten, 1977).

a. leave as is

b. Several parameters for rehabilitation psychology research need to be established to improve evidence-based intervention and therapy in this field (Tate, 2001, 2006; Tate, Findley, Dijkers, Nobunaga, & Karunas, 1999). Personality changes may also occur later in life (Neugarten, 1973, 1977; Neugarten & Hagestad, 1976).

c. Several parameters for rehabilitation psychology research need to be established to improve evidence-based intervention and therapy in this field (Tate, 2001; Tate, 2006; Tate, Findley, Dijkers, Nobunaga, & Karunas, 1999). Personality changes may also occur later in life (Neugarten, 1973, 1977; & Hagestad, 1976).

d. Several parameters for rehabilitation psychology research need to be established to improve evidence-based intervention and therapy in this field (Tate, 2001, 2006; & Findley, Dijkers, Nobunaga, & Karunas, 1999). Personality changes may also occur later in life (Neugarten, 1973, Neugarten & Hagestad, 1976; ibid., 1977).

APA CODES: 6.11–6.21
answer: b
TP-FAMILIARIZATION

When citing a specific part of a source, be sure to give

a. the authors' names.

b. the year of publication.

c. a page number, paragraph number, or nearby heading and paragraph number if a quotation is cited.

d. all of the above.

APA CODES: 6.11–6.21
answer: d
TP-FAMILIARIZATION

Edit the following for the citation of a reference in text:

The acquisition of knowledge about human behavior and the development and continued use of relational skills have the potential to enhance functioning in personal and family lives (e.g., Guy, 1987; Norcross & Aboyoun, 1994).

a. leave as is

b. The acquisition of knowledge about human behavior and the development and continued use of relational skills have the potential to enhance functioning in personal and family lives (e.g., Norcross & Aboyoun, 1994; Guy, 1987).

c. The acquisition of knowledge about human behavior and the development and continued use of relational skills have the potential to enhance functioning in personal and family lives (e.g., Guy, 1987, Norcross & Aboyoun, 1994).

d. The acquisition of knowledge about human behavior and the development and continued use of relational skills have the potential to enhance functioning in personal and family lives (e.g., Guy: 1987; Norcross & Aboyoun: 1994).

APA CODES: 6.11–6.21
answer: a
TP-PRACTICE

Edit the following for the citation of a reference in text:

In three studies with college students, self-esteem was not longitudinally related to depression (Butler, A. C., et al., 1994; Lakey, B, 1988; Roberts, J. E., & Gotlib, I. H., 1997), and in a study of adolescents, self-esteem at age 14 did not predict depression at age 18 (Block, J. H., Gjerde, P. F., & Block, J. H., 1991).

    a. leave as is

    b. In three studies with college students, self-esteem was not longitudinally related to depression (Butler et al., 1994; Lakey, 1988; J. E. Roberts & Gotlib, 1997), and in a study of adolescents, self-esteem at age 14 did not predict depression at age 18 (Block, Gjerde, & Block, 1991).

    c. In three studies with college students, self-esteem was not longitudinally related to depression (Butler et al., 1994; Lakey, 1988; J. E. Roberts and Gotlib, 1997), and in a study of adolescents, self-esteem at age 14 did not predict depression at age 18 (Block, Gjerde, and Block, 1991)

    d. In three studies with college students, self-esteem was not longitudinally related to depression (J. E. Roberts & Gotlib, 1997, Butler et al., 1994, Lakey, 1988;), and in a study of adolescents, self-esteem at age 14 did not predict depression at age 18 (Block, Gjerde, & Block, 1991).

APA CODES: 6.11–6.21
answer: b
TP-PRACTICE

Choose the correct citation:

    a. (Birman et al., 2005; Espin, 2006; Falicov, 1998; Hondagneu-Sotelo & Avila, 1997; Perez Foster, 2001)

    b. (Greenleaf, 1977/2002).

    c. (Hondagneu-Sotelo & Avila, 1997; Falicov, 1998)

    d. b and c

    e. a and b

APA CODES: 6.11–6.21
answer: e
TP-PRACTICE

Edit the following for the citation of references in text:

As humans we have an emotional need to experience "belongingness" or "relatedness" (Baumeister & Leary, 1995; see also Reis & Collins, 2000; Burleson, Albrecht, & Sarason, 1994).

    a. leave as is

    b. As humans we have an emotional need to experience "belongingness" or "relatedness" (Baumeister & Leary, 1995; see also Burleson, Albrecht, & Sarason, 1994; Reis & Collins, 2000).

    c. As humans we have an emotional need to experience "belongingness" or "relatedness" (Baumeister and Leary, 1995; see also Burleson, Albrecht, and Sarason, 1994; Reis and Collins, 2000).

    d. As humans we have an emotional need to experience "belongingness" or "relatedness" (Baumeister & Leary, 1995, see also Burleson, Albrecht, & Sarason, 1994, Reis & Collins, 2000).

APA CODES: 6.11–6.21
answer: b
TP-PRACTICE

Edit the following for the citation of a reference in text:

Using a version of Barr et al.'s (2003) SPC procedure, Townsend, 2007, preexposed infants to a new pair (instead of to the same pair) of puppets for 1 hr per day on successive days. One member of each new pair had been preexposed the day before, whereas the other member was novel. In Phase 1, Townsend, 2007, preexposed 6-month-olds to a different pair of puppets on each of 2 days (A + B, B + C).

a. leave as is

b. Using a version of Barr et al.'s (2003) SPC procedure, Townsend (2007) preexposed infants to a new pair (instead of to the same pair) of puppets for 1 hr per day on successive days. One member of each new pair had been preexposed the day before, whereas the other member was novel. In Phase 1, Townsend preexposed 6-month-olds to a different pair of puppets on each of 2 days (A + B, B + C).

c. Using a version of Barr et al.'s (2003) SPC procedure, Townsend (2007) preexposed infants to a new pair (instead of to the same pair) of puppets for 1 hr per day on successive days. One member of each new pair had been preexposed the day before, whereas the other member was novel. In Phase 1, Townsend (ibid.) preexposed 6-month-olds to a different pair of puppets on each of 2 days (A + B, B + C).

d. Using a version of Barr et al.'s (2003) SPC procedure, Townsend (2007) preexposed infants to a new pair (instead of to the same pair) of puppets for 1 hr per day on successive days. One member of each new pair had been preexposed the day before, whereas the other member was novel. In Phase 1, Townsend (see Townsend, 2007) preexposed 6-month-olds to a different pair of puppets on each of 2 days (A + B, B + C).

APA CODES: 6.11–6.21
answer: b
TP-MASTERY 1

Edit the following for the citation of a reference in text:

Connell & Wellborn (1991) have stressed the importance of children's involvement in deciding what they would like to learn and do.

a. leave as is

b. J. P. Connell and J. G. Wellborn (1991) have stressed the importance of children's involvement in deciding what they would like to learn and do.

c. Connell, and Wellborn (1991) have stressed the importance of children's involvement in deciding what they would like to learn and do.

d. Connell and Wellborn (1991) have stressed the importance of children's involvement in deciding what they would like to learn and do.

APA CODES: 6.11–6.21
answer: d
TP-MASTERY 1

Order the citations of two or more works within the same parentheses in order of their

a. appearance in the reference list.

b. importance.

c. dates of publication.

d. status as printed or electronically published works.

APA CODES: 6.11–6.21
answer: a
TP-MASTERY 1

Edit the following for the citation of a specific part of an Internet source:

One explanation might be similar to that of another fibromyalgia study (Verbunt, Pernot, & Smeets, 2008), in which the level of disability participants perceived had more to do with their mental health status and less to do with their physical condition (PDF page 4).

a. leave as is

b. One explanation might be similar to that of another fibromyalgia study (Verbunt, Pernot, & Smeets, 2008), in which the level of disability participants perceived had more to do with their mental health status and less to do with their physical condition (n.p.).

c. One explanation might be similar to that of another fibromyalgia study (Verbunt, Pernot, & Smeets, 2008), in which the level of disability participants perceived had more to do with their mental health status and less to do with their physical condition (Discussion section, para. 1).

d. One explanation might be similar to that of another fibromyalgia study (Verbunt, Pernot, & Smeets, 2008), in which the level of disability participants perceived had more to do with their mental health status and less to do with their physical condition (http://www.hqlo.com/content/pdf/1477-7525-6-8.pdf).

APA CODES: 6.11–6.21
answer: c
TP-MASTERY 1

Cite personal communications that are not archived or recoverable

a. in the text.

b. in the reference list.

c. Do not cite personal communications.

d. Do a and b.

APA CODES: 6.11–6.21
answer: a
TP-MASTERY 1

From the examples below, identify the correct forms of citation:

a. In the United States, the American Cancer Society (2007) estimated that about 59,940 cases of melanoma would be diagnosed in 2007.

b. One could conclude that the longer the spacing gap, the greater the long-term retention of previously learned material (Rohrer & Pasher, 2007).

c. In 1997, Purcell found that large social gatherings could compound the difficulty of making new friends.

d. All of the above are correct.

APA CODES: 6.11–6.21
answer: d
TP-MASTERY 2

Edit the following for the citation of the first mention of a reference in text:

For example, Steinberg, Lamborn, Dornbusch, and Darling (1992) demonstrated that parental involvement had a greater impact on school performance when coupled with authoritative parenting styles.

a. leave as is

b. For example, Steinberg, Lamborn, Dornbusch, & Darling (1992) demonstrated that parental involvement had a greater impact on school performance when coupled with authoritative parenting styles.

c. For example, Steinberg, et al. (1992) demonstrated that parental involvement had a greater impact on school performance when coupled with authoritative parenting styles.

d. For example, Steinberg et al. (1992) demonstrated that parental involvement had a greater impact on school performance when coupled with authoritative parenting styles.

APA CODES: 6.11–6.21
answer: a
TP-MASTERY 2

Edit the following for the citation of references in text:

The study showed that among workers employed in natural resource, construction, and maintenance occupations, 12.3% of workers employed in farming, forestry, and fishing occupations and 8.1% of those in construction and extraction occupations were classified as working poor (see Table 4; U.S. Department of Labor, 2009; for complete data.)

a. leave as is

b. The study showed that among workers employed in natural resource, construction, and maintenance occupations, 12.3% of workers employed in farming, forestry, and fishing occupations and 8.1% of those in construction and extraction occupations were classified as working poor (see Table 4: U.S. Department of Labor, 2009, for complete data.)

c. The study showed that among workers employed in natural resource, construction, and maintenance occupations, 12.3% of workers employed in farming, forestry, and fishing occupations and 8.1% of those in construction and extraction occupations were classified as working poor (see Table 4; U.S. Department of Labor, 2009, for complete data.)

d. The study showed that among workers employed in natural resource, construction, and maintenance occupations, 12.3% of workers employed in farming, forestry, and fishing occupations and 8.1% of those in construction and extraction occupations were classified as working poor (see Table 4, U.S. Department of Labor, 2009, for complete data.)

APA CODES: 6.11–6.21
answer: d
TP-MASTERY 2

When a work has more than two authors and fewer than six authors, cite

a. all of the authors every time the reference occurs in text.

b. all of the authors the first time the reference occurs in text; use the surname of the first author followed by *et al.* in subsequent citations.

c. the surname of the first author followed by *et al.* every time the reference occurs in text.

d. none of the above.

APA CODES: 6.11–6.21
answer: b
TP-MASTERY 3

When a reference source is cited in the text,

a. each author's surname must be cited every time a reference occurs in the text when there are two authors of a single work.

b. every author's surname is used only the first time a reference is made when a work has more than two and fewer than six authors.

c. only the first author's surname is used followed by *et al.* every time the reference is made when a work has six or more authors.

d. All of the above are correct.

e. Only b and c are correct.

APA CODES: 6.11–6.21
answer: d
TP-MASTERY 3

Edit the following for the citation of references in text:

Several studies have attempted to explain the construct of temperament (Derryberry & Reed, 2005a, 2005b, in-press-a; Rothbart, 2003a, 2003b).

a. leave as is

b. Several studies have attempted to explain the construct of temperament (Derryberry & Reed, 2005a, b, in-press-a; Rothbart, 2003a, b).

c. Several studies have attempted to explain the construct of temperament (Derryberry & Reed, 2005a; Derryberry & Reed, 2005b; Derryberry & Reed, in-press-a; Rothbart, 2003a; Rothbart, 2003b).

d. Several studies have attempted to explain the construct of temperament (Rothbart, 2003a, 2003b; Derryberry & Reed, 2005a, 2005b, in-press-a).

APA CODES: 6.11–6.21
answer: a
TP-MASTERY 3

Edit the following for the citation of a specific part of a reference in text:

Lock (1999, chap. 3), an anthropologist, also developed the idea that the meaning of illness is a crucial issue in the understanding of health and illness.

a. leave as is

b. Lock (1999, ch. 3), an anthropologist, also developed the idea that the meaning of illness is a crucial issue in the understanding of health and illness.

c. Lock (1999, chapter 3), an anthropologist, also developed the idea that the meaning of illness is a crucial issue in the understanding of health and illness.

d. Lock (1999, Chapter 3), an anthropologist, also developed the idea that the meaning of illness is a crucial issue in the understanding of health and illness.

APA CODES: 6.11–6.21
answer: d
TP-MASTERY 3

From the examples below, identify the correct form of citation:

a. According to McMahon (p. 94), math ability is acquired.

b. McVay and Kane's (2009) findings support the notion that variation in conscious thoughts predict (if not cause) some variation in task performance.

c. In a study completed last year, Scarano found that androgynous women respond to self-worth dilemmas differently than do stereotypic women.

d. Csikai concluded that a coordinated team approach to end-of-life decision making may "possibly lead to increased and earlier referral to hospice" (Conclusion section).

APA CODES: 6.11–6.21
answer: b
TP-MASTERY 4

Edit the following for the citation of a reference in text:

Thus, the relationship between acculturation and ethnic-minority health behavior varies by ethnic group, by health behavior, by gender, and by the two- and three-way interactions of these variables (Landrine & Klonoff, 2004). Such complex data seem largely unintelligible and consequently remain largely peripheral to behavioral health interventions (Landrine & Klonoff).

a. leave as is

b. Thus, the relationship between acculturation and ethnic-minority health behavior varies by ethnic group, by health behavior, by gender, and by the two- and three-way interactions of these variables (Landrine and Klonoff, 2004). Such complex data seem largely unintelligible and consequently remain largely peripheral to behavioral health interventions (Landrine and Klonoff, 2004).

c. Thus, the relationship between acculturation and ethnic-minority health behavior varies by ethnic group, by health behavior, by gender, and by the two- and three-way interactions of these variables (Landrine & Klonoff, 2004). Such complex data seem largely unintelligible and consequently remain largely peripheral to behavioral health interventions (Landrine & Klonoff, 2004).

d. Thus, the relationship between acculturation and ethnic-minority health behavior varies by ethnic group, by health behavior, by gender, and by the two- and three-way interactions of these variables (Landrine & Klonoff: 2004). Such complex data seem largely unintelligible and consequently remain largely peripheral to behavioral health interventions (Landrine & Klonoff: 2004).

APA CODES: 6.11–6.21
answer: c
TP-MASTERY 4

When a work has two authors, cite

a. only one name every time the reference occurs in text.

b. both names the first time the reference occurs in text and only one thereafter.

c. both names every time the reference occurs in text.

d. None of the above is correct.

APA CODES: 6.11–6.21
answer: c
TP-MASTERY 4

Edit the following for the citation of references in text:

This diversity, along with the heavily bicultural context of the South Florida area, makes Miami a fertile background in which to conduct research on acculturation (cf. Coatsworth, Maldonado-Molina, Pantin, & Szapocznik, 2005; Schwartz, Pantin, Sullivan, Prado, & Szapocznik, 2006; Sullivan et al., 2007).

a. leave as is

b. This diversity, along with the heavily bicultural context of the South Florida area, makes Miami a fertile background in which to conduct research on acculturation (cf., Schwartz, Pantin, Sullivan, Prado, & Szapocznik, 2006; Sullivan et al., 2007; Coatsworth, Maldonado-Molina, Pantin, & Szapocznik, 2005).

c. This diversity, along with the heavily bicultural context of the South Florida area, makes Miami a fertile background in which to conduct research on acculturation (cf. Coatsworth et al., 2005; Schwartz, Pantin, Sullivan, Prado, & Szapocznik, 2006; Sullivan, Schwartz, Prado, Pantin, Huang, & Szapocznik, 2007).

d. This diversity, along with the heavily bicultural context of the South Florida area, makes Miami a fertile background in which to conduct research on acculturation (cf. Sullivan et al., 2007; Schwartz, Pantin, Sullivan, Prado, & Szapocznik, 2006; Coatsworth, Maldonado-Molina, Pantin, & Szapocznik, 2005).

APA CODES: 6.11–6.21
answer: a
TP-MASTERY 4

Edit the following for the citation of a specific part of a reference in text:

To help raise public awareness we can encourage industry groups to "develop media awards for positive portrayals of girls as strong, competent, and nonsexualized" (American Psychological Association, 2007).

a. leave as is

b. To help raise public awareness we can encourage industry groups to "develop media awards for positive portrayals of girls as strong, competent, and nonsexualized" (American Psychological Association, http://www.apa.org/pi/wpo/sexualizationrep.pdf).

c. To help raise public awareness we can encourage industry groups to "develop media awards for positive portrayals of girls as strong, competent, and nonsexualized" (American Psychological Association, 2007, p. 45).

d. To help raise public awareness we can encourage industry groups to "develop media awards for positive portrayals of girls as strong, competent, and nonsexualized (p. 45)" (American Psychological Association, 2007).

APA CODES: 6.11–6.21
answer: c
TP-MASTERY 4

Who has the responsibility to ensure that references are accurate and complete?

a. an editor
b. a proofreader
c. peer reviewer
d. an author

APA CODES: 6.22–6.25
answer: d
TP-FAMILIARIZATION

Edit the following for ordering the references in a reference list. Choose the sequence of numbers that indicates the correct order of the four references. (*Note:* The numbers are not part of APA Style but are used here for brevity.)

1. Ben-Zeev, T., & Star, J. (2001). Intuitive mathematics: Theoretical and educational implications. In B. Torff & R. Sternberg (Eds.), *The Educational Psychology Series. Understanding and teaching the intuitive mind: Student and teacher learning* (pp. 29–56). Mahwah, NJ: Erlbaum.

2. Ben-Zeev, T., Duncan, S., & Forbes, C. (2005). Stereotypes and math performance. In J. I. D. Campbell (Ed.), *Handbook of mathematical cognition* (pp. 235–249). New York, NY: Psychology Press.

3. Bender, W. N., Vail, C. O., & Scott, K. (1995). Teachers' attitudes toward increased mainstreaming: Implementing effective instruction for students with learning disabilities. *Journal of Learning Disabilities, 28,* 87–84, 120. doi:10.1177/002221949502800203

4. Bender, W. N. (2005). *Differentiating math instruction: Strategies that work for K–8 classrooms!* Thousand Oaks, CA: Corwin Press.

a. leave as is (i.e., 1, 2, 3, 4)
b. 3, 4, 1, 2
c. 3, 1, 4, 2
d. 4, 3, 2, 1

APA CODES: 6.22–6.25
answer: d
TP-FAMILIARIZATION

Edit the following for the application of APA reference style:

Lassen, S. R., Steele, M. M., & Sailor, W. The relationship of school-wide positive behavior support to academic achievement in an urban middle school. *Psychology in the Schools, 43,* 701–712. (2006). doi:10.1002/pits.20177

a. leave as is

b. Lassen, S. R., Steele, M. M., & Sailor, W. 2006. The relationship of school-wide positive behavior support to academic achievement in an urban middle school. *Psychology in the Schools, 43,* 701–712. doi:10.1002/pits.20177

c. Lassen, S. R., Steele, M. M., & Sailor, W. (2006) The relationship of school-wide positive behavior support to academic achievement in an urban middle school. *Psychology in the Schools, 43,* 701–712. doi:10.1002/pits.20177

d. Lassen, S. R., Steele, M. M., & Sailor, W. (2006). The relationship of school-wide positive behavior support to academic achievement in an urban middle school. *Psychology in the Schools, 43,* 701–712. doi:10.1002/pits.20177

APA CODES: 6.22–6.25
answer: d
TP-FAMILIARIZATION

Edit the following for the application of APA reference style:

> Real Academia Española. (2001). *Diccionario de la lengua española, 22nd ed.* [Dictionary of the Spanish language]. Madrid: Author.

a. leave as is

b. Real Academia Española. (2001). *Diccionario de la lengua española* [Dictionary of the Spanish language, 22nd ed.]. Madrid, Spain: Author.

c. Real Academia Española. (2001). *Diccionario de la lengua española* [Dictionary of the Spanish language] (22nd ed.). Madrid, Spain: Author.

d. Real Academia Española. (2001). *Diccionario de la lengua española* [Dictionary of the Spanish language: Twenty-second edition]. Madrid, Spain: Author.

APA CODES: 6.22–6.25
answer: c
TP-FAMILIARIZATION

If no author is given for a source, put the source in the correct order in the reference list by

a. moving the title to the author position and alphabetizing by the first significant word of the title.

b. beginning the entry with the word *Anonymous* and alphabetizing as if this were the author's name.

c. moving the journal title or publishing house to the author position and alphabetizing by the first significant word of the name.

d. Doing none of the above.

APA CODES: 6.22–6.25
answer: a
TP-PRACTICE

In a reference list, when ordering several works by the same first author,

a. place single-author entries before multiple-author entries.

b. write "ibid." for the first author's name after the first entry.

c. order them alphabetically by the name of the journal.

d. do all of the above.

APA CODES: 6.22–6.25
answer: a
TP-PRACTICE

Edit the following for ordering the references in a reference list. Choose the sequence of numbers that indicates the correct order of the four references. (Note: The numbers are not part of APA Style but are used here for brevity.)

1. Steege, M. W., Brown-Chidsey, R., & Mace, F. C. (2002). Best practices in evaluating interventions. In A. Thomas & J. Grimes (Eds.), *Best practices in school psychology IV* (pp. 517–534). Washington, DC: National Association of School Psychologists.

2. Steege, M. W., & Brown-Chidsey, R. (2005). Functional behavioral assessment: The cornerstone of effective problem solving. In R. Brown-Chidsey (Ed.), *Assessment for intervention: A problem solving approach* (pp. 131–154). New York, NY: Guilford.

3. Stokes, T. F., & Osnes, P. G. (1988) The developing applied technology of generalization and maintenance. In R. Horner, G. Dunlap, & R. L. Koegal (Eds.), *Generalization and maintenance: Life-style changes in applied settings* (pp. 5–19). Baltimore, MD: Brookes.

4. Stokes, T. (1992). Discrimination and generalization. *Journal of Applied Behavior Analysis, 25,* 429–432.

a. leave as is (i.e., 1, 2, 3, 4)
b. 2, 1, 3, 4
c. 2, 1, 4, 3
d. 3, 2, 1, 4

APA CODES: 6.22–6.25
answer: c
TP-MASTERY 1

The general rule to follow in alphabetizing surnames that contain articles and prepositions (e.g., Ibn Abdulaziz, von Helmholtz) is to

a. alphabetize letter by letter.
b. always treat the prefix as part of the middle name.
c. treat the prefix as part of the surname if it is commonly used that way or as part of the middle name if it is not customarily used that way.
d. a and c are correct.

APA CODES: 6.22–6.25
answer: d
TP-MASTERY 1

A reference list

a. cites all works supportive of or contradictory to the text.
b. is a synonym for bibliography.
c. should include only the references cited anywhere in the article.
d. should never be used in short articles.

APA CODES: 6.22–6.25
answer: c
TP-MASTERY 2

Edit the following for ordering the references in a reference list. Choose the sequence of numbers that indicates the correct order of the four references. (Note: The numbers are not part of APA Style but are used here for brevity.)

1. Chamberlin, M. T., & Zawojewski, J. (2006). A worthwhile mathematical task for students and their teachers. *Mathematics Teaching in the Middle School, 12,* 82–87.

2. Chamberlin-Quinlisk, C. R. (2005). Across continents or across the street: Using local resources to cultivate intercultural awareness. *Intercultural Education, 16,* 469–479.

3. Chamberlin, S. A., Buchanan, & M. Vercimak, D. (2007). Serving twice-exceptional preschoolers: Blending gifted education and early childhood special education practices in assessment and program planning. *Journal for the Education of the Gifted, 30,* 372–394.

4. Chamberlin, S. A. (2008). An examination of articles in gifted education and multicultural education journals. *Journal for the Education of the Gifted, 32,* 86–99.

a. leave as is (i.e., 1, 2, 3, 4)
b. 1, 4, 3, 2
c. 1, 2, 4, 3
d. 2, 1, 4, 3

APA CODES: 6.22–6.25
answer: b
TP-MASTERY 2

The reference list at the end of a journal article

a. includes personal communications, such as letters, memoranda, and informal electronic communications.
b. provides the information necessary to identify and retrieve each source.
c. includes only references that document the article and provide recoverable data.
d. b and c.
e. all of the above.

APA CODES: 6.22–6.25
answer: d
TP-MASTERY 3

Edit the following for ordering the references in a reference list. Choose the sequence of numbers that indicates the correct order of the four references. (Note: The numbers are not part of APA Style but are used here for brevity.)

1. Allport, G. W. (1930–1967). Correspondence. Gordon W. Allport Papers (HUG 4118.10), Harvard University Archives, Cambridge, MA.

2. Allport, G. W. (1979). *The nature of prejudice* (25th anniversary ed.). Cambridge, MA: Addison-Wesley. (Original work published 1954)

3. Allport, G. W. (2001). Introduction. In S. Akhilananda, *Hindu psychology: Its meaning for the West* (pp. ix–x). London, England: Routledge. (Original work published 1948)

4. Allport, G. W., & Ross, M. J. (1967). Personal religious orientation and prejudice. *Journal of Personality and Social Psychology, 5,* 432–443.

a. leave as is (i.e., 1, 2, 3, 4)
b. 3, 2, 1, 4
c. 4, 2, 3, 1
d. 1, 3, 2, 4

APA CODES: 6.22–6.25
answer: a
TP-MASTERY 3

Reference entries

a. may consist of the author's name only, if the bibliography is totally complete.
b. may contain only the author's name and title of publication, if the bibliography is totally complete.
c. should be complete and correct.
d. should be updated periodically if they contain URLs.
e. c and d are correct

APA CODES: 6.22–6.31
answer: e
TP-MASTERY 4

Edit the following for ordering the references in a reference list. Choose the sequence of numbers that indicates the correct order of the four references. (Note: The numbers are not part of APA Style but are used here for brevity.)

1. McKenzie, B., & Over, R. (1983). Young infants fail to imitate facial and manual gestures. *Infant Behavior and Development, 6,* 85–96.

2. Martin, G. B., & Clark, R. D. (1982). Distress crying in neonates: Species and peer specificity. *Developmental Psychology, 18,* 3–9.

3. Maurer, D. (2005). Neonatal synesthesia: A reevaluation. In C. K. Mondloch & L. C. Robertson (Eds.), *Synesthesia: Perspectives from cognitive neuroscience* (pp. 193–213). New York, NY: Oxford University Press.

4. Meltzoff, A. N. (2007). The "like me" framework for recognizing and becoming an intentional agent. *Acta Psychologica, 124,* 26–43.

a. leave as is (i.e., 1, 2, 3, 4)
b. 3, 4, 2, 1
c. 3, 2, 4, 1
d. 2, 3, 1, 4

APA CODES: 6.22–6.25
answer: d
TP-MASTERY 4

Edit the following for the application of APA reference style:

Von Ledebur, S. C. (2007). Optimizing knowledge transfer by new employees in companies. *Knowledge Management Research & Practice* (Advance publication). doi:10.1057/palgrave.kmrp.8500141

a. leave as is

b. Von Ledebur, S. C. (2007). Optimizing knowledge transfer by new employees in companies. *Knowledge Management Research & Practice.* Advance online publication. doi:10.1057 /palgrave.kmrp.8500141

c. Von Ledebur, S. C. (2007). Optimizing knowledge transfer by new employees in companies. *Knowledge Management Research & Practice.* Retrieved from advance online publication. doi:10.1057/palgrave.kmrp.8500141

d. Von Ledebur, S. C. (2007). Optimizing knowledge transfer by new employees in companies. *Knowledge Management Research & Practice* [Advance online publication]. doi:10.1057 /palgrave.kmrp.8500141

d. Von Ledebur, S. C. (2007). Optimizing knowledge transfer by new employees in companies. *Knowledge Management Research & Practice.* Advance Online Publication. DOI:10.1057/palgrave.kmrp.8500141

APA CODES: 6.22–7.01
answer: b
TP-MASTERY 4

Edit the following for the application of APA reference style:

Marshall-Pescini, S., & Whiten, A. (2008). Social learning of nut-cracking behavior in East African sanctuary-living chimpanzees (*Pan troglodytes schweinfurthii*) (Supplemental material). *Journal of Comparative Psychology, 122,* 186–194. doi. 10.1037/0735-7036.122.2.186

a. leave as is

b. Marshall-Pescini, S., & Whiten, A. (2008). Social learning of nut-cracking behavior in East African sanctuary-living chimpanzees (*Pan troglodytes schweinfurthii*) [Supplemental material]. *Journal of Comparative Psychology, 122,* 186–194. doi. 10.1037/0735-7036.122.2.186

c. Marshall-Pescini, S., & Whiten, A. (2008). Social learning of nut-cracking behavior in East African sanctuary-living chimpanzees (*Pan troglodytes schweinfurthii*): Supplemental material. *Journal of Comparative Psychology, 122,* 186–194. doi. 10.1037/0735-7036.122.2.186

d. Marshall-Pescini, S., & Whiten, A. (2008). Social learning of nut-cracking behavior in East African sanctuary-living chimpanzees (*Pan troglodytes schweinfurthii*) [*Supplemental material*]. *Journal of Comparative Psychology, 122,* 186–194. doi. 10.1037/0735-7036.122.2.186

APA CODES: 6.22–7.01
answer: b
TP-MASTERY 4

Edit the following for the application of APA reference style:

Guimard, P., & Florin, A. (2007). *Les évaluations des enseignants en grande section de maternelle sont-elles prédictives des difficultés de lecture au cours préparatoire?* [Are teacher ratings in kindergarten predictive of reading difficulties in first grade?]. *Approche Neuropsychologique des Apprentissages chez l'Enfant, 19,* 5–17.

a. leave as is

b. Guimard, P., & Florin, A. (2007). Les évaluations des enseignants en grande section de maternelle sont-elles prédictives des difficultés de lecture au cours préparatoire? [Are teacher ratings in kindergarten predictive of reading difficulties in first grade?]. *Approche Neuropsychologique des Apprentissages chez l'Enfant, 19,* 5–17.

c. Guimard, P., & Florin, A. (2007). Les évaluations des enseignants en grande section de maternelle sont-elles prédictives des difficultés de lecture au cours préparatoire? ("Are teacher ratings in kindergarten predictive of reading difficulties in first grade?") *Approche Neuropsychologique des Apprentissages chez l'Enfant, 19,* 5–17.

d. Guimard, P., & Florin, A. (2007). Les Évaluations des Enseignants en Grande Section de Maternelle Sont-elles Prédictives des Difficultés de Lecture au Cours Préparatoire? [Are Teacher Ratings in Kindergarten Predictive of Reading Difficulties in First Grade?]. *Approche Neuropsychologique des Apprentissages chez l'Enfant, 19,* 5–17.

APA CODES: 6.27–6.31
answer: b
TP-MASTERY 1

A reference list entry should have

a. the author's surname and initials in inverted order (e.g., McMahon, P. M.).
b. the journal article DOI if available
c. the author's surname only.
d. only a and b.

APA CODES: 6.27–6.31
answer: d
TP-MASTERY 2

Edit the following for the application of APA reference style:

Sillick, T. J., & Schutte, N. S. (2006). Emotional intelligence and self-esteem mediate between perceived early parental love and adult happiness. E-Journal of Applied Psychology, 2(2), 38–48. Retrieved from http://ojs.lib.swin.edu.au/index.php/ejap

a. leave as is

b. Sillick, T. J., & Schutte, N. S. (2006). Emotional intelligence and self-esteem mediate between perceived early parental love and adult happiness. *E-Journal of Applied Psychology, 2*(2), 38–48. Retrieved from http://ojs.lib.swin.edu.au/index.php/ejap

c. Sillick, T. J., & Schutte, N. S. (2006). Emotional intelligence and self-esteem mediate between perceived early parental love and adult happiness. E-Journal of Applied Psychology, 2(2), 38–48. [HTML file]

d. Sillick, T. J., & Schutte, N. S. (2006). Emotional intelligence and self-esteem mediate between perceived early parental love and adult happiness. *E-Journal of Applied Psychology, 2*(2), 38–48. (no DOI)

APA CODES: 6.27–6.31
answer: b
TP-MASTERY 2

In entries in the reference list,

  a. periods are used to separate major elements (e.g., names of authors, dates, titles).

  b. a comma is used to separate the name of a periodical from volume and page number information.

  c. brackets are used to indicate nonroutine information that is important for identification and retrieval.

  d. punctuation may vary in format according to the type of source.

  e. All of the above are correct.

APA CODES: 6.27–7.01
answer: e
TP-MASTERY 1

Edit the following for formatting a reference entry:

Axelman, A., & Shapiro, J. L. (2007). Does the solution warrant the problem? [Review of the DVD *Brief therapy with adolescents*, produced by APA, 2007]. *PsycCRITIQUES, 52*(51). doi:10.1037/a0009036

  a. leave as is

  b. Axelman, A., & Shapiro, J. L. (2007). Does the solution warrant the problem? [Review of the DVD *Brief therapy with adolescents*, produced by APA, 2007]. *PsycCRITIQUES, 52*(51). doi:10.1037/a0009036.

  c. Axelman, A., & Shapiro, J. L. (2007). Does the solution warrant the problem? [Review of the DVD *Brief therapy with adolescents*, produced by APA, 2007]. PsycCRITIQUES, 52(51). doi:10.1037/a0009036

  d.   Axelman, A., & Shapiro, J. L. (2007). Does the solution warrant the problem? [Review of the DVD *Brief therapy with adolescents*, produced by APA, 2007]. *PsycCRITIQUES 52*(51). doi:10.1037/a0009036

APA CODES: 6.27–7.01
answer: a
TP-MASTERY 1

Edit the following for the application of APA reference style:

Bronfenbrenner, U. (1970). *Two worlds of childhood: U.S. and U.S.S.R.* New York, NY: Russell Sage Foundation.

  a. leave as is

  b. Bronfenbrenner, U. *Two worlds of childhood: U.S. and U.S.S.R.* New York, NY: Russell Sage Foundation. (1970).

  c. Bronfenbrenner, U. (1970). "Two worlds of childhood: U.S. and U.S.S.R." New York, NY: Russell Sage Foundation.

  d. Bronfenbrenner, U. (1970). *Two Worlds of Childhood: U.S. and U.S.S.R.* New York, NY: Russell Sage Foundation.

APA CODES: 6.27–7.02
answer: a
TP-MASTERY 3

What is the digital object identifier or DOI?

  a. a unique alphanumeric string assigned by a registration agency (the International DOI Foundation).

  b. a unique identifier that should only be used if the URL is too long.

  c. a unique identifier that identifies content and provides a persistent link to its location on the Internet.

  d. both a and c.

  e. none of the above.

APA CODE: 6.31
answer: d
TP-FAMILIARIZATION

A digital object identifier is generally located

    a. on the first page of the electronic or print version of an article, near the copyright notice.

    b. in a footnote on the first page of an electronic or print version of an article.

    c. on the database landing page for the article.

    d. all of the above.

    e. a and c.

APA CODE: 6.31
answer: e
TP-PRACTICE

Edit the following for the application of APA reference style:

Herbst-Damm, K. L., & Kulik, J. A. (2005). Volunteer support, marital status, and the survival times of terminally ill patients. *Health Psychology, 24,* 225–229. DOI.10.1037/0278-6133.24.2.225

    a. Leave as is

    b. Herbst-Damm, K. L., & Kulik, J. A. (2005). Volunteer support, marital status, and the survival times of terminally ill patients. *Health Psychology, 24,* 225–229. doi:10.1037/0278-6133.24.2.225

    c. Herbst-Damm, K. L., & Kulik, J. A. (2005). Volunteer support, marital status, and the survival times of terminally ill patients. *Health Psychology, 24,* 225–229. 10.1037/0278-6133.24.2.225

    d. Herbst-Damm, K. L., & Kulik, J. A. (2005). Volunteer support, marital status, and the survival times of terminally ill patients. *Health Psychology, 24,* 225–229. [doi:10.1037/0278-6133.24.2.225]

APA CODE: 7.01
answer: b
TP-PRACTICE

Edit the following for the application of APA reference style:

Laplace, P.-S. (1951/1814). *A philosophical essay on probabilities* (F. W. Truscott & F. L. Emory, Trans.). New York, NY: Dover. (Original work published 1814)

    a. leave as is

    b. Laplace, P.-S. (1951). *A philosophical essay on probabilities* (F. W. Truscott & F. L. Emory, Trans.). (Original work published 1814). New York, NY: Dover.

    c. Laplace, P.-S. (1951). *A philosophical essay on probabilities* (F. W. Truscott & F. L. Emory, Trans.). New York, NY: Dover. (Original work published 1814)

    d. Laplace, P.-S. (1951). [*A philosophical essay on probabilities*] (F. W. Truscott & F. L. Emory, Translators.). New York, NY: Dover. (Original work published 1814)

APA CODE: 7.02
answer: c
TP-PRACTICE

Edit the following for the application of APA reference style:

Haybron, D. M. (2008). Philosophy and the science of subjective well-being. In Eid, M. & Larsen, R. J. (Eds.), *The science of subjective well-being* (pp. 17–43). New York, NY: Guilford Press.

a. leave as is

b. Haybron, D. M. (2008). *Philosophy and the science of subjective well-being.* In M. Eid & R. J. Larsen (Eds.), *The science of subjective well-being* (pp. 17–43). New York, NY: Guilford Press.

c. Haybron, D. M. (2008). "Philosophy and the science of subjective well-being." In M. Eid & R. J. Larsen (Eds.), The science of subjective well-being (pp. 17–43). New York, NY: Guilford Press.

d. Haybron, D. M. (2008). Philosophy and the science of subjective well-being. In M. Eid & R. J. Larsen (Eds.), *The science of subjective well-being* (pp. 17–43). New York, NY: Guilford Press.

APA CODE: 7.02
answer: d
TP-MASTERY 4

Edit the following for the application of APA reference style:

Thomas, N. (Ed.). (2002). *Perspectives on the community college: A journey of discovery* [Monograph]. Retrieved from http://eric.ed.gov/

a. leave as is

b. Thomas, N. (Ed.). (2002). Perspectives on the community college: A journey of discovery [Monograph]. Retrieved from http://eric.ed.gov/

c. Thomas, N. (Ed.). (2002). *Perspectives on the community college: A journey of discovery* [Monograph]. No publisher or DOI available.

d. Thomas, N. (Ed.). (2002). Perspectives on the community college: A journey of discovery. Monograph. Retrieved from http://eric.ed.gov/

APA CODE: 7.02
answer: a
TP-MASTERY 4

Edit the following for the application of APA reference style:

Katz, I., Gabayan, K., & Aghajan, H. (2007). A Multi-Touch Surface Using Multiple Cameras. In J. Blanc-Talon, W. Philips, D. Popescu, & P. Scheunders (Eds.), *Lecture Notes in Computer Science: Vol. 4678. Advanced Concepts for Intelligent Vision Systems* (pp. 97–108). Berlin, Germany: Springer-Verlag. doi:10.1007/978-3-540-74607-2_9

a. leave as is

b. Katz, I., Gabayan, K., & Aghajan, H. (2007). A multi-touch surface using multiple cameras. In J. Blanc-Talon, W. Philips, D. Popescu, & P. Scheunders (Eds.), *Lecture Notes in Computer Science: Vol. 4678. Advanced Concepts for Intelligent Vision Systems* (pp. 97–108). Berlin, Germany: Springer-Verlag. doi:10.1007/978-3-540-74607-2_9

c. Katz, Gabayan, & Aghajan. (2007). A multi-touch surface using multiple cameras. In Blanc-Talon, Philips, Popescu, & Scheunders (Eds.), *Lecture Notes in Computer Science: Vol. 4678. Advanced Concepts for Intelligent Vision Systems* (pp. 97–108). Berlin, Germany: Springer-Verlag. doi:10.1007/978-3-540-74607-2_9

d. Katz, I., Gabayan, K., & Aghajan, H. (2007, December). A multi-touch surface using multiple cameras. In J. Blanc-Talon, W. Philips, D. Popescu, & P. Scheunders (Eds.), *Lecture Notes in Computer Science: Vol. 4678. Advanced Concepts for Intelligent Vision Systems*. Berlin, Germany: Springer-Verlag. doi:10.1007 /978-3-540-74607-2_9

APA CODE: 7.04
answer: b
TP-PRACTICE

Edit the following for the application of APA reference style:

Van Nuys, D. (Producer). (2007, December 19). *Shrink rap radio* [Audio podcast]. Retrieved from http://www.shrinkrapradio.com/

a. leave as is

b. Van Nuys, D. (2007, December 19). *Shrink rap radio* [Audio podcast]. Retrieved from http://www.shrinkrapradio.com/

c. Van Nuys, D. (Producer). (2007, December 19). *Shrink rap radio*. Audio podcast. Retrieved from http://www.shrinkrapradio.com/

d. Van Nuys, D. (Producer). (December 19). *Shrink rap radio* [Audio podcast]. Retrieved from http://www.shrinkrapradio.com/

APA CODE: 7.07
answer: a
TP-PRACTICE

When typing a paper,

a. double-space after headings and between paragraphs and reference list citations; single-space elsewhere.

b. double-space throughout the paper; single- or one-and-a-half spacing may be used in tables or figures.

c. single-space between the lines of table headings.

d. double-space everything except triple-space after major headings.

APA CODE: 8.03
answer: b
TP-FAMILIARIZATION

Edit the following by selecting the correct spacing and margin arrangement for the first sentence of a paragraph:

The mating and social behaviors of many species change dramatically when they are removed from their natural environments, whether to be domesticated or to be exhibited in zoos.

a. leave as is

b.   The mating and social behaviors of many species change dramatically when they are removed from their natural environments, whether to be domesticated or to be exhibited in zoos.

c.   The mating and social behaviors of many species change dramatically when they are removed from their natural environments, whether to be domesticated or to be exhibited in zoos.

d. The mating and social behaviors of many species change dramatically when they are removed from their natural environments, whether to be domesticated or to be exhibited in zoos.

APA CODE: 8.03
answer: b
TP-FAMILIARIZATION

Changes to proofs should not include

a. corrections of production errors.
b. updates to reference citations.
c. rewritten text the author would like to insert.
d. corrections to changes in meaning in text.

APA CODE: 8.03
answer: c
TP-FAMILIARIZATION

Which kind of spacing should not be used anywhere in a manuscript?

a. single-spacing
b. double-spacing
c. triple-spacing
d. all of the above

APA CODE: 8.03
answer: c
TP-PRACTICE

The right margin should

a. have divided words to achieve an even margin.
b. not have divided words and may be uneven.
c. have a 1-in. (2.54-cm) space rather than a 2-in. (5.08-cm) space.
d. have divided or undivided words to achieve a clean line.

APA CODE: 8.03
answer: c
TP-PRACTICE

The correct order of manuscript pages is

a. abstract, text, tables, figures, references, appendices
b. text, references, tables, figures, abstract, appendices
c. abstract, text, references, tables, figures, appendices
d. abstract, text, appendices, references, tables, figures

APA CODE: 8.03
answer: c
TP-PRACTICE

Edit the following for line spacing:

Experiment 1

Method

    Participants. The participants were 44 sets of parents who were bringing their firstborn infant children to a well-baby clinic in a university hospital. The ages of the parents ranged from 19 to 38 years.

a. leave as is

b.

Experiment 1

Method
    Participants. The participants were 44 sets of parents who were bringing their firstborn infant children to a well-baby clinic in a university hospital. The ages of the parents ranged

from 19 to 38 years.

c.

Experiment 1

Method

    Participants. The participants were 44 sets of parents who were bringing their firstborn

infant children to a well-baby clinic in a university hospital. The ages of the parents ranged

from 19 to 38 years.

d.

Experiment 1

Method

    Participants. The participants were 44 sets of parents who were bringing their

firstborn infant children to a well-baby clinic in a university hospital. The

ages of the parents ranged from 19 to 38 years.

APA CODE: 8.03
answer: d
TP-MASTERY 1

Margin size

    a. depends on the style of the typeface.

    b. should always be 1 in. (2.54 cm) at the top, bottom, and sides of the paper.

    c. depends on what section of the paper is being typed.

    d. should be 2 in. (5.08 cm) at the top and bottom and 1/2 in. (1.27 cm) at the left and right sides.

APA CODE: 8.03
answer: b
TP-MASTERY 1

Indentation at paragraphs

    a. is not necessary if there is triple-spaced typing between paragraphs.

    b. should be less than 0.5 in (1.27 cm).

    c. is not necessary if block-style typing format is used for the entire page.

    d. is required in all but a few instances.

APA CODE: 8.03
answer: d
TP-MASTERY 1

The use of a uniform typeface and font size

    a. enhances readability for the reviewer.

    b. should not be used for the reference list.

    c. allows the publisher to estimate the page length.

    d. a and c.

APA CODE: 8.03
answer: d
TP-MASTERY 2

Edit the following by selecting the correct spacing arrangement:

Effects of Academic Stress on Interpersonal Relationships
of Male and Female Students
Whatever the academic standards of a college or university, there always seem to be students who do not meet the standards.

    a. leave as is

    b.

Effects of Academic Stress on Interpersonal Relationships
of Male and Female Students

Whatever the academic standards of a college or university there always seem to be students who do not meet the standards.

    c.

Effects of Academic Stress on Interpersonal Relationships
of Male and Female Students

Whatever the academic standards of a college or university there
always seem to be students who do not meet the standards.

    d.

Effects of Academic Stress on Interpersonal Relationships
of Male and Female Students

Whatever the academic standards of a college or university there
always seem to be students who do not meet the standards.

APA CODE: 8.03
answer: a
TP-MASTERY 2

Identify the numbering error in the following example of the first page of text of a manuscript that has a title page and an abstract page:

Running head: UNDERGRADUATE HELPING SKILLS TRAINING   3

a. The numbering is correct.
b. The first text page is numbered with a 1.
c. A number is not put on the first page.
d. Page numbers are typed flush with the left margin.

APA CODE: 8.03
answer: a
TP-MASTERY 2

A uniform, serif typeface

a. should be used for all text, with the exception of figures.
b. helps the publisher estimate the article length.
c. improves readability.
d. all of the above.

APA CODE: 8.03
answer: d
TP-MASTERY 3

Edit the following by selecting the correct spacing:

Naturalistic Observation of the Duration and Distribution
of Sleep Across the Life Span

Although individual differences within each age group are certainly recognized, our society has general notions about the sleep patterns—duration and distribution—of people at different ages.

a. leave as is

b.

Naturalistic Observation of the Duration and Distribution

of Sleep Across the Life Span

Although individual differences within each age group are certainly recognized, our society has general notions about the sleep patterns—duration and distribution—of people at different ages.

c.

Naturalistic Observation of the Duration and Distribution
of Sleep Across the Life Span

Although individual differences within each age group are certainly recognized, our society has general notions about the sleep patterns—duration and distribution—of people at different ages.

d.

Naturalistic Observation of the Duration and Distribution
of Sleep Across the Life Span

Although individual differences within each age group are certainly recognized, our society has general notions about the sleep patterns—duration and distribution—of people at different ages.

APA CODE: 8.03
answer: d
TP-MASTERY 3

Edit the following for numbering of an abstract page:

Running head: PROCRASTINATION
1

a. leave as is
b. Change the page number 1 to the number 2.
c. The page number is correct, but it should not be typed flush with the right margin.
d. The page number is correct, but the short title should not appear on the abstract page.

APA CODE: 8.03
answer: b
TP-MASTERY 3

Use a typeface that

a. is uniform.
b. enhances readability.
c. allows the publisher to estimate article length.
d. all of the above.

APA CODE: 8.03
answer: d
TP-MASTERY 4

Edit the following by selecting the correct spacing arrangement:

Method

Participants and Procedure

This study was part of a larger project designed to explore civic attitudes and behaviors among diverse youth. Recruited for participation were 304 students from four high schools in the Northeast between 2000 and 2002.

a. leave as is
b.
Method

Participants and Procedure

This study was part of a larger project designed to explore civic attitudes and behaviors among diverse youth. Recruited for participation were 304 students from four high schools in the Northeast between 2000 and 2002.

c.
Method

Participants and Procedure

This study was part of a larger project designed to explore civic attitudes and behaviors among diverse youth. Recruited for participation were 304 students from four high schools in the Northeast between 2000 and 2002.

d.
Method

Participants and Procedure

This study was part of a larger project designed to explore civic attitudes and behaviors among diverse youth. Recruited for participation were 304 students from four high schools in the Northeast between 2000 and 2002.

APA CODE: 8.03
answer: d
TP-MASTERY 4

Concerning page numbers,

    a. number your pages consecutively starting with the title page.

    b. place the numbers in the center of each page at the top margin.

    c. if a page is inserted after numbering is complete, number the inserted page with an a (e.g., 6a).

    d. pages used for figures are not numbered.

    e. a and d are correct.

APA CODE: 8.03
answer: e
TP-MASTERY 4

When typing a reference list,

    a. begin it after the last word of the Discussion section on the same page.

    b. single-space each reference but double-space in between references.

    c. double-space all reference entries.

    d. indent all lines of each reference except the first line at least 0.5 in (1.27 cm)

    e. c and d are correct.

APA CODE: 8.03
answer: e
TP-MASTERY 4

RESEARCH REPORT MASTER TEST FILE

A report of an empirical study usually includes an introduction and sections called Method, _____, and Discussion.

   a. Results
   b. Bibliography
   c. Statement of the Problem
   d. Conclusion

APA CODES: 1.01–1.06
answer: a
RR-MASTERY 1

When writing a report of original research, the sections should reflect the

   a. order of importance.
   b. relation to each other.
   c. stages of the research process.
   d. none of the above.

APA CODES: 1.01–1.06
answer: c
RR-MASTERY 2

Which of the following must identify the variables or theoretical issues under investigation and the relationship between them?

   a. the first sentence of the introduction section
   b. the conclusion of the Discussion section
   c. the title of the report
   d. the first table that is cited

APA CODES: 2.01–2.03
answer: c
RR-MASTERY 4

The abstract of an article should be

   a. a brief, comprehensive summary of the contents of the article.
   b. about 75 to 100 words long.
   c. an evaluation of the research report.
   d. all of the above.

APA CODES: 2.01–2.04
answer: a
RR-MASTERY 1

The abstract of a report of an empirical study should describe

   a. the problem, participants, essential features of the study method, basic findings, and conclusions.
   b. raw data statements with conclusions.
   c. conclusions not found in the text of the report.
   d. *F* values, degrees of freedom, and probability levels.

APA CODES: 2.01–2.04
answer: a
RR-MASTERY 2

The abstract should be formatted as

   a. a single paragraph in block format.
   b. one or more paragraphs with the first line indented.
   c. a single paragraph with the first line indented.
   d. more than one paragraph with space between paragraphs.

APA CODES: 2.01–2.04
answer: a
RR-MASTERY 4

Journal article reporting standards were developed to

    a. make it easier to generalize across fields.

    b. provide a degree of comprehensiveness in the information routinely included in reports of empirical investigations.

    c. help decision makers in policy and practice understand how research was conducted and what was found.

    d. allow techniques of meta-analysis to proceed more efficiently.

    e. all of the above.

APA CODES: 2.01–2.08
answer: e
RR-MASTERY 3

A research report usually includes an introduction and sections called _____, Results, and Discussion.

    a. Method

    b. Bibliography

    c. Statement of the Problem

    d. Hypotheses

APA CODES: 2.01–2.08
answer: a
RR-MASTERY 3

An abstract of a literature review or meta-analysis should describe

    a. the problem or relation(s) under investigation.

    b. type(s) of participants included in primary studies.

    c. basic findings, including effect sizes and confidence intervals and/or statistical significance levels.

    d. all of the above.

    e. a and b.

APA CODES: 2.01–2.08
answer: d
RR-MASTERY 3

When citing references in the introduction,

    a. include an exhaustive historical account.

    b. cite select studies pertinent to the issue under investigation.

    c. refer the reader to reviews if they are available.

    d. stick to print sources rather than electronic sources.

    e. b and c.

APA CODES: 2.01–2.08
answer: e
RR-MASTERY 3

Examples of supplemental materials that are included in online supplemental archives are

    a. lengthy computer code.

    b. detailed description of a complex piece of equipment.

    c. audio or video clips.

    d. a and c.

APA CODES: 2.01–2.13
answer: d
RR-MASTERY 2

A good abstract

    a. needs to be dense with information.

    b. should include information that does not appear in the body of the manuscript.

    c. should be written in the present tense.

    d. all of the above.

APA CODES: 2.04–2.05
answer: a
RR-MASTERY 4

The introduction section of a research report should

   a. include a thorough historical review of the literature.
   b. define all of the terms that would be unintelligible to a reader with no previous exposure to the field.
   c. present the importance of the problem to be explored and specific hypotheses and objectives.
   d. be clearly labeled.

APA CODES: 2.05–2.06
answer: c
RR-MASTERY 1

When animals are the subjects in a study, it is not usually necessary to report

   a. the name and location of the supplier.
   b. genus, species, and strain number.
   c. their age, sex, weight, and physiological condition.
   d. the cost of maintaining them.

APA CODES: 2.05–2.06
answer: d
RR-MASTERY 1

Before writing the introduction section, consider the following questions:

   a. How do hypotheses and research design relate to one another?
   b. What are the theoretical and practical implications of the study?
   c. What statistical tests were used?
   d. all of the above.
   e. a and b.

APA CODES: 2.05–2.06
answer: e
RR-MASTERY 2

When describing participants in your research, you should

   a. give specific demographic characteristics such as age; sex; ethnic and/or racial group; level of education; and socioeconomic, generation, or immigrant status.
   b. describe the procedures for selecting participants, including sampling method.
   c. report whether the participants were provided incentives used to increase compliance.
   d. do all of the above.

APA CODES: 2.05–2.06
answer: d
RR-MASTERY 2

Before writing the introduction, questions to bear in mind include the following:

   a. Why is this problem important?
   b. How does the study relate to previous work in the area?
   c. What are the theoretical and practical implications of the study?
   d. How do the study's hypotheses and research design relate to one another?
   e. all of the above

APA CODES: 2.05–2.06
answer: e
RR-MASTERY 4

The Method section should be described in enough detail to

   a. permit a reader to evaluate the plausibility of your hypotheses.
   b. permit an experienced investigator to replicate your study.
   c. allow a perfect duplication of your investigation.
   d. allow an editor to judge the external validity of your study.

APA CODES: 2.06–2.07
answer: b
RR-MASTERY 3

In the Results section, you should

   a. summarize collected data.

   b. discuss the analytic treatment of data.

   c. discuss the implications of the findings.

   d. do all of the above.

   e. a and b.

APA CODES: 2.06–2.07
answer: e
RR-MASTERY 3

The subsections of the Method section generally include

   a. introduction, procedures, and design.

   b. procedures, tests, and participants.

   c. participants, apparatus, and procedure.

   d. none of the above.

APA CODES: 2.06–2.11
answer: c
RR-MASTERY 4

In the Method section, the procedures section often includes descriptions of

   a. sampling procedures and sample size and precision.

   b. experimental manipulations or interventions used and how they were delivered.

   c. a summary of the collected data and analysis performed on that data.

   d. all of the above

   e. a and b.

APA CODES: 2.06–2.11
answer: e
RR-MASTERY 4

An analysis of variance on your 2×2 design has revealed two main effects without an interaction effect (fewer errors were made with easy tasks, and 6-month-olds did better than 1-month-olds in all tasks). In planning your Results section, the best alternative from among the possibilities is to include

   a. no figure.

   b. one figure to show the main effect of age.

   c. a simple table showing the main effect means.

   d. both a table and a figure.

APA CODES: 2.06–2.11
answer: a
RR-MASTERY 4

The Discussion section should begin with

   a. a statement regarding implications for future research.

   b. a statement of the support or nonsupport of your original hypothesis.

   c. a reformulation of the important points of the paper.

   d. an analysis of the flaws in your study.

APA CODES: 2.06–2.11
answer: b
RR-MASTERY 4

In the Discussion section, an interpretation of the results should take into account

   a. sources of potential bias and other threats to internal validity.

   b. the imprecision of measures.

   c. the overall number of tests or overlap among tests.

   d. other limitations or weaknesses of the study.

   e. all of the above.

APA CODES: 2.06–2.11
answer: e
RR-MASTERY 4

The Discussion section generally includes

a. a statement of support or nonsupport of all original hypotheses.

b. a discussion of similarities and differences between your results and the results of others.

c. an interpretation of the results that takes into account sources of potential bias.

d. does all of the above.

e. b and c.

APA CODES: 2.07–2.08
answer: d
RR-MASTERY 3

Results are sometimes difficult to read and understand; therefore, it is useful to

a. summarize the collected data and the analysis performed on those data relevant to the discourse that is to follow.

b. introduce the reader to statistical theory before you report the results of even basic statistical analyses.

c. let the statistics drive the logic of your Results section, not the logic you developed in your introduction (i.e., your hypotheses).

d. report raw data, descriptive statistics, and the results of inferential analyses.

APA CODES: 2.07–2.11
answer: a
RR-MASTERY 1

Speculation is permitted in the Discussion section if it is

a. faithful to the intuition of the authors.

b. related closely and logically to empirical data or theory.

c. expressed verbosely and eloquently.

d. none of the above.

APA CODES: 2.07–2.11
answer: b
RR-MASTERY 1

In a paper that integrates several experiments, you should

a. not combine the discussion with the description of results.

b. have only one Results section for all of the experiments.

c. make it at least twice as long as a one-experiment study.

d. include a comprehensive general discussion of all of the work.

APA CODES: 2.07–2.11
answer: d
RR-MASTERY 1

When reporting inferential statistical tests, include the

a. obtained magnitude or value of the test statistic.

b. degrees of freedom.

c. exact p value.

d. all of the above.

APA CODES: 2.07–2.11
answer: d
RR-MASTERY 2

For experimental and quasi-experimental designs, always include in the Results section

   a. a description of the flow of participants through the study.
   b. the total number of participants recruited into the study and the number of participants assigned to each group.
   c. the number of participants who did not complete the experiment or crossed over to other conditions and explain why.
   d. all of the above.
   e. a and c.

APA CODES: 2.07–2.11
answer: d
RR-MASTERY 2

The Discussion section is a part of the report in which you can

   a. discuss theory independent of your results.
   b. interpret your results and discuss their implications.
   c. discuss relevant related literature.
   d. reformulate and repeat points already made.

APA CODES: 2.07–2.11
answer: b
RR-MASTERY 2

In a paper that integrates several experiments, you should

   a. not try to relate the experiments to each other.
   b. have only one Results section for all of the experiments.
   c. include a comprehensive general discussion of all the work.
   d. make it at least twice as long as a one-experiment study.

APA CODES: 2.07–2.11
answer: c
RR-MASTERY 2

Choose the correct format for the use of three levels of headings:

   a.

   Experiment 2

   Method

   Participants.

   b.

   METHOD

   Procedure

   Pretraining Period.

   c.

   Method

   Procedure

   Participants.

   d.

   Method

   Procedure

   Pretraining period.

APA CODES: 3.02–3.03
answer: d
RR-MASTERY 1

Edit the following by selecting the correct arrangement of headings:

Method

Subjects

Procedure

Results

Discussion

a. leave as is

b.

Method

Subjects.

Procedure.

Results

Discussion

c.

Method

Subjects

Procedure

Results

Discussion

d.

Method

Subjects

Procedure

Results

Discussion

APA CODES: 3.02–3.03
answer: c
RR-MASTERY 2

Edit the following by selecting the correct arrangement of headings:

Results

Pretraining Phase

 Accuracy.

a. leave as is

b.

RESULTS

Pretraining Phase

 Accuracy.

c.

Results

Pretraining Phase

 Accuracy.

d.

Results

Pretraining Phase

 Accuracy.

APA CODES: 3.02–3.03
answer: d
RR-MASTERY 3

Past tense is usually appropriate for describing

a. previous experiments.
b. the literature review.
c. a procedure if the discussion is of past events.
d. all of the above.

APA CODES: 3.05–3.06
answer: d
RR-MASTERY 1

Consistency of verb tense helps to smooth expression. Select the preferred match of paper section with verb tense from the choices below:

a. conclusion: present tense
b. literature review: present tense
c. Results: past tense
d. Method: past tense
e. all of the above except b

APA CODES: 3.05–3.06
answer: e
RR-MASTERY 2

On the basis of verb tense, in which part of a report is the following text segment likely to appear?

College students judged time differently than did college faculty. Faculty were more accurate in judging the amount of time required to do academic tasks.

a. Method
b. hypotheses
c. Results
d. conclusion

APA CODES: 3.05–3.06
answer: c
RR-MASTERY 4

Consistency of verb tense helps to ensure smooth expression. Select the preferred match of section with verb tense from the following choices:

a. conclusion: present tense
b. literature review: present tense
c. Results: past tense
d. Method: past tense
e. a, c, and d

APA CODES: 3.05–3.06
answer: e
RR-MASTERY 3

The present tense is usually appropriate when you are

a. presenting past research.
b. describing the demographic details of the subjects.
c. discussing implications of the results and presenting conclusions.
d. describing the results.
e. The present tense is never used.

APA CODES: 3.05–3.06
answer: c
RR-MASTERY 3

Informal verb use such as *the participant felt that,* colloquial expressions such as *write up,* or approximations of quantity such as *quite a large part*

    a. have a place in serious scientific writing.
    b. add warmth to dull scientific prose.
    c. reduce word precision and clarity.
    d. can be used to enhance communication.
    e. are more acceptable in written than in oral communication.

APA CODES: 3.07–3.10
answer: c
RR-MASTERY 4

Which of the following examples represents correct hyphenation?

    a. *t*-test results
    b. pro-Freudian
    c. 2-, 3-, and 10-min trials
    d. all of the above

APA CODES: 4.12–4.13
answer: d
RR-MASTERY 1

Edit the following for capitalization:

On Day 2 of Experiment 3, the students read Chapter 2 of their textbook, which described Eriksonian Life Span Theory and Life History Theory.

    a. leave as is
    b. *Day* and *Experiment* do not need to be capitalized.
    c. *Chapter* does not require capitalization.
    d. *Life Span Theory* and *Life History Theory* should not be capitalized.

APA CODES: 4.14–4.20
answer: d
RR-MASTERY 1

Capitalize

    a. the word *factor* when it is followed by a number (e.g., Factor 6).
    b. nouns that precede a variable.
    c. names of conditions or groups in an experiment.
    d. all of the above.
    e. none of the above.

APA CODES: 4.14–4.20
answer: a
RR-MASTERY 1

Which of the following examples demonstrates correct use of capitalization?

    a. Trial 3 and Item 4
    b. trial *n* and item *x*
    c. Chapter 4
    d. Table 2 and Figure 3
    e. all of the above.

APA CODES: 4.14–4.20
answer: e
RR-MASTERY 2

Edit the following for capitalization of statistical and mathematical copy:

A 2 × 2 × 3 (Sex of Participant × Sex of Target × Activity Profile) analysis of variance was performed on the attractiveness scores.

a. leave as is
b. A 2 × 2 × 3 (sex of participant × sex of target × activity profile) analysis of variance was performed on the attractiveness scores.
c. A 2 (Sex of Participant) × 2 (Sex of Target) × 3 (Activity Profile) analysis of variance was performed on the attractiveness scores.
d. A 2 (Sex of participant) × 2 (Sex of target) × 3 (Activity profile) analysis of variance was performed on the attractiveness scores.

APA CODES: 4.14–4.20
answer: a
RR-MASTERY 2

Edit the following for capitalization of names of variables, factors, or effects:

In light of the fact that both Baseline and Intervention Effect factors are qualified by gender, a full presentation of the moderated findings follows.

a. leave as is
b. The words *Baseline* and *Intervention Effect* should not be capitalized.
c. The word *Factors* should be capitalized.
d. The word *factor* is not capitalized when followed by a number.

APA CODES: 4.14–4.20
answer: a
RR-MASTERY 2

Identify the example with incorrect use of capitalization:

a. The conclusion is obvious: forgiveness is not granted to the stronger partner in an inequitable relationship.
b. The Method section of the article described the Asian sample, which included 30 Chinese and 45 Vietnamese persons.
c. The article referred to the associate learning model.
d. The items were taken from the Depression scale of the Minnesota Multiphasic Personality Inventory—2 (Butcher, Dahlstrom, Graham, Tellegen, & Kaemmer, 1989).

APA CODES: 4.14–4.20
answer: a
RR-MASTERY 3

Edit the following for capitalization of experimental conditions:

The Sex-education and No-sex-education groups were then asked to view a film on the ethics of physical intimacy.

a. leave as is
b. The names of experimental conditions or groups should not be capitalized.
c. All nouns following hyphens should be capitalized.
d. The word *groups* also should be capitalized.

APA CODES: 4.14–4.20
answer: b
RR-MASTERY 3

In table headings and figure captions,

    a. capitalize only the first word and proper nouns.

    b. capitalize all major words.

    c. do not capitalize any words.

    d. capitalization will depend on the message you wish to convey.

APA CODES: 4.14–4.20
answer: a
RR-MASTERY 4

Edit the following for the capitalization of names of experimental conditions:

Participants in the tobacco-chewing therapy condition and in the no-therapy control condition then each received two wads of chewing tobacco.

    a. leave as is

    b. The names of experimental conditions should always be capitalized.

    c. The names of treatments such as *two wads* should be capitalized.

    d. Because *chewing tobacco* is a commercial term, it should be capitalized.

APA CODES: 4.14–4.20
answer: a
RR-MASTERY 4

Which of the following should not be italicized?

    a. *a priori*

    b. 1973, *26,* 46–77

    c. $F(l, 53) = 10.03$

    d. *Journal of Experimental Psychology*

APA CODE: 4.21
answer: a
RR-MASTERY 4

In general, use abbreviations

    a. if the reader is more familiar with the abbreviation than with the complete word or words being used.

    b. for all units of time.

    c. if considerable space can be saved and repetition avoided.

    d. Answers a and c of the above are correct.

    e. All of the above are correct.

APA CODES: 4.22–4.30
answer: d
RR-MASTERY 1

Abbreviations appearing in several figures or tables

    a. must be explained in the figure caption or table note for every figure or table in which they are used.

    b. must be explained in the figure caption or table note of only the first figure or table in which they are used.

    c. should be explained only in the text.

    d. need not be explained.

APA CODES: 4.22–4.30
answer: a
RR-MASTERY 2

The abbreviations S, E, and O (for subject, experimenter, and observer, respectively)

   a. are treated the same as other abbreviations in the text.
   b. are not used in APA articles.
   c. should be used only in table notes and figure captions.
   d. None of the above is correct.

APA CODES: 4.22–4.30
answer: b
RR-MASTERY 3

The abbreviations S, E, and O (for subject, experimenter, and observer, respectively)

   a. should always be used in articles.
   b. should be used only in journals that deal with physiological aspects of psychology.
   c. should be used only in the Method section.
   d. are not used in APA articles.

APA CODES: 4.22–4.30
answer: d
RR-MASTERY 4

Edit the following for the expression of numbers:

The participants were tested on items from 10 seven-point scales, and results included 2 two-way interactions.

   a. leave as is
   b. The participants were tested on items from ten 7-point scales, and results included two 2-way interactions.
   c. The participants were tested on items from ten seven-point scales, and results included two two-way interactions..
   d. The participants were tested on items from ten 7-point scales, and results included 2 two-way interactions.

APA CODES: 4.31–4.38
answer: d
RR-MASTERY 1

Edit the following for the expression of numbers:

Procedural errors occurred while 2 rats in the drug condition and 3 rats in the placebo condition were being tested.

   a. leave as is
   b. Procedural errors occurred while 2.0 rats in the drug condition and 3.0 rats in the placebo condition were being tested.
   c. Procedural errors occurred while two rats in the drug condition and three rats in the placebo condition were being tested.
   d. Procedural errors occurred while two (2) rats in the drug condition and three (3) rats in the placebo condition were being tested.

APA CODES: 4.31–4.38
answer: c
RR-MASTERY 1

Edit the following for the expression of numbers:

The 3-dimensional conceptualization allows for 8 possible dyadic relationships.

a. leave as is

b. The 3-dimensional conceptualization allows for eight possible dyadic relationships.

c. The three-dimensional conceptualization allows for eight possible dyadic relationships.

d. The three-dimensional conceptualization allows for 8 possible dyadic relationships.

APA CODES: 4.31–4.38
answer: c
RR-MASTERY 1

Edit the following for the expression of numbers:

There were twenty 6-year-olds, eighteen 10-year-olds, and twenty-four 14-year-olds.

a. leave as is

b. There were 20 6-year-olds, 18 10-year-olds, and 24 14-year-olds.

c. There were 20 six-year-olds, 18 ten-year-olds, and 24 fourteen-year-olds.

d. There were twenty six-year-olds, eighteen 10-year-olds, and twenty-four 14-year-olds.

APA CODES: 4.31–4.38
answer: a
RR-MASTERY 1

Edit the following for the expression of ordinal numbers:

The 6th and 12th graders in each of the treatment conditions returned for a 5th session in which the performance measures were taken.

a. leave as is

b. The sixth and 12th graders in each of the treatment conditions returned for a fifth session in which the performance measures were taken.

c. The sixth and twelfth graders in each of the treatment conditions returned for a fifth session in which the performance measures were taken.

d. The 6th and 12th graders in each of the treatment conditions returned for a fifth session in which the performance measures were taken.

APA CODES: 4.31–4.38
answer: b
RR-MASTERY 1

When using decimal numbers,

a. use a zero is before the decimal point with numbers that are less than 1 when the statistic can exceed 1 (e.g., 0.23 cm, Cohen's $d = 0.70$, 0.48 s).

b. never use a zero before the decimal point (.05).

c. check with the editor of each specific APA journal.

d. use a zero before a decimal fraction when the statistic cannot be greater than 1.

APA CODES: 4.31–4.38
answer: a
RR-MASTERY 1

Edit the following for the presentation of numbers:

In comparison with girls, boys were rated as having higher levels of externalizing symptoms at first grade, $t(1,364) = 2.00, p < .01, d = 0.11$.

a. leave as is

b. In comparison with girls, boys were rated as having higher levels of externalizing symptoms at first grade, $t(1364) = 2.00, p < .01, d = 0.11$.

c. In comparison with girls, boys were rated as having higher levels of externalizing symptoms at first grade, $t(1.364K) = 2.00, p < .01, d = 0.11$.

APA CODES: 4.31–4.38
answer: b
RR-MASTERY 1

Edit the following for the expression of numbers:

Study 1 showed that 3 times as many students studied abroad in the current year than did in the past 6 years.

a. leave as is

b. Study 1 showed that three times as many students studied abroad in the current year than did in the past 6 years.

c. Study 1 showed that three times as many students studied abroad in the current year than did in the past six years.

APA CODES: 4.31–4.38
answer: a
RR-MASTERY 2

Edit the following for the expression of numbers:

The survey had a sampling error of four %.

a. leave as is

b. The survey had a sampling error of four percent.

c. The survey had a sampling error of 4%.

d. The survey had a sampling error of 4 percent.

APA CODES: 4.31–4.38
answer: c
RR-MASTERY 2

Edit the following for the expression of numbers:

To test the program, we sought schools which at least one fourth of the students did not finish the year above grade level on the criterion measure.

a. leave as is

b. To test the program, we sought schools in which at least 1/4 of the students did not finish the year above grade on the criterion measure.

c. To test the program, we sought schools in which at least 1/4th of the students did not finish the year above grade level on the criterion measure.

d. To test the program, we sought schools in which at least one-fourth of the students did not finish the year above grade level on the criterion measure.

APA CODES: 4.31–4.38
answer: a
RR-MASTERY 2

Edit the following for the expression of numbers:

Each client was asked to describe his or her actual and ideal selves on 16 5-point rating scales.

 a. leave as is
 b. Each client was asked to describe his or her actual and ideal selves on sixteen five-point rating scales.
 c. Each client was asked to describe his or her actual and ideal selves on sixteen 5-point rating scales.
 d. Each client was asked to describe his or her actual and ideal selves on 16 five-point rating scales.

APA CODES: 4.31–4.38
answer: c
RR-MASTERY 2

Edit the following for the expression of decimal fractions:

The dots appeared simultaneously on the screen, .5 cm apart.

 a. leave as is
 b. The dots appeared simultaneously on the screen, 0.5 cm apart.
 c. The dots appeared simultaneously on the screen, .50 cm apart.

APA CODES: 4.31–4.38
answer: b
RR-MASTERY 2

Edit the following for the expression and punctuation of numbers:

A content analysis was performed on 1,480 episodes of soap operas that had been televised in the preceding 5 years.

 a. leave as is
 b. A content analysis was performed on 1480 episodes of soap operas that had been televised in the preceding 5 years.
 c. A content analysis was performed on 1,480 episodes of soap operas that had been televised in the preceding five years.
 d. A content analysis was performed on 1480 episodes of soap operas that had been televised in the preceding five years.

APA CODES: 4.31–4.38
answer: a
RR-MASTERY 2

Edit the following for the expression of numbers and scientific abbreviations:

The stimulus presentations were separated by a masking field that lasted for 2 ms.

 a. leave as is
 b. The stimulus presentations were separated by a masking field that lasted for two milliseconds.
 c. The stimulus presentations were separated by a masking field that lasted for 2 mss.

APA CODES: 4.31–4.38
answer: a
RR-MASTERY 3

Edit the following for the expression of numbers:

Each critical word was preceded by zero, one, two, or three priming words in the list.

a. leave as is
b. Each critical word was preceded by zero, 1, 2, or 3 priming words in the list.
c. Each critical word was preceded by 0, 1, 2, or 3 priming words in the list.
d. Each critical word was preceded by zero (0), one (1), two (2), or three (3) priming words in the list.

APA CODES: 4.31–4.38
answer: c
RR-MASTERY 3

Edit the following for the expression of numbers:

Each participant evaluated each of the 12 social portraits on each of 6 dimensions.

a. leave as is
b. Each participant evaluated each of the twelve social portraits on each of six dimensions.
c. Each participant evaluated each of the 12 social portraits on each of six dimensions.
d. Each participant evaluated each of the twelve social portraits on each of 6 dimensions.

APA CODES: 4.31–4.38
answer: c
RR-MASTERY 3

Edit the following for the expression of numbers:

There were 20 4-person teams in each leadership-style condition.

a. leave as is
b. There were twenty four-person teams in each leadership-style condition.
c. There were 20 four-person teams in each leadership-style condition.
d. There were twenty 4-person teams in each leadership-style condition.

APA CODES: 4.31–4.38
answer: c
RR-MASTERY 3

Edit the following for the expression of decimal fractions:

The correlation between scores on the two measures of job satisfaction was .84.

a. leave as is
b. The correlation between scores on the two measures of job satisfaction was 0.84.
c. The correlation between scores on the two measures of job satisfaction was 84×10^{-2}.
d. The correlation between scores on the two measures of job satisfaction was .8400.

APA CODES: 4.31–4.38
answer: a
RR-MASTERY 3

Edit the following for the expression of numbers:

Experiment I was a normative study to determine the reactions of hospital staff members to different diseases and illnesses.

   a. leave as is

   b. Experiment One was a normative study to determine the reactions of hospital staff members to different diseases and illnesses.

   c. Experiment 1 was a normative study to determine the reactions of hospital staff members to different diseases and illnesses.

   d. Experiment one was a normative study to determine the reactions of hospital staff members to different diseases and illnesses.

APA CODES: 4.31–4.38
answer: c
RR-MASTERY 3

Edit the following for the expression of numbers:

The tones were presented at 6,000 Hz for varying durations.

   a. leave as is

   b. The tones were presented at 6000 Hz for varying durations.

   c. The tones were presented at 6×10^3 Hz for varying durations.

APA CODES: 4.31–4.38
answer: b
RR-MASTERY 3

The general rule on expressing numbers is

   a. use words to express all numbers.

   b. use numerals to express all numbers.

   c. use numerals to express numbers 10 and above and words to express numbers below 10.

   d. use numerals to express numbers in tables and graphs and words to express numbers in the text.

APA CODES: 4.31–4.38
answer: c
RR-MASTERY 4

Edit the following for the expression of numbers:

The number of times the client used *I* in each therapy sessions is shown in Figure Two.

   a. leave as is

   b. The number of times the client used *I* in each therapy session is shown in Figure II.

   c. The number of times the client used *I* in each therapy session is shown in Figure 2.

   d. The number of times the client used *I* in each therapy session is shown in Figure two.

APA CODES: 4.31–4.38
answer: c
RR-MASTERY 4

Edit the following for the expression of numbers:

The investigation compared the effectiveness of 3 methods for disseminating health information in 8 locations in the local community.

a. leave as is

b. The investigation compared the effectiveness of three methods for disseminating health information in 8 locations in the local community.

c. The investigation compared the effectiveness of three methods for disseminating health information in eight locations in the local community.

d. The investigation compared the effectiveness of 3 methods for disseminating health information in eight locations in the local community.

APA CODES: 4.31–4.38
answer: c
RR-MASTERY 4

Edit the following for the expression of numbers:

Sixty percent of the victims' closest relatives, but only twenty-eight percent of the victims themselves, showed signs of anxiety and stress on the delayed tests.

a. leave as is

b. Sixty percent of the victims' closest relatives, but only 28% of the victims themselves, showed signs of anxiety and stress on the delayed tests.

c. 60% of the victims' closest relatives, but only 28% of the victims themselves, showed signs of anxiety and stress on the delayed tests.

d. Sixty percent (60%) of the victims' closest relatives, but only 28% of the victims themselves, showed signs of anxiety and stress on the delayed tests.

APA CODES: 4.31–4.38
answer: b
RR-MASTERY 4

Edit the following for the expression of ordinal numbers:

The sequence of events changed on the fourth trial.

a. leave as is

b. The sequence of events changed on the 4th trial.

c. The sequence of events changed on the IVth trial.

APA CODES: 4.31–4.38
answer: a
RR-MASTERY 4

Edit the following for the expression of decimal fractions:

The four-subtest battery added to this prediction, $R^2 = .21$, $\Delta R^2 = .09$, $F(4, 144) = 3.56$, $p = 0.004$, 95% CI [.10, .32].

a. leave as is

b. The four-subtest battery added to this prediction, $R^2 = .21$, $\Delta R^2 = .09$, $F(4, 144) = 3.56$, $p = .004$, 95% CI [.10, .32].

c. The four-subtest battery added to this prediction, $R^2 = .21$, $\Delta R^2 = .09$, $F(4, 144) = 3.56$, $p = .0040$, 95% CI [.10, .32].

APA CODES: 4.31–4.38
answer: b
RR-MASTERY 4

Edit the following for the expression of numbers:

The differential treatments were implemented on Trial 2.

a. leave as is
b. The differential treatments were implemented on Trial II.
c. The differential treatments were implemented on Trial Two.
d. The differential treatments were implemented on trial two.

APA CODES: 4.31–4.38
answer: a
RR-MASTERY 4

Edit the following for the punctuation of numbers:

We counted the number of times that incumbent and nonincumbent candidates referred to themselves and their opposition in a total of 1663 speeches during the 1984 and the 1988 political campaigns.

a. leave as is
b. We counted the number of times that incumbent and nonincumbent candidates referred to themselves and their opposition in a total of 1,663 speeches during the 1,984 and the 1,988 political campaigns.
c. We counted the number of times that incumbent and nonincumbent candidates referred to themselves and their opposition in a total of 1,663 speeches during the 1984 and the 1988 political campaigns.

APA CODES: 4.37–4.38
answer: c
RR-MASTERY 4

Physical measurements should be expressed in

a. metric units.
b. traditional nonmetric units.
c. units of the original measurement.
d. physical units.

APA CODES: 4.39–4.40
answer: a
RR-MASTERY 1

Which of the following is correctly expressed?

a. 13 cms
b. 313 cm.
c. 31 cm
d. 313 cms.

APA CODES: 4.39–4.40
answer: c
RR-MASTERY 1

Experimenters who use instruments that record measurements in nonmetric units

a. should report the measurement as recorded.
b. may report the nonmetric units but must also report the SI (metric) equivalents.
c. can report either the nonmetric units or the SI (metric) equivalents.
d. None of the above is correct.

APA CODES: 4.39–4.40
answer: b
RR-MASTERY 2

Spell out the metric unit

    a. when the unit does not appear with a numeric value.

    b. when the unit appears with a numeric value.

    c. in table headings.

    d. None of the above is correct.

APA CODES: 4.39–4.40
answer: a
RR-MASTERY 2

The APA policy on the use of metric units in writing states that

    a. because of the complex nature of the metric system, it should be used only for publication in international journals.

    b. the metric system is used in journals if possible; when not possible, nonmetric units must also be accompanied by their equivalents (in parentheses) in the International System of Units.

    c. either system, metric or nonmetric, is acceptable.

    d. the use of nonmetric units is completely unacceptable.

APA CODES: 4.39–4.40
answer: b
RR-MASTERY 4

Edit the following for citing the source of a statistic in text:

A one-way analysis of variance (see any standard statistics text) was used to assess the effect of drug dosage.

    a. leave as is

    b. A one-way analysis of variance was used to assess the effect of drug dosage.

    c. A one-way analysis of variance (Grimm & Yarnold, 2000) was used to assess the effect of drug dosage.

APA CODES: 4.41–4.47
answer: b
RR-MASTERY 2

Include formulas for

    a. new or rare statistics or mathematical expressions.

    b. a statistical or mathematical expression essential to a paper.

    c. all statistics and mathematical expressions.

    d. a and b.

    e. none of the above.

APA CODES: 4.41–4.47
answer: d
RR-MASTERY 2

Edit the following for the presentation of statistics:

High-school GPA statistically predicted college mathematics performance, $R^2 = .12$, $F(1, 148) = 20.18$, $p < .001$, 95% CI [.02, .22].

    a. leave as is

    b. High-school GPA statistically predicted college mathematics performance, $R^2 = .12$, $F(df = 1, 148) = 20.18$, $p < .001$, 95% CI [.02, .22].

    c. High-school GPA statistically predicted college mathematics performance, $R^2 = .12$, $F(1, 148) = 20.18$, $p < 0.001$, 95% CI (.02, .22).

    d. High-school GPA statistically predicted college mathematics performance, $R^2 = .12$, $F(1/48) = 20.18$, $p < .001$, 95% CI [.02, .22].

APA CODES: 4.41–4.47
answer: a
RR-MASTERY 2

Edit the following for the presentation of statistics:

The volunteers who appeared for the orientation session (sample size = 120) were then randomly assigned to one of the three conditions.

a. leave as is

b. The volunteers who appeared for the orientation session (N = 120) were then randomly assigned to one of the three conditions.

c. The volunteers who appeared for the orientation session (N = 120) were then randomly assigned to one of the three conditions.

d. The volunteers who appeared for the orientation session (n = 120) were then randomly assigned to one of the three conditions.

APA CODES: 4.41–4.47
answer: c
RR-MASTERY 2

When you include statistics from another source in a research report, cite the reference

a. for less common statistics.

b. for statistics used in a controversial way.

c. when the statistic itself is the focus of an article.

d. all of the above.

APA CODES: 4.41–4.47
answer: d
RR-MASTERY 3

Edit the following for citing the source of a statistic in text:

A chi-square test (Grimm & Yarnold, 2000) was used to compare the preference distributions for girls and boys.

a. leave as is

b. A chi-square test (see any standard statistics text) was used to compare the preference distributions for girls and boys.

c. A chi-square test was used to compare the preference distributions for girls and boys.

APA CODES: 4.41–4.47
answer: c
RR-MASTERY 3

Edit the following for the presentation of statistics:

The one-degree-of-freedom contrast of primary interest (the mean difference between Conditions 1 and 2) was also statistically significant at the specified .05 level, $t(df = 177) = 3.51, p < .001$, $d = 0.65$, 95% CI [0.35, 0.95].

a. leave as is

b. The one-degree-of-freedom contrast of primary interest (the mean difference between Conditions 1 and 2) was also statistically significant at the specified .05 level, $t_{177} = 3.51$, $p < .001, d = 0.65$, 95% CI [0.35, 0.95].

c. The one-degree-of-freedom contrast of primary interest (the mean difference between Conditions 1 and 2) was also statistically significant at the specified .05 level, $t(177) = 3.51$, $p < .001, d = 0.65$, 95% CI [0.35, 0.95].

d. The one-degree-of-freedom contrast of primary interest (the mean difference between Conditions 1 and 2) was also statistically significant at the specified .05 level, $t = 3.51, p < .001, d = 0.65$, 95% CI [0.35, 0.95].

APA CODES: 4.41–4.47
answer: c
RR-MASTERY 3

Edit the following for the presentation of statistics:

High-school GPA statistically predicted college mathematics performance, $R^2 = .12$, $F(1, 148) = 20.18$, $p < .001$, 95% CI (.02, .22).

   a. leave as is

   b. High-school GPA statistically predicted college mathematics performance, $R^2 = .12$, $F(1, 148) = 20.18$, $p < .001$, 95% CI [LL = .02, UL = .22].

   c. High-school GPA statistically predicted college mathematics performance, $R^2 = .12$, $F(1, 148) = 20.18$, $p < .001$, 95% CI [.02, .22].

   d. High-school GPA statistically predicted college mathematics performance, $R^2 = .12$, $F(1, 148) = 20.18$, $p < .001$, 95% CI [.02; .22].

APA CODES: 4.41–4.47
answer: c
RR-MASTERY 3

Edit the following for the presentation of statistics:

The applicants in the support condition ($n = 18$) were given a training course in resume writing and interview techniques.

   a. leave as is

   b. The applicants in the support condition (n = 18) were given a training course in resume writing and interview techniques.

   c. The applicants in the support condition ($N = 18$) were given a training course in resume writing and interview techniques.

   d. The applicants in the support condition (sample size = 18) were given a training course in resume writing and interview techniques.

APA CODES: 4.41–4.47
answer: a
RR-MASTERY 3

Edit the following for typing statistical and mathematical copy:

The four-subtest battery added to this prediction, $R^2 = .21$, $\Delta R^2 = .09$, F(4, 144) = 3.56, p = .004, 95% CI [.10, .32].

   a. leave as is

   b. The four-subtest battery added to this prediction, $R^2 = .21$, $\Delta R^2 = .09$, $F(4, 144) = 3.56$, $p = .004$, 95% CI [.10, .32].

   c. The four-subtest battery added to this prediction, $R^2 = .21$, delta$R^2 = .09$, $F(4,144) = 3.56$, $p = .004$, 95% CI [.10, .32].

   d. The four-subtest battery added to this prediction, $R^2 = .21$, $\Delta R^2 = .09$, $F(4, 144)=3.56$, $p=.004$, 95% CI [.10, .32].

APA CODES: 4.41–4.47
answer: b
RR-MASTERY 3

Edit the following for the typing of statistical copy:

The one-degree-of-freedom contrast of primary interest (the mean difference between Conditions 1 and 2) was also statistically significant at the specified .05 level, $t(177) = 3.51$, $p < .001$, $d = 0.65$, 95% CI (0.35, 0.95).

a. leave as is

b. The one-degree-of-freedom contrast of primary interest (the mean difference between Conditions 1 and 2) was also statistically significant at the specified .05 level, $t(177) = 3.51$, $p<.001$, $d=0.65$, 95% CI [0.35, 0.95].

c. The one-degree-of-freedom contrast of primary interest (the mean difference between Conditions 1 and 2) was also statistically significant at the specified .05 level, $t(177) = 3.51$, $p <.001$, $d = 0.65$, 95% CI [0.35, 0.95].

d. The one-degree-of-freedom contrast of primary interest (the mean difference between Conditions 1 and 2) was also statistically significant at the specified .05 level, $t(177) = 3.51$, $p < .001$, $d = 0.65$, 95% CI [0.35,0.95].

APA CODES: 4.41–4.49
answer: c
RR-MASTERY 1

Edit the following for the citation of a statistic in text:

A t test for related means was used to compare the number of targets found by birds in the experimental group with the number found by their yoked partners.

a. leave as is

b. A t test for related means (Grimm & Yarnold, 2000) was used to compare the number of targets found by birds in the experimental group with the number found by their yoked partners.

c. A t test for related means (see any standard statistics reference work) was used to compare the number of targets found by birds in the experimental group with the number found by their yoked partners.

APA CODES: 4.41–4.49
answer: a
RR-MASTERY 1

Edit the following for the presentation of a formula:

We used a t test to compare the frequencies of heterosexual intercourse per month by heterosexual and bisexual men.

a. leave as is

b. We used a t test (t = difference between means/standard error of difference between means) to compare the frequencies of heterosexual intercourse per month by heterosexual and bisexual men.

c. We used a t test [$t = (M_H - M_B)$/standard error of difference between means] to compare the frequencies of heterosexual intercourse per month by heterosexual and bisexual men.

d. We used a t test $[(M_H - M_B)/(SE_{M_H - M_B})]$ to compare the frequencies of heterosexual intercourse per month by heterosexual and bisexual men.

APA CODES: 4.41–4.49
answer: a
RR-MASTERY 1

When presenting an inferential statistic in text, give

    a. sample sizes.

    b. cell means.

    c. standard deviations.

    d. all of the above.

    e. none of the above.

APA CODES: 4.41–4.49
answer: d
RR-MASTERY 1

Edit the following for the use of statistical symbols:

We first conducted a pilot study to determine the % of participants who could complete the task with different time limits.

    a. leave as is

    b. We first conducted a pilot study to determine the percentage of participants who could complete the task with different time limits.

    c. We first conducted a pilot study to determine the % age of participants who could complete the task with different time limits.

    d. We first conducted a pilot study to determine the percentage (%) of participants who could complete the task with different time limits.

APA CODES: 4.41–4.49
answer: b
RR-MASTERY 1

Which of the following should be used to designate the number of members in a part of a total sample?

    a. N

    b. n

    c. n

    d. N

APA CODES: 4.41–4.49
answer: b
RR-MASTERY 1

Choose the correct format for presenting a confidence interval:

    a. M = 30.5 cm, 99% CI [18.0, 43.0] cm

    b. M = 30.5 cm, 99% CI (18.0, 43.0)

    c. M = 30.5 cm, 99% CI (18.0, 43.0) cm

    d. M = 30.5 cm, 99% CI [18.0, 43.0]

APA CODES: 4.41–4.49
answer: d
RR-MASTERY 1

Formulas for statistics should be given

    a. at all times.

    b. for common statistics and for a statistic that is used only once in the article.

    c. for a statistic not yet widely known or for one that is the focus of the article.

    d. None of the above is correct.

APA CODES: 4.41–4.49
answer: c
RR-MASTERY 4

Edit the following for the presentation of formulas:

The participants were divided into high and low self-monitors by a median split (*Mdn* = 50th percentile).

a. leave as is

b. The participants were divided into high and low self-monitors by a median split (*Mdn* = 50th %ile).

c. The participants were divided into high and low self-monitors by a median split [*Mdn* = (n + 1)/2].

d. The participants were divided into high and low self-monitors by a median split.

APA CODES: 4.41–4.49
answer: d
RR-MASTERY 4

Which of the following is the correct way to present a statistic in text?

a. *t* = 3.51(177), *p*< .001, *d* = 0.65, 95% CI [0.35, 0.95]

b. *t* = *3.51(177)*, *p* <.001, *d* = 0.65, 95% CI [0.35, 0.95]

c. *t*(177) = 3.51, *p*<.001, *d* = 0.65, 95% CI [0.35, 0.95]

d. any of the above

e. none of the above

APA CODES: 4.41–4.49
answer: e
RR-MASTERY 4

Edit the following for the presentation of statistics:

The means for the no-treatment, placebo, and drug conditions were 8.8, 7.2, and 4.6, respectively.

a. leave as is

b. The means for the three conditions were 8.8, 7.2, and 4.6.

c. The means for the three conditions were 8.8, 7.2, and 4.6, respectively.

APA CODES: 4.41–4.49
answer: a
RR-MASTERY 4

Edit the following for the expression of statistical terms:

The *M*s for the alcohol and no-alcohol conditions were 18.4 and 13.6, respectively.

a. leave as is

b. The means for the alcohol and no-alcohol conditions were 18.4 and 13.6, respectively.

c. The MEANS for the alcohol and no-alcohol conditions were 18.4 and 13.6, respectively.

d. The $\overline{Xs}$ for the alcohol and no-alcohol conditions were 18.4 and 13.6, respectively.

APA CODES: 4.41–4.49
answer: b
RR-MASTERY 4

Edit the following for typing statistical and mathematical copy:

High school GPA statistically predicted college mathematics performance, $R^2 = .12$, $F(1, 148) = 20.18$, $p < .001$, 95% Confidence Interval [.02, .22].

    a. leave as is

    b. High-school GPA statistically predicted college mathematics performance, $R^2 = .12$, $F(1, 148) = 20.18$, $p < .001$, 95% CI [.02, .22].

    c. High-school GPA statistically predicted college mathematics performance, $R^2 = .12$, $F(1, 148) = 20.18$, $p< .001$, 95% CI [.02, .22].

    d. High-school GPA statistically predicted college mathematics performance, $R^2 = .12$, $F(1,148) = 20.18$, $p < .001$, 95% CI [.02, .22].

APA CODES: 4.41–4.49
answer: b
RR-MASTERY 4

In scientific writing, the dominant function of graphical displays is

    a. decoration.

    b. communication.

    c. storage.

    d. calculation.

    e. exploration.

APA CODES: 5.01–5.06
answer: b
RR-MASTERY 4

Design your graphical display with the reader in mind by

    a. placing items that are to be compared next to each other.

    b. placing labels so that they clearly abut the elements they are labeling.

    c. using fonts large enough to be read without magnification.

    d. all of the above.

APA CODES: 5.01–5.06
answer: d
RR-MASTERY 4

Tables should be numbered in the order

    a. in which they are first mentioned in the text.

    b. that seems most logical to the author.

    c. that seems most logical to an editor.

    d. any of the above

APA CODES: 5.01–5.06
answer: a
RR-MASTERY 4

From the following examples, select the correct way to refer to a figure in text:

    a. see the figure above.

    b. see the figure on page 14.

    c. see Figure 2.

    d. see Figure 2 above on page 14.

APA CODES: 5.01–5.06
answer: c
RR-MASTERY 4

Edit the table below for tabular presentation:

Table 6

Mean Imagined Scores of Students Reporting an Out-of-Body Experience

Condition	Imaginal scores
Visual	7.1
Auditory	4.0

  a. Means should be carried out to two decimal places.

  b. No standard deviations are given.

  c. Results consisting of only two means should be presented in the text, not in a table.

  d. b and c

APA CODES: 5.07–5.19
answer: d
RR-MASTERY 1

Tables should be

  a. integral to the text but understandable in isolation.

  b. referred to but not duplicated in the text.

  c. referred to in text by their numbers.

  d. all of the above.

APA CODES: 5.07–5.19
answer: d
RR-MASTERY 1

Every table should have a title that is

  a. brief.

  b. clear.

  c. explanatory.

  d. all of the above.

APA CODES: 5.07–5.19
answer: d
RR-MASTERY 1

Which of the following abbreviations need not be explained in table headings or table notes?

  a. abbreviations of technical terms

  b. standard abbreviations for nontechnical terms

  c. group names

  d. none of the above

APA CODES: 5.07–5.19
answer: b
RR-MASTERY 1

A specific note to a table

  a. refers to a particular column or individual entry.

  b. is indicated by a superscript uppercase letter.

  c. is placed within the body of the table.

  d. does none of the above.

APA CODES: 5.07–5.19
answer: a
RR-MASTERY 1

A table should be used

  a. whenever numbers are involved.

  b. when an article is more than five pages.

  c. when it supplements rather than duplicates text.

  d. for all of the above.

APA CODES: 5.07–5.19
answer: c
RR-MASTERY 2

Identify tabular presentation error(s) in the following:

Table 3

Estimated Distance (cm) for Letter and Digit Stimuli

		95% CI	
Condition	*M (SD)*	*LL*	*UL*
Letters	14.5 (28.6)	5.4	23.6
Digits	31.8 (33.2)	21.2	42.4

a. Table 3 should be Table III.
b. CI, *LL,* and *UL* need to be defined in a table note.
c. Centimeters should be spelled out in the table title.
d. b and c

APA CODES: 5.07–5.19
answer: b
RR-MASTERY 2

For all tables within one paper, use

a. the same terminology.
b. similar formats.
c. the same title.
d. a and b.

APA CODES: 5.07–5.19
answer: d
RR-MASTERY 2

A table title should be

a. brief but explanatory.
b. clear and reflect basic content of the table.
c. detailed about all independent and dependent variables.
d. a and b are correct.

APA CODES: 5.07–5.19
answer: d
RR-MASTERY 2

The left-hand column of a table (the *stub*) has a heading (the *stubhead*) that usually describes the

a. elements in that column.
b. dependent variables.
c. independent variables.
d. data.
e. a and c.

APA CODES: 5.07–5.19
answer: e
RR-MASTERY 2

When reporting confidence intervals in a table, you can

a. use brackets as in text.
b. use the same confidence level throughout the paper.
c. give upper and lower limits in separate columns.
d. all of the above.

APA CODES: 5.07–5.19
answer: d
RR-MASTERY 2

Tables should be used for

    a. any data relevant to the article.

    b. important data directly related to the content of the article.

    c. any data presented in the text.

    d. all of the above.

APA CODES: 5.07–5.19
answer: b
RR-MASTERY 3

Tables should be an integral part of the text yet designed to be understood in isolation. To accomplish this end,

    a. use extensive footnotes (one third of a page).

    b. explain all but the most common statistical abbreviations.

    c. cite the table in the text by saying "in the above table."

    d. put tables in an appendix.

    e. do all of the above.

APA CODES: 5.07–5.19
answer: b
RR-MASTERY 3

For all tables within one paper, use

    a. the same terminology.

    b. similar formats.

    c. similar titles.

    d. a and b.

APA CODES: 5.07–5.19
answer: d
RR-MASTERY 3

The left-hand column of a table (the *stub*) usually lists

    a. mean values.

    b. the major independent variables.

    c. decked heads.

    d. none of the above.

APA CODES: 5.07–5.19
answer: b
RR-MASTERY 3

The body of a table

    a. always contains data that are rounded off to the number of decimal places the precision of measurement justifies.

    b. contains columns of data even if those data can be easily calculated from other columns.

    c. contains words or numerical data.

    d. does all of the above.

    e. a and c.

APA CODES: 5.07–5.19
answer: e
RR-MASTERY 3

A table should be used

    a. whenever data analyses are involved.

    b. when an article is more than 1,200 words long.

    c. when it compresses data and allows relationships to be seen that are not readily seen in text.

    d. all of the above

APA CODES: 5.07–5.19
answer: c
RR-MASTERY 4

Tables should be an integral part of the text, yet be readable alone. To accomplish this end,

a. use extensive footnotes (one third of a page).
b. explain all but the most common statistical abbreviations in the table title or table notes.
c. cite the table in the text by saying "in the above table."
d. put tables in an appendix.
e. all of the above

APA CODES: 5.07–5.19
answer: b
RR-MASTERY 4

Table numbers and titles should be typed

a. centered in uppercase and lowercase letters.
b. single-spaced at the top of the table.
c. flush left in uppercase and lowercase letters.
d. a and b

APA CODES: 5.07–5.19
answer: c
RR-MASTERY 4

The column spanner of a table

a. is a thick line used to mark the top of the table.
b. is used exclusively to list the dependent variables.
c. is used to identify the entries in the vertical columns in the body of the table.
d. should be no more than 20 characters wide.

APA CODES: 5.07–5.19
answer: c
RR-MASTERY 4

The body of a table

a. always contains data rounded off to the nearest tenth.
b. contains columns of data even if those data can be easily calculated from other columns.
c. contains words or numerical data.
d. does all of the above.

APA CODES: 5.07–5.19
answer: c
RR-MASTERY 4

Table notes

a. are placed below the bottom rule of a table.
b. explain table data or provide additional information.
c. acknowledge the source of a reprinted table.
d. do all of the above.
e. do none of the above.

APA CODES: 5.07–5.19
answer: d
RR-MASTERY 4

A probability note to a table

a. includes an explanation of abbreviations.
b. begins with a superscript lowercase letter *a*.
c. indicates how asterisks and other symbols are used in a table to indicate *p* values.
d. a and b

APA CODES: 5.07–5.19
answer: c
RR-MASTERY 4

When reporting confidence intervals in a table,

    a. use brackets as in text.

    b. use parentheses.

    c. give upper and lower limits in separate columns.

    d. do not state the confidence level.

    e. a and c.

APA CODES: 5.14–5.16
answer: e
RR-MASTERY 3

Which of the following is the correct order of notes in a table?

    a. specific, probability, general

    b. general, specific, probability

    c. general, probability, specific

    d. none of the above.

APA CODES: 5.14–5.16
answer: b
RR-MASTERY 3

When inserting rules in tables,

    a. limit the use of rules.

    b. use horizontal and vertical rules to separate rows and columns throughout.

    c. you may substitute appropriately positioned white spaces for rules.

    d. a and c.

    e. all of the above.

APA CODE: 5.17
answer: d
RR-MASTERY 3

When checking whether data are effectively presented in your table, what question should you *not* ask yourself?

    a. Should this table be vertically displayed?

    b. Is the table necessary?

    c. Does every column have a heading?

    d. Are confidence intervals reported for all major point estimates?

    e. all of the above

APA CODE: 5.19
answer: a
RR-MASTERY 1

Figure captions

    a. serve as the explanation and as the title of the figure.

    b. should describe the contents of the figure in a brief sentence or phrase.

    c. should include explanations of units of measurement, symbols, and abbreviations not included in the legend.

    d. all of the above.

APA CODES: 5.20–5.23
answer: d
RR-MASTERY 2

Which type of figure typically displays the relationship between two quantitative indices?

    a. maps

    b. graphs

    c. charts

    d. all of the above

APA CODES: 5.20–5.24
answer: b
RR-MASTERY 3

What factors weigh against using a figure?

a. It duplicates elements of the paper.
b. It complements text and reduces lengthy discussions.
c. It cannot be produced in a way that captures essential information features without visually distracting detail.
d. Answers a and c are correct.
e. Answers a and b are correct.

APA CODES: 5.20–5.30
answer: d
RR-MASTERY 1

What kind of figure generally displays nonquantitative information such as the flow of subjects through a process?

a. photograph
b. chart
c. map
d. drawing
e. graph

APA CODES: 5.20–5.30
answer: b
RR-MASTERY 1

Which of the following is essential in presenting electrophysiological, radiological, and other genetic data?

a. clear and complete labeling.
b. limiting the number of different shadings.
c. type style.
d. all of the above.

APA CODES: 5.20–5.30
answer: a
RR-MASTERY 1

The word *figure* refers to

a. maps.
b. graphs and charts.
c. drawings.
d. all of the above.

APA CODES: 5.20–5.30
answer: d
RR-MASTERY 2

A figure is not necessary if it

a. augments text.
b. duplicates text.
c. eliminates lengthy discussion from the text.
d. does none of the above.

APA CODES: 5.20–5.30
answer: b
RR-MASTERY 2

A figure legend should be positioned

a. within the figure.
b. to the left of the figure.
c. below the figure.
d. above the figure.

APA CODES: 5.20–5.30
answer: a
RR-MASTERY 2

A good figure caption

    a. describes the figure in detail no matter how lengthy it becomes.

    b. should refer the reader to a place in the text for explanation of the figure.

    c. is concise but explanatory.

    d. does none of the above.

APA CODES: 5.20–5.30
answer: c
RR-MASTERY 3

What kind of lettering should be used in a figure?

    a. serif typeface

    b. simple, sans serif typeface

    c. boldface 16-point type

    d. boldface 6-point type

    e. a and c

APA CODES: 5.20–5.30
answer: b
RR-MASTERY 3

Which of the following is the correct ordering of manuscript sections in a research report?

    a. Method, Results, tables, Discussion

    b. References, tables, figures

    c. author notes, figures, figure captions, tables

    d. none of the above

APA CODES: 5.20–5.30
answer: b
RR-MASTERY 3

A good figure

    a. conveys only essential facts.

    b. is easy to understand.

    c. is prepared in the same style as similar figures in the same article.

    d. is all of the above.

APA CODES: 5.20–5.30
answer: d
RR-MASTERY 4

A figure caption

    a. functions as the title of the figure.

    b. does not need to include abbreviations and symbols defined in the text.

    c. includes acknowledgments that a figure is reproduced from another source.

    d. is all of the above.

    e. a and c

APA CODES: 5.20–5.30
answer: e
RR-MASTERY 4

Select the figure caption that does not explain its figure effectively:

    a. *Figure 1.* Videocamera effects.

    b. *Figure 4.* Varimax rotation of factors.

    c. *Figure 2.* Outpatient and inpatient contrasts.

    d. All of the above.

APA CODES: 5.23–5.24
answer: d
RR-MASTERY 1

Which part of a research report should not always begin on a new page?

a. abstract
b. References
c. Method
d. a and b

APA CODE: 8.03
answer: c
RR-MASTERY 1

The title page includes the title,

a. author byline and abstract.
b. author byline, institutional affiliation, running head, and the page number 1.
c. author byline, institutional affiliation, running head, the page number 1, and author note.
d. author byline, institutional affiliation, and abstract.

APA CODE: 8.03
answer: c
RR-MASTERY 1

Choose the correct statement about the placing of a table in a manuscript:

a. Type the table in full exactly in the place in the text where it should be printed.
b. Type the table on the back of the page that first refers to it.
c. Try to type all of the tables on the same page.
d. Type each table on a separate page.

APA CODE: 8.03
answer: d
RR-MASTERY 1

Which of the following is the correct ordering of manuscript sections in a research report?

a. title page, abstract, introduction
b. Method, Results, Discussion
c. References, figures, tables
d. a and b

APA CODE: 8.03
answer: d
RR-MASTERY 2

A running head to be used in a research report should be

a. centered at the bottom of the title page in all uppercase letters.
b. flush left at the top of the title page in all uppercase letters.
c. centered at the bottom of the title page in uppercase and lowercase letters.
d. flush right at the bottom of the title page in all uppercase and lowercase letters.

APA CODE: 8.03
answer: b
RR-MASTERY 2

Which of the following should be placed on a separate page of a manuscript?

a. the abstract
b. appendices
c. figure captions
d. all of the above
e. a and b

APA CODE: 8.03
answer: e
RR-MASTERY 4